NATURE'S ARISTOCRACY

Legacies of Nineteenth-Century
American Women Writers

SERIES EDITORS
Sharon Harris, *University of Connecticut*
Karen Dandurand, *Indiana University of Pennsylvania*

BOARD OF EDITORS
Martha Cutter, *University of Connecticut-Storrs*
France Smith Foster, *Emory University*
Susan K. Harris, *University of Kansas*
Mary Kelley, *University of Michigan*
Venetria Patton, *Purdue University*
Karen Sanchez-Eppler, *Amherst College*
Elizabeth Young, *Mt. Holyoke College*

Miss Jennie Collins. *Frank Leslie's Sunday Magazine*, October 1887. Courtesy of General Research Division, New York Public Library, Astor, Lenox, and Tilden Foundations.

NATURE'S ARISTOCRACY

or

Battles and Wounds in Time of Peace

A PLEA FOR THE OPPRESSED

Jennie Collins

Edited and with an introduction by Judith A. Ranta

UNIVERSITY OF NEBRASKA PRESS
Lincoln and London

© 2010 by the Board of Regents
of the University of Nebraska
All rights reserved. Manufactured in
the United States of America.

LIBRARY OF CONGRESS
Cataloging-in-Publication Data
Collins, Jennie, 1828–1887.
Nature's aristocracy, or, Battles and
wounds in time of peace: a plea for the
oppressed / Jennie Collins ;
edited and with an introduction
by Judith A. Ranta.
p. cm.
— (Legacies of nineteenth-century
American women writers)
Includes bibliographical references.
ISBN 978-0-8032-1934-2
(pbk. : alk. paper)
I. Ranta, Judith A., 1953–
II. Title. III. Title: Battles and
wounds in time of peace.
PS1359.C5627N38 2010
305.5'620973—dc22
2009045364

Designed and set in
Minion Pro by
A. Shahan

Contents

Acknowledgments
vii

Editor's Introduction
ix

A Note on the Text
xli

Nature's Aristocracy;
or, Battles and Wounds in
Time of Peace: *A Plea
for the Oppressed*
1

Notes
209

Acknowledgments

This kind of recovery project would not be possible without the assistance of staffs at research libraries and archives. The editor extends grateful thanks to the librarians of the New York Public Library's Humanities and Social Sciences Library, Boston Public Library, the New England Historic Genealogical Society Library, the New York Genealogical and Biographical Society Library, Columbia University Law Library, New York University's Bobst and Tamiment Libraries, and the Manchester Historic Association. Carol Harris at Temple University Library's Special Collections, Conwellana-Templana Department, contributed her expertise and interest in Jennie Collins. Appreciation is due to Steven F. Kruger of the City University of New York, for his interest in discussing the introduction; to David S. Reynolds, also of the City University of New York, for reading and commenting on the introduction; and to the series editors and staff at the University of Nebraska Press.

Editor's Introduction

Jennie Collins wrote *Nature's Aristocracy; or, Battles and Wounds in Time of Peace: A Plea for the Oppressed* at a time when questions about the meaning of work and about relations between labor and capital were being passionately debated. During the headlong post-bellum expansion of American industry, people struggled to understand the changing workplace. One journalist wrote in 1869, "It is becoming more and more plain, and being more and more freely admitted, that this fundamental question of the rights of labor, and its just relations to capital, is crowding other issues aside, and, with the financial issue, promises very shortly to usurp the chief and most intense thought of the time" ("Labor Question").

In response to her era's tumultuous pressures, Collins created a varied text that can be difficult to categorize because it encompasses multiple genres. On the one hand, it is autobiographical, drawing upon her decades of employment in such working-class occupations as textile mill operative, domestic servant, and garment shop tailoress. *Nature's Aristocracy* reflects as well Collins's achievements as a labor rights orator and activist described by a contemporary as "the chosen champion and apostle of the Eastern Workingwomen" ("Visitors"). The text also includes fictionalized narratives of workers' experiences, so it occupies a middle ground between fiction and nonfiction. While it is the first attempt by a U.S. author of any class background or gender to produce an extended overview of working-class life, *Nature's Aristocracy* appears to have been modified and even distorted in places by its editor, Russell H. Conwell (1843–1925). Nonetheless, animated by a profound concern for the working poor, Collins produced a groundbreaking book on the perennially vexed problem of class in America.

BIOGRAPHICAL

Jane "Jennie" Collins was born in 1828 in Amoskeag, a New Hampshire factory village now part of Manchester.[1] Although in adulthood she was usually known as Jennie, her given name was Jane. Collins's early life is shrouded in some mystery. Records of her birth and forebears have apparently not been preserved, so her exact birth date and parents' names are unknown.[2] Even Ellen R. Robson, a friend who had known Collins for twenty-five years preceding Collins's death, contended that "whether she [Collins] had or had not a family . . . she never said" ("In Memory").

Several obituaries note that Collins had often claimed Spanish and Scottish descent, "her small figure and dark face being the legacy of the one blood, and her great energy and indomitable will the gift of the other" ("Obituary: Jennie Collins, the Friend"; "Obituary Record"). Her "Spanish" ethnic characteristics, unusual for an early nineteenth-century New Englander, may have contributed to her empathy for marginalized groups such as slaves and fallen women. After her father died of consumption when she was two years old, Collins's mother either passed away soon after or was unable to care for her three children, so Collins was sent to live with her Quaker grandmother. Robson asserts that Collins "passed her girlhood in one of the mill towns on the Merrimac" ("In Memory").

Following her grandmother's death, fourteen-year-old Collins was obliged to support herself. Although the biographical writings contend that she worked first in Lawrence, Massachusetts, and later in Lowell, she may have begun working closer to home in the mills of Amoskeag or Manchester.[3] As reflected in *Nature's Aristocracy*, the hardships of mill work made a deep impression on her while threatening her fragile health. Sometime in the 1850s she became a nurse and domestic in the family of Judge John Lowell of Boston. While one newspaper writer claims that Collins "sought a position as nurse in a rich family, 'wishing,' as she said, 'to see what kind of an affair life was to the rich,'" it seems just as likely that she wanted to avoid further exposure to unhealthy mill conditions (P., L.C.). About 1860 she began working in Boston garment shops as a vest maker, first for a firm located in the Old State House and then, from 1861 to 1870, for Macullar, Williams & Parker, a manufacturer and retailer of men's and boys' clothing.

In her scant free time, Collins took advantage of evening classes and other educational and cultural opportunities, which led her to believe that she possessed talents beyond those needed for the factory and shop. She studied history and politics and, according to one nineteenth-century journalist, was recognized by her coworkers and employers for "her vivacity and the excellence of her understanding, and her faculty of earnest discussion of the subjects in which she was interested" ("Obituary: Jennie Collins," *Boston Morning Journal*). One such subject was slavery, to which Collins early assumed a fervent and outspoken opposition. She was chosen to lead an evening class on English history and also taught children of deceased Civil War soldiers ("Collins, Jennie"). In their spare time, Collins and her garment shop mates conducted charitable work aiding Union soldiers.

In 1868 Collins began speaking publicly on labor and women's concerns, as well as on behalf of political candidates. She was the only woman to speak at a meeting of the Ward Eight Grant Club in Boston, where she advocated the election of Ulysses S. Grant, Charles Sumner, and William Claflin ("Political"). Moreover, one obituary contends that Collins was first to urge that women be allowed into the halls of the state legislature ("Jennie Collins Dead"). Also in 1868, she made her first important public address during a debate in Boston's Washington Hall, where she "advocat[ed] woman's rights from the working woman's standpoint in such a plain, beautiful and yet masterly way that she carried her audience by storm" ("Obituary: Jennie Collins, the Friend"). Her fame soon began to spread. In the next several years she spoke at many labor and women's events, often to great acclaim, promoting such causes as the eight-hour day, child labor reform, and improved wages and working conditions for women. In April 1869 she became one of three provisional directors of the Boston Working Women's League.

Due to her renown as a feminist and labor rights leader, Collins was invited to address the January 1870 convention of the National Woman Suffrage Association.

Collins began speaking on Boston Common in the summer of 1870, but her gatherings met with opposition. As a *Boston Daily Advertiser* reporter observes, "It is said that some of the politicians, whose hostility she had aroused, complained to the aldermen and the meetings were discontinued" ("Obituary: Jennie Collins, the Friend").[4] Thereafter Collins committed more of her energy to charitable endeavors, although she continued lifelong to speak, write, or act on behalf of the causes she cherished, especially women's suffrage and labor rights. Never marrying, she was able to dedicate herself wholly to her work, forming many enduring friendships, particularly among women. During the later years of her life, Collins lived in the home of Mrs. Eveline J. (Damon) Pillsbury, a widow, and Pillsbury's brother.

On July 25, 1870, Collins established Boffin's Bower, a charity aiding Boston's poor and working women. To support her work, she obtained donations from large employers of women, such as her former workplace Macullar, Williams & Parker, and from other sources. She devoted herself to such efforts even though she knew, as she wrote in *Nature's Aristocracy*, that philanthropy does not change the system responsible for poverty and workers' oppression (49–50). Boffin's Bower provided several comfortable rooms where working women could relax and enjoy reading material, a piano, an employment bureau, meals for those in need, and limited lodging. Recreational programs and instruction in such skills as machine sewing were offered. Margaret Allen observes that in founding and managing Boffin's Bower, Collins pioneered in settlement house work before college-educated women entered the field in the 1880s (105).

In November 1870 Collins published her only monograph, *Nature's Aristocracy*. The writing of this book, which must have spanned some considerable time before the founding of Boffin's Bower, offers evidence of what one journalist called "the feeling which she acknowledged [in the later 1860s] of adopting a literary rather than a philanthropic career" ("Obituary: Jennie Collins," *Boston Morning Journal*). Collins's literary ambitions were shared by many factory women, such as those who wrote for the *Lowell Offering* (1840–45) and other such workers' periodicals. As an occupation requiring few material resources and pursued successfully by poor women, including Lydia Sigourney, Harriet Jacobs, and Lucy Larcom, authorship appealed powerfully to factory women.

In her speaking, writing, and philanthropic work, Collins drew strength from Spiritualism, an enormously popular grassroots religious and social movement that was an offshoot of Christianity. Spiritualists embraced the occult belief that the dead can communicate with the living through specially gifted—often female—mediums. Many Spiritualists supported labor and women's rights, which made the movement especially attractive to women and the working classes. Ann Braude contends in *Radical Spirits: Spiritualism and Women's Rights in Nineteenth-Century America*, "Spiritualism became a major—if not *the* major—vehicle for the spread of woman's rights ideas in mid-century America" (57).

Collins's obituary in Boston's *Banner of Light*, a major Spiritualist paper, suggests how important Spiritualism was for her. The anonymous writer recalls that Collins had visited the office in 1872 and confided that "she was unquestionably a spirit-medium, and was 'told by the angels' to enter upon the special mission in which she was engaged" ("Decease"). In *Nature's Aristocracy*, Collins hints at her capacity as a medium, contending that through her text's composition "the shades of the hungry, toil-killed, and heart-shattered men and women shall tell their tales to the world in death, as they told them to me in life" (11). Collins also suggests her sense of divine mission when she encourages her readers to undertake charitable visits to poor people's wretched homes, as she herself had done and would continue doing. Her narrator advises readers not to fear, "resting assured that God has called you to a noble work, and will not leave you without protection" (24). Her sense of possessing a spiritual mission allowed Collins to overcome fears. According to Braude, "With the encouragement of spirits, women did things that they themselves believed women could not do. . . . Spirit presence helped women overcome internal doubts as well as external sanctions" (83). Collins's Spiritualist beliefs thus strengthened her to step outside her social position as a working-class woman to become a labor leader, author, and manager of a charity.

Collins continued contributing prolifically to newspapers and other periodicals, as well as publishing annual reports of Boffin's Bower activities. On July 20, 1887, she died at a friend's home in Brookline, Massachusetts, of the respiratory ailment that had long afflicted her. She is buried in Walnut Hills Cemetery, Brookline, where the epitaph on her simple grave marker reads (in part): "Jennie Collins / The Working Girls' Friend / And / Founder of Boffin's Bower."

SIMPLE TALES OF REAL LIFE:
A CRITICAL DISCUSSION OF THE TEXT

Collins structures *Nature's Aristocracy* loosely around the argument that nineteenth-century U.S. society has developed unnaturally, deviating from the ideals set forth by the nation's founders, who had taken steps to prevent the development of a corrupt aristocracy like those left behind in Europe. The authors of the U.S. Constitution, for instance, attempted to limit the development of an American aristocracy by forbidding the use of titles of nobility (see Article I, Section 9). Nonetheless, by the mid-nineteenth century, in Collins's view, a moneyed aristocracy has gained an ascendancy that stifles many citizens' aspirations and abilities. People possessing special virtues and talents—that is, natural aristocrats—can be found in all social strata, but their paths are often thwarted by what Collins calls "the usurping line of money-kings" (154).

In her treatment of the concept of nature's aristocracy, Collins contributes to an ongoing American discussion about class and wealth, responding to arguments advanced by prominent leaders and intellectuals such as Thomas Jefferson, Ralph Waldo Emerson, and Theodore Parker. With her deep roots in working-class communities, Collins also draws from the oral and written traditions created by workers themselves. Going back at least to the 1830s, American mill workers and other laborers had produced prose, fiction, poetry, songs, and many kinds of protest writings to express their experience and concerns. Throughout the nineteenth century, workers in major industrial communities published their own periodicals.[5] As a worker and especially as a labor activist, Collins would have been well acquainted with these literary traditions.

Phrases such as "nature's aristocracy," "natural aristocracy," and "nature's noblemen" appear quite commonly in late eighteenth- and nineteenth-century writings on both sides of the Atlantic. These terms usually denote an inborn superiority of character, intellect, or physical appearance not attributable to the possessor's familial inheritance. With the founding of the United States, "nature's aristocracy" and similar terms took on new connotations.

For Thomas Jefferson and other early Americans, the new republic offered unprecedented opportunities for nature's aristocrats to gain the opportunities and power they deserved. Influenced by Aristotle's recommendation that society be governed by an aristocracy of the most virtuous, Jefferson formulated his own ideas about natural and pseudo-aristocracy in letters exchanged with John Quincy Adams and in his *Autobiography*, all published in several editions before 1870. Writing to Adams, Jefferson "agree[s] . . . that there is a natural aristocracy among men. The grounds of this are virtue and talents." He admits, however, that "there is also an artificial aristocracy, founded on wealth and birth, without either virtue or talents" ("To John Adams" 223). In his autobiography, Jefferson further explains his objections to artificial aristocracy, contending that "an aristocracy of wealth, [is] of more harm and danger, than benefit, to society" (36). Instead, Jefferson hopes to promote "the aristocracy of virtue and talent, which nature has wisely provided for the direction of the interests of society, and scattered with equal hand through all its conditions" (36–37). He considers such an aristocracy "essential to a well-ordered republic" (37). In his home state of Virginia, Jefferson successfully proposed laws changing patterns of inheritance and spreading public education, which he believed "laid the axe to the foot of pseudo-aristocracy" ("To John Adams" 225).[6]

Similarly, in her first chapter Collins shows how nature has scattered her nobility among all social groups. She contends, however, that rather than Jefferson's "well-ordered republic," the United States more nearly resembles a haphazardly constructed building, much in need of "rebuilding" (13). During the Civil War, Collins writes, when soldiers from various regions of the United States became acquainted, "they found everywhere the same great gulf between the rich and the poor which the founders of the nation had hoped to cover with the laws against titles and hereditary aristocracy" (186). She shows that those natural aristocrats born among the poor and laboring classes often find it quite impossible to escape the quagmire of poverty and wretched working conditions.

Ralph Waldo Emerson further developed the notion of an American aristocracy of nature. In 1836 he began composing and delivering a lecture, "Natural Aristocracy," published posthumously in 1884 under the title "Aristocracy," assigned by his executor. Emerson herein argues that although people prefer to believe that human virtues and talents are passed from one generation to another, in fact nature, personified as a capricious feminine power, chooses to disperse her gifts among individuals of all social strata (33). Money, power, and family name are meaningless to her. Although human institutions such as governments can err in their choice of favorites, "Nature makes none [mistakes]" (36). Authentic natural "aristocracy is the class eminent by personal qualities" (38).

While Emerson acknowledges the economic disparities among various social groups, admitting that he "know[s] how steep the contrast of condition looks; such excess here and such destitution there," he minimizes the significance of these contrasts. He assures the reader that "the revolution of things . . . is sure to bring home the opportunity to every one" (46). He thus brushes aside the hardships and impediments to class mobility that so distress Collins. In *Nature's Aristocracy* she shows again and again that opportunities are more often denied to poor people than brought home to them.

While Collins lacks Emerson's optimism regarding social conditions, she shares the Transcendentalist veneration for nature and nature's God. In her conception of nature, which is invoked rather than explained in *Nature's Aristocracy*, Collins draws from Transcendentalism and even more from Spiritualism. In the foundational Transcendentalist essay, "Nature" (1836), Emerson contends that nature restores our humanity. The narrator explains, "The tradesman, the attorney comes out of the din and craft of the street, and sees the sky and the woods, and is a man again. In their eternal calm, he finds himself" (13). Emerson argues that truth, beauty, and other virtues originate in nature, while suffering results when people lose touch with nature. Collins likewise looks to nature for the correction of social evils. As her narrator remarks, "In a true and natural state of society there would be no paupers who deserved charity" (143). Although she does not specify just how a "natural state of society" might be attained, Collins echoes the Transcendentalists' hopeful faith in nature's essential goodness.

Spiritualist conceptions of nature, given Spiritualism's widespread popularity among working-class people, probably influenced Collins's thinking even more than Transcendentalism. In terms that almost replicate some of the central ideas of *Nature's Aristocracy*, Messer-Kruse argues that "among Spiritualism's most cherished beliefs was its view that all of nature, and, indeed, all creation, was harmonious. Human suffering and injustice, therefore, was the effect of the operation of human institutions or customs that subverted the natural order" (16). Collins apparently also believed in such underlying harmony, although she wrote much more clearly and viscerally of society's troubles.

The first chapter of *Nature's Aristocracy* establishes nature's authority and abhorrence for inherited, unnatural aristocracy. The narrator explains, "Nature hates every aristocracy but her own, and she is ever at work trying to restore to the throne her own line of nobles, which the dollar and family pride have deposed" (13). Although nature possesses unquestionable authority, people "will not go to Nature and learn of her" (163), so she is not always successful in seeing her chosen aristocrats placed in suitable positions. Current social conditions, Collins argues, often see "these branches of the royal line defeated and disheartened by the never-ending persecution of the arrogant-wealthy" (15). In her suggestion that the solution to these problems lies in human efforts such as *"practical co-operation* between the laborer and the capitalist," women's suffrage, and labor organizing, Collins rejects Jefferson's faith in "a well-ordered republic" and Emerson's confidence in "the revolution of things" to rectify class oppression (207).

As several of her contemporaries observe, Collins was much more influenced by Theodore Parker, who was a reformer as well as a Transcendentalist. According to Margaret Allen, Collins greatly esteemed Theodore Parker (114). Rachel Ray similarly observes that Parker "was the man after her [Collins's] own heart, to whom she reverently listened, while the great truths of religion and humanity, the fatherhood of God and the brotherhood of man, which he preached, sank deep into her soul" (401). In *Nature's Aristocracy*, Collins includes Parker among the natural aristocrats who like herself had overcome obstacles while rising to prominence. As she writes, "Theodore Parker in his early life, while picking berries to purchase his first Latin Grammar, and working at odd jobs to obtain the rudiments of an education, . . . showed unmistakable evidence of his natural ability" (168). Besides identifying with his youthful struggles, Collins must have been inspired by his social-reform sermons, such as "A Sermon of the Perishing Classes" (1846) and "A Sermon of Poverty" (1849).

Parker's willingness to challenge Bostonians' hypocrisy inspired Collins to comparable courage. In "A Sermon of the Perishing Classes," Parker exposes the terrible plight of the city's poor, declaring, "This class of men are perishing; yes, perishing in the nineteenth century; perishing in Boston, wealthy, charitable Boston; . . . and perishing all the worse because they die slow, and corrupt by inches" (203). Collins as well is not afraid to expose the corruption of wealthy Bostonians, as when her narrator remarks that the word "charity" "is applied to anything and everything which a rich man may do to gain praise" (142).

But Collins departs in her own way from Parker's example. Whereas he pleads—however passionately—on behalf of the poor in the aggregate, Collins's mission is to make them individuals. Tired of being only another of the faceless lower class, Collins insists upon her own and her characters' subjectivity. In chapter 1 when discussing her purposes in writing *Nature's Aristocracy*, Collins explains that she intends to adhere "always to the simple tales of real life which have occurred within the limit of my personal acquaintance" (15). The text's grounding in Collins's "personal acquaintance" with people she has known in "real life" ensures that her own subjectivity and as much of her characters' individuality as can be conveyed through the narrative remain central. *Nature's Aristocracy* allows the little-heard voices of poor women to be represented, such as the aggrieved mill weaver contemplating an impending strike who tells Collins, "I have come near to the conclusion that it is better to stay out and starve in the sunshine than to work and famish in those musty shades [i.e., in the mills]" (137). The weaver thus expresses her determination in the face of limited, disagreeable options.

The curious subtitle of *Nature's Aristocracy* sounds less curious when considered in light of Civil War memories and the writings of Collins's contemporaries. In chapter 11, "Among the 'Strikers,'" Collins links the subtitle's first part, "Battles and Wounds in Time of Peace," to labor struggles. Referring to the 1859 Lynn, Massachusetts, shoemakers' strike, Collins writes, "Then came a hard-fought battle, such as sometimes startle communities in time of peace, and in which there are more wounded and killed than there are in time of war. It was labor against capital" (125). Writing in the wake of the Civil War's turmoil and carnage, Collins works to elicit support for labor causes by arguing that they are as urgent as those that prompted the war. She also insinuates that what appear to be times of peace are just the opposite for workers caught in the war between capital and labor.

The image of industrialism's march, with its consequent class stratification, as a kind of war is found in the work of other mid-nineteenth-century U.S. writers. The narrator of Rebecca Harding Davis's novel *Margret Howth: A Story of To-Day* (1861), set in the Indiana woolen mills, takes the reader into these "vulgar American" scenes, imploring,

> I want you to go down into this common, every-day drudgery, and consider if there might not be in it also a great warfare.

... Men and women, lean-jawed, crippled in the slow, silent battle, are in your alleys, sit beside you at your table; its martyrs sleep under every green hill-side. (6–7)

Theodore Parker's "A Sermon of the Perishing Classes" views with alarm the condition of Boston's poor. At several points, Parker compares their plight to a battle or war. His narrator asks, "What shall become of the children of such men [i.e., the poor]? They stand in the fore-front of the battle, all unprotected as they are; a people scattered and peeled, only a miserable remnant reaches the age of ten!" (203–4). Collins employs the war metaphor, as does Davis, in order to represent the experiences of individual contestants in the battle.

Nature's Aristocracy conveys not only Collins's views, however, but also those of the editor who contributed to the text. Evidence has not been found to reveal whether the publisher or Collins herself chose Russell H. Conwell to serve as editor. Collins's warm dedication of the book to Conwell's wife, Jane (Jennie) P. Hayden Conwell (1844–1872), suggests that the women were friends, so Russell Conwell may also have been Collins's friend. Indirect but compelling evidence suggests that Conwell made significant changes to Collins's text. Betty T. Bennett in her essay on editing the work of Mary Shelley argues that "editors . . . are indeed critics who influence the reading of an author and a text" (84). Conwell served as the kind of editor, in Bennett's terms, "who 'corrects' the idiosyncrasies of an author" (89).

Even without a named editor, a published book represents a collaborative effort to some degree since the publisher contributes to its creation. Many textual scholars now consider published texts less in terms of an individual author's intentions and efforts than as social productions, involving collaborators, editors, publishers, etc. David Greetham explains that "*social textual criticism* . . . denies the automatic priority traditionally given to authors' intentions, preferring instead to regard textual creation and transmission as a collaborative, social act" (9). For Collins's book, the populist press of Lee and Shepard made an especially suitable publisher. In *Lee and Shepard,*

Publishers for the People, Raymond L. Kilgour contends that they "were more concerned with social and political causes than with literary refinements," seeking "to please the average reader" (v). Given Collins's concern with social conditions that weighed upon common people, she made a good choice in publishing with Lee and Shepard.

Russell Conwell also made a likely candidate for editor, given the ways in which his background and interests resonated with Collins's. His father had been an abolitionist whose house had served as a way station on the Underground Railroad (Persons 367). Like Collins, Conwell had been raised in poverty and had worked his way through school. William C. Higgins contends that "his [Conwell's] experience and taste of the bitterness of poverty aroused in him a burning sympathy with the poor" (79). Furthermore, according to Higgins, while Conwell was living in the Boston area in the 1860s and early 1870s, "he often made political speeches, and was the especial favorite of the workingmen" (83). Also during this period, he freely gave legal advice and assistance to "any deserving poor person" (Higgins 80–81). He earned a law degree but also worked as a schoolteacher, journalist, editor, author, lecturer, and finally a pastor and the founder of Temple College (now Temple University), Philadelphia. He lived and worked in the Boston area in the 1860s and early 1870s, when he must have made Collins's acquaintance.

In biographies of Conwell, no mention is made of Jennie Collins or his editing of *Nature's Aristocracy*. Publisher's advertisements, however, give Conwell an unexpectedly large measure of credit for the book. Lee and Shepard published *Nature's Aristocracy* simultaneously with Conwell's first book, *Why and How: Why the Chinese Emigrate, and the Means They Adopt for the Purpose of Reaching America* (1870). In an advertisement for *Nature's Aristocracy* appended to *Why and How*, Lee and Shepard present Collins's book as published "uniform with" Conwell's and as coming "from the pen of Colonel Russell H. Conwell." Describing him as "so well known as an orator and lecturer" and "the most fascinating word-painter of the day," Lee and Shepard evidently hoped to boost sales of Collins's book by linking it with him (284).

Although Collins was well known as a labor orator and lecturer in her own right, Lee and Shepard's advertisements neglect to mention this. Since she was a working-class woman possessing little formal education, Lee and Shepard evidently considered her achievements less significant than Conwell's. The advertisement indicates little of the quality of Collins's writing, briefly characterizing *Nature's Aristocracy* as "so interesting a volume" and, in terms that suggest the titillation to be derived from Collins's discussion of working women's seductions, "a thrilling book" (284). At the back of *Nature's Aristocracy* (1870), a corresponding advertisement for *Why and How* stresses Conwell's achievements, contending that he "as a lecturer and writer has won a most enviable reputation" (323).

Despite Collins's and Conwell's shared interests in the poor and oppressed, he apparently exercised a heavy hand in editing *Nature's Aristocracy*. While circumstantial evidence strongly suggests that Collins's words were altered by Conwell, direct evidence—such as "authors' working manuscripts and printer's-copy manuscripts," which Joel Myerson contends often exist for canonical American authors—in Collins's case has apparently not been preserved (357). I have not been able to locate any of Collins's manuscripts or personal writings. Since she was a working-class woman with a dubious past as a labor agitator, records of her life and writing were likely considered less important for preservation.[7]

The nature of Conwell's editorial contribution is implied in a review of *Nature's Aristocracy* appearing in the *Revolution*. Disappointed in the book, the anonymous reviewer writes, "Instead of her [Collins's] quaint, crisp, powerful expressions, we have every thing toned down, smoothed, and the corners rubbed off, until with its little stories of good men and women it reads like an old-fashioned Sunday-school book. In truth, it has been not the work of Jennie Collins, but of those she called in to assist her" ("Book Table"). The *Revolution*'s other contents reveal that Collins was well acquainted with its editors, such as Susan B. Anthony and Elizabeth Cady Stanton, who had invited Collins to address the January 1870 convention of the National Woman Suffrage Association, so they may have known more of the details of *Nature's Aristocracy*'s creation.

A comparison of Collins's journalistic contributions with the text of *Nature's Aristocracy* shows that there is some truth to the *Revolution* reviewer's claims. Collins's periodical writings address some of the topics found in *Nature's Aristocracy*. Since these pieces were either unedited or little edited, they may well come closer to representing Collins's own voice. At least they suggest that Collins's unmediated literary voice differed from that of *Nature's Aristocracy*. Writing to the *Commonwealth* in October 1870, Collins sketches factory women's typical experience, a subject similarly treated in chapter 11, part 2 of *Nature's Aristocracy*. The *Commonwealth* piece reads in part as follows:

> She [the factory operative] eats in a crowd; she goes to work in a crowd; she passes the day in another crowd. She has no yesterday; no to-morrow. She looks forward to no time; but the moment the hand of the clock points to 12, she runs down stairs. The same experience is repeated day after day. . . . In the afternoon she carries up her cloth to the desk, thinking how soon she will have money to pay the last of her doctor's bill. Neither her employer nor their hard-hearted agent see the look of despair upon her face as she reads a written notice informing her that her wages, after a certain date, will be "reduced ten per cent." Her first thought is to go elsewhere, but the black flag is raised against her. The slave was pursued by the bloodhounds in the Southern swamps; the "discharge" pursues the operative—more civil, but it amounts to the same thing. On the whole, she makes up her mind to stay where she is. . . . Saturday she has earned for the week $4, working eleven hours per day. When she hears of a death she wishes it was herself. ("Mrs. Child")

Here Collins provocatively argues that factory working conditions are just as much an evil as southern slavery. Mill operatives are not even allowed to express discontent by resigning, since the blacklist holds them in a captivity little different from that imposed on slaves. This passage's most intense and graphic terms—"hard-hearted agent," "black flag," "bloodhounds," "Southern swamp"—do not appear in the corresponding passage of *Nature's Aristocracy* or indeed anywhere in the text. While Collins does liken mill work to slavery at several points in *Nature's Aristocracy* (see pp. 121, 123, 126), these passages lack the intense imagery of the *Commonwealth* piece. Since it appeared in print just prior to the November 1870 release of *Nature's Aristocracy*, Collins may have been trying to publish material that she knew Conwell had expunged from the text.

Likewise, in a letter to the *Revolution* published January 13, 1870, Collins comments on factory life generally and, more specifically, on the 1869 factory women's strike against the Cocheco Manufacturing Company of Dover, New Hampshire, for imposing a wage reduction:

> Before the operative puts on her apron, she is obliged to go to the counting-room and sign a contract, one of the most despotic codes that was ever issued in a free country, called a regulation paper. . . . As the corporations have boarding-houses for their operatives, poverty has driven large numbers of them back to those living tombs. . . . Allowing that stock was low in the market, no reduction was made in the salary of the agent and the supernumeraries (the dry pumps). The *men* [mill management] in the factories produce nothing. If the stock is low in the market why not let the men and women share the consequences equally. . . . Fifteen years ago a similar strike took place in Manchester, N.H. They appointed a committee to wait on the agent. He refused to meet them, but instead, sent the mayor out to read the riot act, but the women were afraid of the bullets from the cotton chivalry, so they went back [to work]. Fifteen years have elapsed, the working women have the platform and tongues to use, and no man now dares to come into an orderly meeting and read the riot act. We working women will wear fig-leaf dresses before we will patronize the Cocheco Company. ("New England Factories")

Comparing these statements to passages in *Nature's Aristocracy*, especially chapter 11 part 7, which addresses the Dover strike, and chapter 11 part 2, reveals that Collins's most vivid *Revolution* terminology ("one of the most despotic codes . . . ever issued in a free country," "living tombs," "dry pumps," "bullets from the cotton chivalry," "fig-leaf dresses," etc.) is missing entirely from *Nature's Aristocracy*. As the *Revolution* reviewer argues, Collins's "quaint, crisp, powerful expressions" do indeed seem to have been "rubbed off" from *Nature's Aristocracy* by Conwell and/or unnamed others who assisted Collins ("Book Table").

Why would Conwell have altered Collins's words? His own writings offer some clues. In his book about Boston's Great Fire of 1872, Conwell praises Collins's humanitarian efforts aiding poor women but adds that she was "sometimes misguided, and at others too enthusiastic" (*History* 186). In the nineteenth century, the word "enthusiastic" connoted something closer to "fanatical" or other such terms describing overly emotional people lacking good judgment.

In another of his books, *Woman and the Law: A Comparison of the Rights of Men and Rights of Women before the Law* (1875), Conwell argues at length against some of the ideas expressed in *Nature's Aristocracy* but without mentioning Collins's name or the title of the work. He contends, for instance, that women's suffrage—one of Collins's most cherished causes—would not cure social evils or even help women. Conwell also reveals his displeasure with some of women's ways of speaking and behaving. In one passage, Conwell's narrator objects to the "folly, bordering on great sin," of women's penchant for "idle gossip" and "reading trashy novels" (60). His exasperated narrator asks, "Is there culture in slang phrases?," implying that women are more prone to using such slipshod language (61). Editing *Nature's Aristocracy*, Conwell was able to "correct," or in some measure compensate for, Collins's injudiciousness and unkempt slang expressions.

Not only was Collins's writing female writing, but it also had its roots in working-class folkways. While Conwell had experienced poverty and at times worked on behalf of poor laboring people, his life experience differed in important ways from Collins's. Whereas she had entered the mills by age fourteen, Conwell had attended Wilbraham Academy, Yale College, and law school in Albany, New York. After working on his family's farm in childhood and in a hotel during his year at Yale, he never again held anything resembling a working-class job (Persons 367). As a teenager, Conwell had traveled to Europe, earning his passage by laboring on a cattle steamer (Bjork 5). While his experience reflects his pluck and intelligence, it also owes much to his privilege as a white male, privilege beyond the reach of a working-class woman such as Collins. Conwell's experience had distanced him from the harsh working conditions that were so familiar to, and vexing for, Collins. His more extensive formal education had taught him the value of considering questions and issues in a calm, disinterested manner and in standard (non-slang) language.

Reports of Collins's speeches given near the time of the publication of *Nature's Aristocracy*, as well as other newspaper pieces written by her, also suggest that Conwell moderated the rhetoric of Collins's book.[8] Having heard Collins speak about working women's problems at the National Woman Suffrage Association Convention in January 1870, the newspaper columnist "Olivia" (Emily Edson Briggs) writes,

> In the obscurest place on the platform sits the genius of the convention, Jennie Collins, the factory girl of New England, with her sad, hungry face. You can only remember the eyes, which look as if there was something fierce and awful behind them ready to spring out and bite.... She painted the hideous lives of the 48,000 factory girls of Massachusetts. Her presence breathed the print of the nails. She made you hear the whir of the machinery.... Miss Collins abused General Grant, abused the Republican party, but the audience was under her spell and did not raise a dissenting voice. A young girl in the audience spoke loud enough to be heard by those around her, "Isn't she a frightful woman?" It was the savage looking out of the New England factory prison. (143, 145)

To some middle-class white Americans, such as Briggs, Collins's views and manner of speaking were perceived as frightening and "savage" (although Briggs does acknowledge the power of Collins's presence and oratory). Another newspaper writer similarly observes that Collins's "first efforts were crude and sharp-edged, with that element of fierceness that is so apt to repel cultured people" ("Boston").

These journalists' views reflect the era's incipient social Darwinism, which considered poor people mental and physical inferiors who deserved their lives of hard labor and confinement.[9] Collins's crudity, savagery, and ferocity thus served as markers of, and grounds for, her inferior social standing. Moreover, Collins's dark coloring may have evoked for Briggs images of Native American "savages." Collins's work may be fruitfully compared with the writings of nineteenth-century Native American women discussed in Cari M. Carpenter's *Seeing Red: Anger, Sentimentality, and American Indians*, "who were met not only with these stereotypes of 'savage' rage but with social proscriptions against female anger" (2). Not only was Collins's anger a dangerous female anger, but it was the even more fearsome rage of the oppressed working classes.

For genteel writers such as Briggs, it is almost as though Collins were speaking a foreign language. And in a sense she was. As a worker and labor reformer, Collins had been steeped in the often fiercely angry traditions of labor reform rhetoric, with which many middle-class Americans would have been unacquainted. Written by a Lowell factory worker and labor activist, Amelia's "Some of the Beauties of Our Factory System—Otherwise, Lowell Slavery," published in Lowell in 1845, resonates interestingly with Collins's *Commonwealth* and *Revolution* pieces quoted above. Amelia writes,

> She [the factory woman] soon finds herself once more within the confines of that close noisy apartment [her mill workroom], and is forthwith installed in her new situation—first, however, premising that she has been sent to the Countingroom, and receives therefrom a Regulation paper, containing the rules by which she must be governed while in their employ; and lo! . . . for in addition to the tyranous [sic] and

oppressive rules which meet her astonished eyes, she finds herself compelled to remain for the space of twelve months ... however strong the wish for dismission; thus, in fact, constituting herself a slave, a very slave to the caprices of him for whom she labors.... they [the mill management] *may* [author's emphasis] deign to bestow upon them [the workers] what is in common parlance termed, a "regular discharge;" thus enabling them to pass from one prison house to another. Concerning this precious document, it is only necessary to say, that it very precisely reminds one of that which the dealers in human flesh at the South are wont to give and receive as the transfer of one piece of property from one owner to another. (5)

Likening factory work to slavery, northern writers such as Amelia and Collins hoped to elicit the support of the many antislavery New Englanders. For Amelia the regulation paper consists of "tyranous [*sic*] and oppressive rules," while for Collins it is "one of the most despotic codes ... ever issued in a free country." Both writers draw from a tradition of fervid labor discourse. David S. Reynolds argues that beginning in the 1840s American labor reformers developed "a fiery rhetoric filled with grotesque imagery aimed at unmasking 'idle' and 'depraved' aristocrats" (81). Amelia and Collins attempt to show that the mills, often touted as beehives of invigorating industry, actually resemble something more like prisons or slave plantations. With this unmasking, writers such as Amelia and Collins hoped, for one, to motivate middle-class citizens to join them in working for reform.

Although Conwell apparently muted some of the intense rhetoric of *Nature's Aristocracy*, the text still retains some strong expressions of anger. Collins's narrator voices indignation at those who oppress the poor, while she humanizes the poor by presenting sympathetic, often sentimental stories of their lives and struggles. Like the nineteenth-century women's texts discussed in Linda M. Grasso's *Artistry of Anger: Black and White Women's Literature in America, 1820–1860*, *Nature's Aristocracy* contributes to "public expressions of anger [that] inform the larger culture that the individual or group are human beings of consequence who are seeking attention, respect, and equal rights and privileges" (12). Collins works to counteract her society's tendency to denigrate laboring people as less intelligent, less virtuous, and thus less deserving of respect and justice.

In *Nature's Aristocracy*, Collins's anger spares neither sex. She holds a special disdain for wealthy mill owners who hide their exploitation of workers behind charitable efforts, such as the founding of rest homes for aged and ill laborers. Her narrator avers, "It is dreadful to think that when a man gives back to his victims, in a provision for 'an institution,' a part of the sum of which he deliberately robbed them, he is to be lauded to the skies as an example of mortal perfection" (143). Collins employs a combination of sarcasm, as seen in this passage and others, and sentimentality in the text's "tales" similar to that found in the nineteenth-century Native authors examined by Carpenter. As Carpenter writes, "Alice Callahan, Pauline Johnson, and Sarah Winnemucca each employ a sentimentality in which sarcasm and irony mark anger" (127). For Collins, the sarcasm of calling some well-to-do men "example[s] of mortal perfection" is a way of pulling them down from a height of false superiority from which they wrongly look down upon laborers.

Collins just as often vents sarcastic anger at privileged women. In chapter 2, "The Beggars," her narrator describes how domestic servants work in the early morning preparing breakfast and sometimes feeding the poor who come around begging, while "the puny house-dolls . . . lay above stairs sleeping in down and damask" (22). Such pampering renders these women not only physically weak but also ignorant of important realities, such as the poverty in their midst. Collins's narrator chides them, "Ah, ye drawing-room beauties and afternoon belles, ye cannot see the phases of life which the kitchen-girl sees" (21). While exposing the "belles'" heartlessness, Collins's irony reverses the social positions of these women, placing the "kitchen-girl" in a place of superiority vis-à-vis the "belle" who ordinarily looks down on her.

These angry passages raise the question of whether such writing would not more readily alienate middle- and upper-class readers than elicit their support for labor causes. This leads to the deeper question of who exactly was Collins's intended audience. Some contemporary reviewers assume that Collins's book was meant primarily for readers like herself. As a *Lowell Daily Citizen and News* writer avers, *Nature's Aristocracy*'s "free, flowing style . . . is calculated to interest the general reader, and especially the large class who claim the honorable title of laborers" ("Jennie Collins's Book"). While the angry passages must have particularly gratified working-class readers, the text's sentimental "tales" seem more targeted to middle- and upper-class readers, who would presumably identify with the characters' sensitivity and refinement. The text lacks a clear sense of its intended audience, possibly a result of Conwell's editorial contribution.

Nature's Aristocracy alternates angry rhetoric with the more covertly persuasive strategies of sentimentality. Mary Louise Kete's work on sentimentality in literature has identified some of its components. Sentimentality's overriding concern, Kete argues, is with "express[ing] the utopian impulse to abolish boundaries and expand community" (545). In her sentimental tales of the suffering poor, Collins strives to reconnect these people to the community that has debased and exploited them. She thus works to heal the "broken bonds" that along with "lost homes, [and] lost families" are Kete's "three signal topics of sentimentality" (545).

Collins employs sentimental diction and rhetoric to evoke sympathy for her subjects. Her narrator compares the poor tailoress Annie Masdon to a flower, drawing from the floral imagery so popular in the nineteenth century. In an extended metaphor, Collins writes that Annie Masdon

> was born a flower; and her sweet disposition, delicate feelings, fine discernment and mental liveliness were a part of her constitutional nature. . . . Like the flowers, she ever looked upward, and from her humble position saw more of heaven than did thousands who could look down upon her. (59)

With such images of beauty and innocence, Collins counters the genteel perception of poor women as coarse and dissolute. In a striking reversal of the expected, she shows that the tailoress's abject social position affords her spiritual advantages compared to those "who could look down upon her." Collins thus challenges readers who have scorned such women to change their views and welcome the world's Annie Masdons into their community.

Collins works especially hard to humanize sentimentally the despairing women assailed by the temptations of prostitution. In the story of the fallen "shop-girl," Wellie Wallace, Collins employs sentimentality's special rhetorical trope, the apostrophe. According to Kete, apostrophe, or "direct address to an abstraction or one to an absent person," is the quintessential feature of sentimental literature, one that "dramatizes the existence of multiple registers of imagined reality" (545). In commenting on her formerly refined coworker's fall into a life of sin, Collins's narrator interrupts the narrative to address Wellie's absent presence numerous times. The narrator interjects near the beginning, "Dear Wellie, how I loved you! ... what a halo of holy light seemed to surround you wherever you went!" (37). Collins thus brings Wellie closer to the reader, who might previously have preferred to maintain distance from such a woman. By unreservedly displaying her love for Wellie, Collins also demonstrates that a working-class woman like herself is capable of refined sentiment.

Collins's sentimental strategies probably owe more to the popular British novelist Charles Dickens than to anyone else. Several periodical writers remark on her admiration for Dickens, her favorite author ("Jennie Collins Dead"). Collins named her charity "Boffin's Bower" after the home of the poor but virtuous Mr. and Mrs. Noddy Boffin in Dickens's *Our Mutual Friend* (1865). An article appearing in the *Woman's Journal* explains that Collins chose the name as "an appreciation of the great novelist and his labors in the behalf of the poor" ("Boffin's Bower"). During a visit to England, according to one journalist, Collins "laid a wreath ... on the bust of Charles Dickens in Westminster Abbey as her tribute to his memory" ("Without Ostentation"). Collins held an annual service at Boffin's Bower to commemorate Dickens's death and to honor his work.

Not only did Dickens write with great sympathy about the poor, but he also engaged in benevolent work on their behalf, such as helping to found and manage the Home for Homeless Women in London. Such efforts must have been inspiring for Collins. She expressed some of her appreciation when she lectured in Boston's Music Hall in September 1870, not long after Dickens's death, "on Charles Dickens as a labor reformer." According to a brief newspaper account, "She [Collins] was certain that Mr. Dickens would have defended the laboring men in the measures which they are taking in this country against their employers. No more striking example of what is occurring today can be found than his description of 'hard times'" ("Jennie Collins's Lecture"). She alludes to Dickens's novel *Hard Times* (1854), which indeed shows great concern for oppressed mill workers. As reported, however, Collins curiously overlooks the novel's unflattering representation of the labor activist, Slackbridge. Despite Collins's experience as a labor leader, *Nature's Aristocracy* frequently assumes, in accord with much of Dickens, that individual acts of Christian charity, rather than social reforms, offer the surest remedy for poverty and other social ills. For instance, she relates in chapter 13 the story of the wealthy Pennsylvania banker who through his personal attention and charity transforms the lives of some poor neighbors. Her admiring narrator exclaims, "What more could man do?" (165).

Collins often viewed her writing and charitable work through the lens of Dickens's fiction, particularly his sentimental characterizations. In *Nature's Aristocracy*'s chapter "The Beggars," Collins's representation of stray children pressed into begging by a corrupt adult owes much to such scenes in Dickens's *Oliver Twist* (1838). She later penned a newspaper article entitled "'Little Nell': An Appeal for Something to Do, Which Should Be Answered" after the heroine, Little Nell, of Dickens's *Old Curiosity Shop* (1841). Dickens's sentimentality is most often associated with characters such as Little Nell, who embody youthful innocence, purity, and love.

In his work on sentimentality in Dickens, Fred Kaplan argues that such characterizations are intended to evoke and strengthen in readers what many Victorians believed were humanity's "innate moral sentiments" (4). Rooted in eighteenth-century moral philosophy, the belief in moral sentiments sprang from a view of human nature's essential goodness. Dickens thus hoped that such protracted sentimental scenes as the death of Little Nell, one of his most famous scenes, "would stir the world's conscience as well as its fears. The suppressed and the exploited would benefit" (Kaplan 50). In "'Little Nell'" Collins presents a case from Boffin's Bower who she believes "is a perfect prototype of 'Little Nell.'" She recounts the experience of an orphaned adolescent girl selflessly struggling to support her four younger siblings. After their landlord evicted the family, Collins wrote this article hoping that a reader would offer "a situation" for the eldest girl. Like Dickens's representation of Little Nell, Collins hoped that her sentimental account of these poor children's undeserved suffering would activate the moral sentiments of her readers, who would offer assistance.

Dickens's sentimental representation of the death of Little Nell influenced the equally well-loved sentimental scene of Little Eva's death in Harriet Beecher Stowe's *Uncle Tom's Cabin, or, Life among the Lowly* (1852). Both novels contributed to Collins's sentimental treatment in *Nature's Aristocracy* of the death of the orphaned cash girl, Viola, who as she expires expresses wishes to receive in heaven a mother, nice clothes, and a doll (54). Collins thus attempts to touch the hearts of female readers who have possessed such advantages and persuade them to extend their sympathies to orphans such as Viola. In her representations of children's suffering, Collins shares in Dickens's view "that fictional presentations of the deaths of children had extraordinary corrective potential. Such deaths appealed powerfully to the moral sentiments . . . because they seem against 'nature' and 'human nature'" (Kaplan 50). In such scenes as Viola's death and her representations of child mill workers, Collins reveals the unnaturalness of society's treatment of poor children and its great need for correction.

Besides advocating individual acts of benevolence, *Nature's Aristocracy* proposes two "remedies" for "some evils . . . resulting from the unnatural condition of society": "*practical co-operation between the laborer and the capitalist, and . . . woman's suffrage*"

(207). On the whole, Collins devotes much less attention to remedies for workers' oppression and related social ills than she gives to representing these problems. Such indefiniteness was common among nineteenth-century reformers. As Timothy Messer-Kruse contends in his study of nineteenth-century labor and other reform movements, *The Yankee International: Marxism and the American Reform Tradition, 1848–1876*, "They [American radicals] approached the problems of labor with a clearer sense of what was wrong with the mushrooming industrial order than of what particular remedies and strategies would work to counter these evils" (43). Collins thus leaves her identification of "remedies" to *Nature's Aristocracy*'s conclusion, where she does not specify how they would work, although she briefly addresses cooperation and woman's suffrage as solutions earlier in the text.

Cooperative or worker-owned factories and stores had been established with varying degrees of success in the United States as early as the 1830s. Workers thereby believed that, according to Steven Leikin, they "could end wage labor and their exploitation by middlemen through economic institutions of their own design" (321). The kinds of large-scale industries in which Collins worked, namely textile and ready-made garment production, were more difficult to make cooperative because they required larger initial investments of capital than laborers possessed.

In chapter 11, Collins seems to have recognized this when she proposes cooperation as a solution. In her brand of cooperation, workers do not own the factories but instead share the profits with the capitalist-owners. This "fair division of the profits" is, she contends, "nothing more than simple justice" (141). This seems to be what Collins means by the "*practical co-operation* between the laborer and the capitalist" proposed at the conclusion of *Nature's Aristocracy*, although she does not specify what was "practical" about it (207). Leikin explains that cooperation was often viewed by nineteenth-century Americans as a pragmatic solution. As he writes, "Cooperation's appeal to working men and women rested in its often perceived practicality" (321). Collins does not explain how capitalists would be persuaded to share their profits with workers, although she seems to assume that her writing of *Nature's Aristocracy* would contribute to moving them by the force of its sentimentality and anger to act upon "simple justice."

Collins devotes her final chapter to a cause she championed throughout her life, women's suffrage. While arguing that the vote was even more important for laboring women than for their more privileged sisters—a view not often heard in suffrage literature, Collins also treats such related subjects as "Woman's Sphere" and an appreciation of Margaret Fuller's life and work. Collins's stance on women's rights was a complex one comprised of what today's feminists would consider progressive and conservative elements. On the one hand, she argues that "women as a class" are not "the mental equals of the men as a class" (195). Yet she maintains that there are exceptional women who possess intelligence or physical strength equal to men's and that these women should not be barred from any position held by men.

The most distinctive feminist contribution of *Nature's Aristocracy* is its emphasis on working women's need for the vote. Collins employs an argument much like that advanced in Sojourner Truth's famous "And Ar'nt *I* a Woman?" speech (1851), which shows that not all women were sheltered in—or confined to—woman's sphere. Collins's narrator contends, "The factory-girl, who enters upon her work when ten or twelve years of age, . . . must work as hard and do her task as well as a man, or, like him, be discharged, without ceremony or apology" (203). While the mill woman is obliged to fend for herself in the public arena, she lacks the means to influence the laws and customs that govern so much of her life. Although she is "treated in every respect like a man" (203), Collins argues that she needs the franchise to obtain some of men's privileges, such as higher wages. *Nature's Aristocracy* thus contributes to our understanding of laboring women's contribution to, and stake in, the women's rights and suffrage movements.

NOTES

1. There is no full-length biography of Collins. The major biographical sources are Collins's obituaries and recent sketches by Hoxie and Buhle.

2. See entries for Jane Collins in U.S. Census Bureau, *Federal Census, 1860*, Massachusetts, Suffolk County, Boston, Ward 8, p. 454; U.S. Census Bureau, *Federal Census, 1870*, Massachusetts, Suffolk County, Boston, Ward 8, p. 77; U.S. Census Bureau, *Federal Census, 1880*, Massachusetts, Suffolk County, Boston, E.D. 710, p. 27. When Collins was young, Amoskeag was part of Goffstown, New Hampshire. Sources examined in the search for Collins's parents' names and her exact birth date include Goffstown NH, Town Clerk, *Town Records, 1749–1843*, unpublished manuscript; Goffstown NH, Town Clerk, "Records of Marriages, Births, and Deaths, 1774–1925," MS; George P. Hadley, *History of the Town of Goffstown*, 2 vols. (Concord: Rumford, 1922–24); Manchester NH, "Town Records, 1806–1868," MS.

3. Although Collins's obituaries assert that she began working at age fourteen, in *Nature's Aristocracy* she writes that "the factory-girl . . . enters upon her work when ten or twelve years of age" (203). From Jennie Collins, *Nature's Aristocracy; or, Battles and Wounds in Time of Peace: A Plea for the Oppressed*. (Subsequent page references from this text will appear in parentheses. The page numbers refer to this volume.) Since Collins was born in the factory village of Amoskeag NH, she might well have begun working there before age fourteen. An entry appearing in James O. Adams, *Directory for the City of Manchester, New Hampshire* (Manchester. Printed at the American Office, 1846), "Collins Jane, S. C. [Stark Corporation] b. [boards] 76, Elm st.," may relate to Jennie Collins (29).

4. For a contemporary announcement of Collins's "deliver[ing] addresses on the Common," see "In Brief," *Boston Daily Advertiser*, July 11, 1870, p. 1.

5. For more about nineteenth-century American workers' literary traditions, see Benita Eisler, ed., *The Lowell Offering: Writings by New England Mill Women (1840–1845)* (New York: Norton, 1997); Philip S. Foner, ed., *American Labor Songs of the Nineteenth Century* (Urbana: University of Illinois Press, 1975); Philip S. Foner, ed., *The Factory Girls: A Collection of Writings on Life and Struggles in the New England Factories of the 1840s by the Factory Girls Themselves* (Urbana: University of Illinois Press, 1977); Judith A. Ranta, *Women and Children of the Mills: An Annotated Guide to Nineteenth-Century American Textile Factory Literature* (Westport CT: Greenwood, 1999).

6. J. R. Pole contends, however, that in the postrevolutionary period, "to Jefferson it was already clear that virtue and talent could lie concealed in ex-

isting social structures" (Jack Richon Pole, *The Pursuit of Equality in American History*, rev. ed. [Berkeley: University of California Press, 1993] 145).

7. Collins's or Conwell's correspondence is not found in Lee and Shepard, *Business Records (1860s–1906)*, American Antiquarian Society (Susan M. Anderson, assistant curator of manuscripts, American Antiquarian Society, e-mail message to author, Feb. 27, 2008), and there are no documents or correspondence concerning Jennie Collins in *Russell Herman Conwell, Papers, 1862–1972*, Temple University Library, Special Collections.

8. See, for instance: "The Crispin Cold Chill," *Boston Daily Advertiser*, June 30, 1870, p. 1; Horace H. Day, "The N.E. Labor-Reform League Convention," *(Boston) Weekly American Workman*, June 12, 1869, pp. 2–4; "Jennie Collins and the Dover Strike," *Revolution*, Dec. 30, 1869, p. 410; "Jennie Collins vs. Parson Fulton," *Boston Herald*, Dec. 20, 1869, p. 2; "Working Women and the Ballot," *Revolution*, Mar. 17, 1870, p. 173.

9. The author thanks Steven F. Kruger for first suggesting this idea.

WORKS CITED

Allen, Margaret Andrews. "Jennie Collins and Her Boffin's Bower." *Charities Review* 2.2 (Dec. 1892): 105–15.

Amelia [possibly Amelia Sargent]. "Some of the Beauties of Our Factory System—Otherwise, Lowell Slavery." *Factory Life as It Is: Factory Tracts Numbers 1 and 2*. 1845. Comp. Helena Wright. Lowell: Lowell, 1982.

Bennett, Betty T. "Feminism and Editing Mary Wollstonecraft Shelley: The Editor And?/Or? the Text." *Palimpsest: Editorial Theory in the Humanities*, ed. George Bornstein and Ralph G. Williams. Ann Arbor: University of Michigan Press, 1993. 67–96.

Bjork, Daniel W. *The Victorian Flight: Russel [sic] Conwell and the Crisis of American Individualism*. Washington: University Press of America, 1979.

"Boffin's Bower." *(Boston) Woman's Journal*, Mar. 25, 1871: 90.

"Book Table." *Revolution*, Jan. 26, 1871: [12].

"Boston." *Chicago Daily Tribune*, Dec. 19, 1875: 10.

Braude, Ann. *Radical Spirits: Spiritualism and Women's Rights in Nineteenth-Century America*. 2nd ed. Bloomington: Indiana University Press, 2001.

Briggs, Emily Edson. *The Olivia Letters: Being Some History of Washington City for Forty Years as Told by the Letters of a Newspaper Correspondent*. New York: Neale, 1906.

Buhle, Mari Jo. "Collins, Jennie." *American National Biography*, ed. John A. Garraty and Mark C. Carnes. New York: Oxford University Press, 1999. 5:251–52.

Carpenter, Cari M. *Seeing Red: Anger, Sentimentality, and American Indians.* Columbus: Ohio State University Press, 2008.

Collins, Jennie. *Annual Report of Boffin's Bower.* Vols. 1–15. Boston: Franklin, 1871–85.

———. "'Little Nell': An Appeal for Something to Do, Which Should Be Answered." *Boston Globe,* Apr. 8, 1879: 2.

———. "Mrs. Child and 'Labor.'" *(Boston) Commonwealth,* Oct. 1, 1870: 2.

———. *Nature's Aristocracy; or, Battles and Wounds in Time of Peace: A Plea for the Oppressed.* Ed. Russell H. Conwell. Boston: Lee and Shepard, 1870.

———. "New England Factories." *Revolution,* Jan. 13, 1870: 19.

———. *Plan for Future Work, in Behalf of the Working Women, June, 1872.* Boston: George L. Keyes, 1872.

"Collins, Jennie." *Appleton's Annual Cyclopedia and Register of Important Events of the Year 1887.* New York: D. Appleton, 1889. 577–78.

Conwell, Russell H. *History of the Great Fire in Boston, November 9 and 10, 1872.* Philadelphia: Quaker City, 1873.

———. *Why and How: Why the Chinese Emigrate, and the Means They Adopt for the Purpose of Reaching America. With Sketches of Travel, Amusing Incidents, Social Customs, &c.* Boston: Lee and Shepard, 1870.

———. *Woman and the Law: A Comparison of the Rights of Men and Rights of Women before the Law.* Boston: Henry L. Shepard, 1875.

———. *Woman and the Law: A Comparison of the Rights of Men and Rights of Women before the Law.* 2nd ed. Philadelphia: Quaker City, 1876.

Davis, Rebecca Harding. *Margret Howth: A Story of To-Day.* 1861. Afterword by Jean Fagan Yellin. New York: Feminist Press, 1990.

"Decease of Jennie Collins." *(Boston) Banner of Light,* July 30, 1887: 4.

Emerson, Ralph Waldo. "Aristocracy." In *The Complete Works of Ralph Waldo Emerson, with a Biographical Introduction and Notes by Edward Waldo Emerson,* centenary ed. Boston: Houghton, Mifflin, 1903–4. 10:29–66.

———. "Nature." In *The Collected Works of Ralph Waldo Emerson,* introduction and notes by Robert E. Spiller, text established by Alfred R. Ferguson. Cambridge: Belknap, 1971. 1:7–45.

Fuller, Margaret. *Woman in the Nineteenth Century: An Authoritative Text, Backgrounds, Criticism.* 1845. Ed. Larry J. Reynolds. New York: Norton, 1998.

Grasso, Linda M. *The Artistry of Anger: Black and White Women's Literature in America, 1820–1860.* Chapel Hill: University of North Carolina Press, 2002.

Greetham, David C. *Textual Scholarship: An Introduction.* New York: Garland, 1994.

Higgins, William C. *Scaling the Eagle's Nest: The Life of Russell H. Conwell of Philadelphia by an Old Army Comrade.* Springfield: James D. Gill, 1889.

Hoxie, Elizabeth F. "Collins, Jennie." *Notable American Women, 1607–1950: A Biographical Dictionary,* ed. Edward T. James. Cambridge: Belknap, 1971. 1:362–63.

"In Memory of Jennie Collins." *Boston Daily Globe,* July 21, 1893: 4.

Jefferson, Thomas. "Autobiography." *The Writings of Thomas Jefferson,* ed. Henry A. Washington. New York: Riker, 1853. 1:1–110.

———. "To John Adams, 28 Oct. 1813." *The Writings of Thomas Jefferson,* ed. Henry A. Washington. New York: Riker, 1854. 6:221–28.

"Jennie Collins Dead." *Boston Daily Globe,* July 21, 1887: 5, evening ed.

"Jennie Collins's Book." *Lowell Daily Citizen and News,* Nov. 23, 1870: 2.

"Jennie Collins's Lecture." *Boston Daily Advertiser,* Sept. 12, 1870: 1.

Kaplan, Fred. *Sacred Tears: Sentimentality in Victorian Literature.* Princeton: Princeton University Press, 1987.

Kete, Mary Louise. "Sentimental Literature." *The Oxford Encyclopedia of American Literature,* ed. Jay Parini. Oxford: Oxford University Press, 2004. 3:545–54.

Kilgour, Raymond L. *Lee and Shepard, Publishers for the People.* Hamden CT: Shoe String, 1965.

"The Labor Question." *(Boston) Banner of Light,* Sept. 18, 1869: 5.

Leikin, Steven. "Cooperation." *Encyclopedia of U.S. Labor and Working-Class History,* ed. Eric Arneson. New York: Routledge, 2007. 1:321–24.

Massachusetts State House, Division of Vital Statistics. Registration of Deaths, Ms. 383, 1887, Boston, p. 272 ("Jennie Collins").

Messer-Kruse, Timothy. *The Yankee International: Marxism and the American Reform Tradition, 1848–1876.* Chapel Hill: University of North Carolina Press, 1998.

Myerson, Joel. "Colonial and Nineteenth-Century American Literature." *Scholarly Editing: A Guide to Research,* ed. D. C. Greetham. New York: MLA, 1995. 351–64.

"Obituary: Jennie Collins." *Boston Morning Journal,* July 22, 1887: 4.

"Obituary: Jennie Collins, the Friend of Working Girls." *Boston Daily Advertiser,* July 22, 1887: 5.

"The Obituary Record. Miss Jennie Collins." *Chicago Daily Tribune,* July 22, 1887: 3.

P., L.C. "Help for the Girls." *Atlanta Constitution,* Jan. 27, 1889: 3.

Parker, Theodore. "A Sermon of Poverty." *Speeches, Addresses, and Occasional Sermons,* comp. Theodore Parker. Boston: Ticknor and Fields, 1861–67. 1:333–63.

———. "A Sermon of the Perishing Classes in Boston." *Speeches, Addresses, and Occasional Sermons*, comp. Theodore Parker. Boston: Ticknor and Fields, 1861–67. 1:185–226.

Persons, Frederick T. "Conwell, Russell Herman." *Dictionary of American Biography*, ed. Allen Johnson and Dumas Malone. New York: Scribner's, 1958. 2:367–68.

"Political: Meeting of Ward Eight Grant Club." *Boston Daily Advertiser*, Oct. 14, 1868: 4.

Ray, Rachel. "The Genius of 'Boffin's Bower.'" *Revolution*, Dec. 29, 1870: 401.

Reynolds, David S. *Beneath the American Renaissance: The Subversive Imagination in the Age of Emerson and Melville*. Cambridge: Harvard University Press, 1988.

"Visitors at the Revolution Office." *Revolution*, Mar. 10, 1870: 155.

"Without Ostentation: The Body of Jennie Collins Is Laid to Rest." *Boston Daily Globe*, July 23, 1887: 1, evening ed.

A Note on the Text

Jennie Collins's text is reproduced from the only edition, which was published in late 1870 by Lee and Shepard of Boston, Massachusetts, and by Lee, Shepard, and Dillingham of New York, New York. The title page is dated 1871, although 1870 is the copyright date, and most published reviews of the book appeared in late 1870 and early 1871. The text as presented here is nearly the same as Collins's, retaining nineteenth-century word spellings and usage. The only changes have been the standardization of capitalization in chapter headings and the correction of a few apparent spelling and punctuation errors. Collins's original notes appear as footnotes within the text of *Nature's Aristocracy*, while the editor's notes follow the conclusion of Collins's text. Abbreviations of state names and other words have been spelled out. The reformatting of the text has caused the inevitable loss of the original text's topical running titles.

NATURE'S ARISTOCRACY

or

Battles and Wounds in Time of Peace

A PLEA FOR THE OPPRESSED

To *Mrs. Jennie Hayden Conwell,*

whose sympathy for the oppressed, kindness to the poor, and lively interest in all that concerns the welfare of woman has been so often shown in words and deeds, the author would affectionately dedicate this volume.

Preface

Duty has often called, and in this book I try to respond. I have attempted but little, and whether that has been accomplished the impartial reader shall determine.

Contents

CHAPTER 1. **Nature's Aristocracy** 11

*Shall I Write?—Unnatural State of Society.—
Needed Reconstruction.—Nature's Aristocracy.
—Her Impartiality.—The Battle of Genius.*

CHAPTER 2. **The Beggars** 16

*Little Lizzie.—Professional Beggars.—Begging as a
Business.—Success in Life.—Marrying a Beggar
for Money.—An Empress in Rags.—Little Applicants for
Food.—"Little Sister's real cold."—The Little Boy's Heroism.*

CHAPTER 3. **One Grade above the Beggars** 24

*Homes of the Poor.—Why They Are Wretched.—Educated
Women in Distress.—The Old Apple-Woman.—The
Soldier's Wife.—Comfort and Plenty in Exchange for
Virtue.—Generosity of a Tailoress.—"Freddie and Mamma
won't cry, will they, Mamma?"—The Sailor's Last Dollar.*

CHAPTER 4. **Crime and Nobility** 36

*Able Criminals.—Fall of Companions.—Wellie's Fate.
—Martha the Actress.—The Able Gambler.—
Loss of Caste.—A Writer in the House of Correction.
—She Is Not Worth Saving.—"The Prisoner's Friend."
—Who Is Responsible for Crime.*

CHAPTER 5. **Newsboys and Bootblacks** *48*

Success in Life.—Their Genius and Education.—Newsboys' "Home."—Dividing the Profits.—You May Borrow, but You Shall Never Pay.

CHAPTER 6. **Shop-Girls** *52*

Who Are Shop-Girls.—Their Condition.—The Little "Cash-Girl."—Female Clerks.—Their Trials.—What Society Owes Them.—The Tailor-Shops.—Acts of Kindness.—Ability of the Shop Hands.

CHAPTER 7. **Journeymen Tailors** *66*

The Troubles of a Tailor.—How Custom Coats Are Made.—Too Much Work, or Too Much Leisure.—Their Pay.—Intellectual Ability.—Oppressive Foremen.—Piece-Makers.—How They Grind the Face of the Poor.

CHAPTER 8. **Servant-Girls** *73*

Why American Girls Prefer the Shops and Factories.—Their Taste and Refinement.—Incidents in Kitchen Life.—The Old Cook.—The Nurse.—The Waiter.—Anecdotes, &c.

CHAPTER 9. **Then and Now of Factory Life** *87*

Spirit of the Age.—Why Servants Are Impudent.—The First Manufacturers.—Treatment of Operatives.—The Factory-Girls.—The Boarding-Houses.—The Golden Age of Factory Life.—The First Factories in New England.—Growth of the System.—Incorporation.—The Factories of England.—The Ten-Hour Bill.—John Bright.—Americans Descending and the English Ascending.—The Operatives Now in American Employ.—History of a Factory Which Prospered with the "Old School" and Failed with the "New."

CHAPTER 10. **How Cotton Is Manufactured —Factory Friendships** *103*

Brotherly Affection.—The Destitute Wife.—The Widow's Trial.—The Country Girl and the Actress.—Drunken Pickard and Bob.

CHAPTER 11. **Among the "Strikers"** 117

*Character of "Strikers."—Homes of Workmen.—
Life of a Factory Girl.—Of Factory Men.—Tailors'
and Telegraph Strikes.—The "Dover Strike."—
Incidents of Factory Life, &c.*

CHAPTER 12. **Charitable Institutions** 142

*What Is Charity?—Wages According to the Profits.—
The Lawrence Calamity.—Charity and Small Wages.
—Cutting Down the Pay of Operatives to Make
Great Donations.—Temporary Relief Not a Permanent
Cure.—"Homes."—Their Uses and Abuses.—How a
"Soldiers' Home" Was Supported.—Incidents, &c.*

CHAPTER 13. **Natural and Unnatural Aristocrats** 162

*Representatives of Nature.—Who Save the Communities.
—Examples of Nobility.—Names of Prominent
American Aristocrats.—The Darker Side of
the Picture.—Anecdotes of Unnatural Aristocracy.
—No Peace with Ill-Gotten Gains.*

CHAPTER 14. **Labor Reform** 183

*Lack of Thought.—How Politicians Lead the People.
—The Lessons of the War.—Organization of a
Labor Reform Party.—No Leaders.—What
the Laborers Demand.—Less Hours.—The Respect
of Thinking Men.—Just Legislation.*

CHAPTER 15. **Woman's Suffrage** 194

*Woman's Rights.—Woman's Sphere.—Using the Talents
Which God Gave Her.—History of the Suffrage Movement
in America.—Margaret Fuller.—Why the Rich Do Not Want
the Ballot.—Who Need It.—Conclusion.*

CHAPTER 1

Nature's Aristocracy

*Shall I Write?—Unnatural State of Society.—
Needed Reconstruction.—Nature's Aristocracy.
—Her Impartiality.—The Battle of Genius.*

1

They are sad tales indeed which I have to tell. Too full of sorrow and suffering, defeats and discouragements, oppression and cruelty to be sought by the gay, and too true to attract the novelist. Yet I must write them. The world shall hear them, though the recollection brings tears and the repetition a shudder. Sad faces! How they crowd upon me now that I open the gate of memory! Lonely wives, oppressed daughters, tearful toilers at needle and loom, broken-hearted victims, and lifeless suicides.

Must I live it over again? Must I look once more into those tearful eyes, and see those outstretched hands? Can I listen to their touching appeals again, even in memory, and feel that I have no bread, no influence, no political power? Yes, God helping me, *I will* write. Yea, I will tread fearlessly back along the thorny path of my short life; and the shades of the hungry, toil-killed, and heart-shattered men and women shall tell their tales to the world in death, as they told them to me in life.[1]

Ah the old Merrimack![2] How he leaps into the foreground, as if the wheels he has turned, the bodies he has floated, and the scraps he has washed away had told him secrets too great to keep! But he must be dumb, or relate his sad history only to the bubble-worn rocks, the sands, and the ocean. For too much is already known.

How often in the spare moments of factory toil I have gazed out at the long windows upon the sombre waves of that river as they rolled unceasingly over the dam, and grew cheerful and gay as they leaped over ledges, and eddied around boulders, and, giggling a moment with the race-way flood, sped on toward the ocean, thoughtless and happy! How many a sigh it wafted away in those long dull days, and how often it reflected faces that longed to make in it their cold bed, eternity only knows. But it flows there now as powerful as ever. Dreamy faces look upon its flood now as they did in the years gone by, and the rattle of shuttle and the crash of gearing still mingle with its wild and hollow roar. I suppose the faces are yet in the windows, though they often change; and that the trembling window-sills support exhausted and agitated operatives as often now as they did years ago. We will peer into them with the reader before we are done, and search for the men and women who, like many in other stations of life, are far below their natural level, living an aimless, useless life, while their inferiors are riding in the parks or dining in their decorated halls. But first we must visit the workshops of the city, the dwellings of the wealthy, the homes of poverty, and the slums of North Street,* that we may point out those persons to whom God has given five talents, and who, by the unnatural condition of society, have been consigned to places where they cannot use even one.[3] Wrecks! mastless and rudderless, swinging around and around in the current of the great maelstrom, and destined to be swallowed up within sight of the land from which they once sailed as well-rigged and well-manned men-of-war, capable of defending the coast and of doing themselves honor.

Strange, strange dispensation! Men that should be kings, in damp, dirty cellars, working at a bench, and women made for queens, now in the dancing-saloon and poorhouse; while the snob, whose brains fit him only for carrying a hod, with women whose natural stations would be at the street-corners sweeping the walks, are found in the beautiful homes of millionnaires and in the responsible offices of government.[4] I would not say that it is always so. For there are

---

North Street: A street in the vilest quarter of Boston.

rich men who are nature's noblemen, and fashionable women of wealth who are well fitted for their station, as there are also workmen that have found their level at the spade, and working-women whose sewing-machines are above their genius. But it is strange that there should be *any* filling positions so far from those to which the God of nature seemed to have assigned them. If you should enter a factory and find the water-wheels in the garret, the heaviest machinery in the seventh story, and the dressing and weave-room in the basement, you would find the machinery and system less out of joint than at present it seems to be in this strange country of ours.[5] The structure of our society is like a building for which the stone were carefully designed and carved, but in the construction of which the masons seized upon whatever block came handiest, without regard to design or fitness, using window-sills for partition walls, capstones for the foundation, and chink-pieces for the corner-stone. What wonder that it cracks under the pressure and jar of labor, frightening its occupants and appalling the spectators! It needs rebuilding! and let us proceed, as the workmen do with the crumbling cathedrals on the Rhine, beginning at the bottom and replacing, piece by piece, the old wall by new until the whole—renewed, though unchanged in general design—with each corner, tie, sill, and cap, shall be one complete and harmonious whole.

2

Nature hates every aristocracy but her own, and she is ever at work trying to restore to the throne her own line of nobles, which the dollar and family pride have deposed. As if to spite the haughty devotees of money, she gives them spendthrifts for sons and daughters, who seldom keep the treasure-chest through the second generation. To the intellectually endowed she often gives idiotic children; to the minister of the gospel, ungodly posterity; and to every anxious father, a son differing, at least in some respect, from the coveted ideal. Great men seldom ever see their own equal in the person of a son. On the other side, the farmer expects an assistant in the field when his child shall be grown, and behold! he soon finds himself the father of a philosopher. The poor mechanic at the anvil dreams of a time when his boy shall stand beside him swinging the hammer as he himself has ever done; but lo! in a few years he finds that Nature has haply deceived him and given him an orator. The humble attendant on belt, shuttle, and loom marks out a factory career for his child, and has no higher ambition than to be the father of an overseer; but when to his wondering eyes he sees the fashioning hand of culture making the bobbin-boy into a man of letters, and sees him the idol of millions, and perhaps a leader in the nation, he is hardly able to convince himself that this prodigy is the same boy for whom he had laid out such an humble plan of life.[6] Nature makes an equal distribution of her favors, and the son of an ignorant or common man is a more acceptable suitor at her feet than is the son of the wealthy and great. There will be but one Napoleon, though his posterity continue in power a hundred years. There will be but one Washington, one Benjamin Franklin, one Florence Nightingale, one Joan of Arc, in their respective family lines. Blood does *not* tell where we will find genius and true greatness; neither will Nature tell us beforehand. For she peers into every habitation, from the lowest hovel to the most princely palace, and, as if she loved practical jokes, she says to her agents, "These parents would have a street-sweep,—give them a general; these would have a carpenter,—give them an inventor; these would have a merchant,—give them a truckman; these would have a prince,—give them a loafer; these would have a king,—give them a hod-carrier." And thus, throughout all the circles and grades of society, she keeps changing the leadership,—raising the lowly, humbling the proud, belittling the great, and dignifying the poor; ever planning to defeat those strenuous human attempts at the establishment of an hereditary aristocracy, and to teach men that in her royal line, and in hers only, are to be found the legitimate noblemen.

Yet, notwithstanding all her attempts and her impartiality, Nature does not always succeed in getting the recognition of her claims to which she is entitled. Mortals do defeat her. Sometimes her chosen men are so inspired by her that they break every bond of custom, prejudice, and pride, and, amid a fearful shower of curses and discouragements, fight their way against the army of human aristocracy until they scale the highest wall of the citadel and stand on its parapets conquerors and kings. Others, regardless of poverty and hardship, buy with their genius a place which money could not purchase, and after years of toil look down from their niche and laugh at the aping aristocrats who are trying to buy wings and attempting to fly on "borrowed pinions" to the seats which the sons of "mechanics" so gracefully fill. But these are the exceptions. In this inconsistent society of ours Genius has a terrible battle to fight, and five chances out of ten he falls fighting on the field, while the usurper treads upon his neck and grinds him in the dust. In every grade of society we find these branches of the royal line defeated and disheartened by the never-ending persecution of the arrogant-wealthy and the conceitedly fortunate. Even beggars and street-sweepers there are, whose graceful forms and intelligent faces indicate nobility. But their courage is not equal to their genius in other respects, the battle has already been lost, and they, with the thousands whom their intellect might have saved, are dejected, ambitionless captives. Of the successful ones it is not my place to write. The world sees them, and the conceited aristocrats envy them. But of the lowly and spirit-broken fugitives, whose just claims for position and influence, and often for a livelihood, have been jostled aside by wickedness and crime, and of whom the world does not so often hear, it is my place, as a lover of justice and humanity, to speak. And it is my purpose to do so considerately, truthfully, and encouragingly, without malice or prejudice, and keeping always to the simple tales of real life which have occurred within the limit of my personal acquaintance.

CHAPTER 2

The Beggars

Little Lizzie.—Professional Beggars.—Begging as a Business.—Success in Life.—Marrying a Beggar for Money.—An Empress in Rags.—Little Applicants for Food.—"Little Sister's real cold." —The Little Boy's Heroism.

1

Poor little Lizzie! How sad she always appeared as she came to the kitchen door and asked for something to eat! I can see her still as I recall her tattered dress, dirty feet, matted hair, fresh red cheeks, and large blue eyes. With all her rags and filth she had the air of a queen,—a queen of moral purity and love. Behind her bright eyes gleamed an intelligence so clear and vivacious that the beholder felt awed, even in the presence of a child.

"What is your name, my little girl?" said I to her one morning.

"Lizzie," said she, in the sweetest, most touching tones that I have ever heard.

"How old are you?"

"Only six years," said she, looking shyly up, as if she wondered what selfish purpose prompted the query.

"Where do you live?"

"In Salem Street," said she, pointing toward it with her pretty little hand. "I am nobody's girl, as my mother was killed by the cars and left nobody to tell who I belonged to.[1] Mrs. McVarney has took me."

"What do you do for Mrs. McVarney?"

"O, I begs."

Poor little thing! so she did beg, not only abroad for money, but at home for food; and although she obtained a considerable quantity of the former, her supply of the latter was limited indeed. I went home with her one day to ascertain why this little queen of natural and intellectual beauty was seen in the street so ragged and dirty, instead of being comfortably cared for and sent regularly to school. I never shall forget that home and the things which I saw there.

It was a tenement-house at the end of a long, dark, filthy alley in the vilest portion of the city, and the rooms occupied by Lizzie's mistress were in the second story, and were reached by a rickety stairway on the outside of the house. There was wretchedness on every side. Bloated faces stared at me from the cellars, chilling curses echoed from the adjoining tenements, base women and baser men quarrelled in the alley, while little half-naked children played in the dirt and laughingly pronounced the most terrible oaths. Lizzie was not with me, because she dare not be the escort of a stranger; but from her description of the locality I easily found the rooms occupied by her mistress. At the door, as I paused a moment to consider the step I was taking and to form an excuse for my visit, I was startled by a series of most piercing shrieks, mingled with curses and the dull "thugs" of heavy blows. The sound proceeded from the room into which the door opened, and without further thought I thrust it open and stepped into the apartment.

In the middle of the wretchedly furnished room stood a thin, bony-framed woman, with flashing black eyes, beating a freckled-faced girl with the broken handle of a wooden ladle. There were five other girls in the room, none of whom were over eight years old, and all looking on with an expression of terror that was most pitiful. When the woman saw me she released the girl, whom she had been holding on tiptoe by her hair, and, turning upon me with the uplifted ladle, demanded who I was and what I wanted. I cannot tell now what passed between us, for I became so excited; I only know that she struck me a blow upon the shoulder, and a policeman came and took her away. But I do remember how the girls clapped their little hands, and with tearful eyes caught hold of my dress, asking, O so pitifully! "Will she come back any more?" And when I asked the poor things what they were all doing there, I received from each little lisping pair of lips the same reply which Lizzie gave me,—"I begs."

They were hungry and nearly naked, their feet were sore and swollen, while their faces and wadded hair were a most disgusting sight.

How pretty they looked, however, and how happy they seemed, when, after a thorough washing and being neatly clothed, they stood together in a row before the police-officer, to testify against their enslaver! Four were orphans, and two were stolen from their parents, and all had been taken and tortured by this vile woman, who made a business of sending out beggars. She taught them fine speeches of a dying mother, and of starvation, and taught them to call on the name of the Lord, and forbade the use of profanity, in order that they might have a pleasing address; and she was successful. These little creatures heeded her lessons so well that they often brought home five dollars in a single day besides boarding themselves on the food they received. If they obtained nothing they were made to go to their bed—which was simply a blanket on the bare floor—without a mouthful to eat. Great was the indignation of the officers and other officials to whom the story came, and a heavy fine with a term in the jail was her sentence. She paid the fine by an order on the bank, which contained seven thousand dollars of her deposits, and after her term had expired she went into the old business again. All her love and pity had been crushed out of her in her younger days by the cruelties of a loved libertine, and no word of kindness or of counsel could find lodging in her broken heart. Once she was an angel of beauty; now an incarnate devil, fit only for cruelty and remorseless oppression. But to her history I may again refer; and I will pass on, by saying that one of the girls is now a teacher in a public school, while, through the opportunities given by benevolent men and women, all the others have become noble women and lights in their social circles.

2

Often have I been surprised at the business tact which I have seen displayed among beggars, and I feel assured that the same economy and shrewdness displayed in a higher scale of business would entitle them to the respect of the mercantile community. Few persons, old or young, ever adopt begging as a business without first being driven into it by starvation or suffering. Yet thousands, after they have once broken their pride and gained the courage, continue in it and lay away money. Some have been known to own fine blocks of stone buildings, and still sit by the street-corners begging. One of the beggars now seen in Boston, and whose face and extended hand are as familiar as the State House, has become so wealthy that a woman last year married him, saying privately to her friends that she "did not love the cripple, but could spend some of his money." One old man who was blind, and who carried about on his breast the placard "I'm blind," died a few months ago with fourteen thousand dollars in bank-stocks hid away in his old waistcoat. He had not only begged, but *speculated*; and in so doing showed a better fitness for a place in State or Wall Street than is exhibited by many who are there.[2] One old sailor, who was forced to beg for food after having been robbed in North Street, conceived the idea of collecting the scraps that were so freely offered him and of selling them to the keepers of swine. He undertook it in company with a boy whom he hired, and began to have such an income that he purchased share after share in a ship. Soon he became sole owner, and could sail as master of his own vessel. One of the wealthiest retail merchants on Broadway was once a beggar, living on kitchen refuse and sleeping on the wharves.[3] Accidentally he found a ten-dollar gold-piece on the pavement, and, investing it in confectionery for a little stand on the street-corner, he started in the mercantile career which has given to himself a princely fortune and to the world a generous supporter of all that is good.

3

I remember a poor beggar-woman, who came to the kitchen door one cold day in the winter of 1858, through whose tattered garments the frosty wind came at will, and in whose features there was such an indication of past refinement that I stared at her with unfeigned surprise. It seemed as if I had seen her before; and her ways were so much like the manners in higher grades of society that I felt as if it was a burlesque or a practical joke made to surprise me or some of my friends. But she shivered in the chilling wind, the frost gathered in her hair, her partially bare feet grew purple with cold, as she asked for a piece of bread to eat. Had she commanded me to order a carriage and take her to a home on Beacon Street, I should have been less surprised than I was to hear her ask for food.[4] Her high forehead and large eyes, prominent nose and close-fitting lips, round chin and broad shoulders, seemed to have been made for an empress; and she carried herself with such unassumed dignity, as she walked into the kitchen in response to my deferential invitation, that I felt convinced that she had been one. And there before the fire and in the soul-cheering warmth of the faces that gathered around, she told her simple story. She was the daughter of a wealthy landholder in Ireland, and was educated in the most polished schools of that island. But she fell in love with a young farmer, and, as her parents opposed the marriage, eloped with him to America. Here they managed to eke out an existence for three years, during which time she had two children. Then came poverty and suffering. Her husband tried to get a place to work in New York, and afterwards in Boston, without avail. The place for Irishmen, *everybody* said, was on the railroad. This work he could not do, on account of his health. Closer grew their poverty and greater became their wants, until at last in his misery, disgusted with wife and children, the husband would accept jobs of work for what liquor he could drink, and, coming home intoxicated, abused them in a most terrible way. Then she tried for work. She could teach, she could sew, she could copy or draft; but nowhere would they take an unrecommended stranger. So in her distress she had become a beggar. When I inquired why she went in such rags when a few stitches would make them more comfortable, she rose to her feet and, taking hold of the ragged skirt, exclaimed, "When I began to beg, this dress was whole. It was the only one I had, and I valued it highly. But I found that the world was a great stage, upon which each character must appear in a proper dress.[5] I was a beggar! and while my dress was whole, my face washed, and my hair combed, no one would give me a farthing.[6] So I tore this dress, disarranged my hair, and rent my shoes that men might believe my story. For appearance or comfort are nothing to me compared with the lives of my dear children. Could I only see those poor things, that are shivering now, with no fire; hungry, and have no food; crying for 'mother,' and she comes not,—ay, could I see them in some safe place of refuge, where no voice should ever say that their mother was a beggar, O how welcome death would be! The snow-bank would be as soft a pillow, or the ocean as warm a bed, as this poor bleeding heart could wish."

I gave her a shawl to cover her bare shoulders, but she put it under her skirt, saying: "Mary or *he* will like it, or I may pawn it; but every comfort which I accept for myself is a curse to me now. I am happiest when freezing, for then I get food for my dear children." So saying, she trod bravely away from the fire, and, like a hero about to charge a fortress, she swept over the threshold into the cold drifting snow. And when I returned from the chilly door-way to the fire, after having watched her fluttering garments as they disappeared around the next corner, I said to myself, "*Many real queens are without a throne, and some are beggars!*"

4

Ah, ye drawing-room beauties and afternoon belles, ye cannot see the phases of life which the kitchen-girl sees, nor learn the value of purity and virtue by a comparison with vice and shame. If you would but go to the kitchen door in the cold winter mornings when that hesitating, gentle rap comes upon the panel, or that timid pull at the bell, and would look into the little pleading faces as they tremblingly ask for food, you would find a field of useful work of more interest than the latest fashion, and of more importance than last night's ball. Many of these beggars, it is true, are impostors, and others are "runners" for men or women who make a business of collecting these contributions. But now and then there comes a face so beautiful, so innocent, so full of anguish, and so like an angel in rags, that you feel like asking her to stay forever. Little boys I have seen at the door whose faces fairly shone with the divine fervor of genius, and whose very walk was indicative of embryo greatness, but upon whose dress and tones the mark of poverty was too apparent to be doubted. Bright little cherubs they were indeed! So much sweeter, nobler, braver, than the puny house-dolls which lay above stairs sleeping in down and damask. Often as I have turned away from listening to the patter of retreating footsteps I have said to myself, "How proud the master and mistress of this house would be if they only had such a son!" Nothing strange would it be if some one of those little beggar-boys should at some time be the successor, if not the heir, of the owner of the mansion, while the legitimate heir, according to the human view, goes as far into poverty as the parents have into wealth and extravagance.

5

I recall two little children who came to the door when a cold rain-storm beat against the windows and covered the trees with glistening sleet. Their little eyes were filled with tears, their fingers numb, and their clothing drenched. Sweet little voices told the maid that they with their mother were turned out of doors, and they had come for a piece of bread. Neither were more than four years old, and it seemed hardly possible that so juvenile a pair could find their way through the back alleys.

"Are you not cold?" said the maid, as she gave them a piece of bread.

"No, ma'am," said the little boy, trying to push his benumbed hands into his trousers pockets, "I'm not cold any; but little sister is *real cold.*"

"Will you come in and warm you by the oven?" asked the maid, at the same time making as if she would lead them in.

"No mind me, ma'am, but please warm little sister," said the brave little fellow, holding his head erect, and looking defiantly up at the storm. "Mother and I don't mind the cold, but little sister here is small."

And the brave little fellow remained on the doorstep like a hero, shivering and aching, having tucked away the piece of bread; and not a murmur escaped his lips while his little sister warmed herself and partook of a hearty meal. He showed no impatience when she came out, but, taking her warm hand, would have trudged away with her, had not the maid, who was "trying" him, called him back and made him understand that it would not be intruding to warm himself at the great oven. Here we learned that his mother was the widow of a mechanic, who, having died a short time before, had left them destitute; and what added tenfold to the hungry little fellow's heroism was the fact, as he reluctantly admitted, that he had tucked away the little piece of bread because he was "'fraid mama had nuthin' t' eat." Wonderful generosity! Providing for his mother and sister, and braving the storm cheerfully, while he himself was hungry and almost freezing! Was not he one of nature's little noblemen? and will he not, if he wins the hard battle against caste and custom, become the "head of the corner"?[7]

CHAPTER 3

One Grade above the Beggars

*Homes of the Poor.—Why They Are Wretched.—
Educated Women in Distress.—The Old Apple-
Woman.—The Soldier's Wife.—Comfort and Plenty
in Exchange for Virtue.—Generosity of a Tailoress.
—"Freddie and Mamma won't cry, will they,
Mamma?"—The Sailor's Last Dollar.*

1

Do you call them dens? You are right; they *are* dens. For most assuredly they are not *homes*, although they may be human dwellings. Ah! how you revolt at the idea of entering those musty attics and those damp and vermin-filled cellars! But the lowest stage of human wretchedness will not be seen without such a sacrifice; so march boldly into the dark passages, the narrow alleys, and the dangerous stairways, resting assured that God has called you to a noble work, and will not leave you without protection. "The poor ye have always with you," said the blessed Redeemer, and it does seem as if we had many more now than ever before, while the necessity for such wretchedness has long since passed.[1] Thousands to-day are eating, sleeping, and working in the bare garrets of old rickety buildings, or gradually drawing in with each painful breath a deadly potion of consumption or rheumatism from the dark cellars of the dirtiest, narrowest, and gloomiest streets of our great cities. Many of them have a bundle of straw for a bed, old clothes for quilts, and nothing for fire. Do you say that the locality seems an appropriate place for such wrecks of humanity? Then let me inquire if they made the locality, or did the locality make them? Is their coarseness a natural necessity? or have their associations and circumstances made them coarse? Is their lack of love and respect a natural defect? or have want and suffering calloused their hearts to every kind emotion? Are they dishonest? Who would not be dishonest when with truth came certain starvation? I tell you to go and see them, and form an opinion of your own. Ask them who robbed or swindled them out of an honest livelihood. Ask them what drunkard consigned them to such prisons. Ask them who broke their loving hearts, and abandoned them to the mercies of the unfeeling world; and fail not to inquire what landlord oppresses them now, or what employer cheats them out of rightful wages. The story will chill your warmest pulse, and tingle down the minutest nerve; and if they relate to you the stories of injustice, crime, and misfortune which they have poured into my reluctant ears, while noting the intellect and ability which lay hid in rags, you will be ready to exclaim with me, "O for the day when God's will shall 'be done on earth as it is in heaven'!"[2] I shall not venture to say that all the poor are such from injustice or from any uncommon misfortune; for some few do appear to have been *born to be poor*, and would be unhappy with plenty of food, clothing, or a pleasant home. "Constitutionally lazy" some of them really are, and to attempt to ameliorate their condition would be to offend their sense of right. But the thousands of natural aristocrats whose station in society is far above these dirty mendicants, and whose niche has never been filled and never can be occupied by another,—they are the subjects of honest, honorable pity. Educated women are to-day in the garrets, working night and day for the food that scarce sustains life, who are well fitted for teachers in our academic institutions.

2

I recall an instance where a woman was found in a lonely garret at the North End of Boston, who at the time she was discovered was working in a cold room with bleeding fingers, patching clothes, and who, when questioned by the Captain of Police who found her, showed a ready knowledge of geometry, Latin, French, and German. She had rather die than beg; and, failing to get a situation in the city before starvation came upon her, she took old clothes to mend, and at no time could she earn enough ahead to pay for a calico dress in which to make renewed attempts at the betterment of her condition.

3

I remember an old apple-woman who used to be well known in the tailor-shops of Washington Street in Boston, and whose face became so familiar to the needle and machine girls that she was looked upon as a friend. Seldom did she come into the shop without finding many purchasers for her fruit and confectionery, and she always had thanks for all who thus favored her. No one knew her history, except that she was a lone widow, for she never spoke of her domestic affairs. The day came when she was missed from the shops, and the absence of her genial face and kind smile cast a gloom over many a poor sewing-girl who had become attached to her. At last, after an interval of several weeks, I met her on Boston Common with her old basket, slowly tottering toward the shops. I stopped her and inquired why she had been absent, although a glance at her pale and wrinkled face and sunken cheeks rendered the question unnecessary. She said that she had been sick, and was out that day for the first time in three weeks. I then asked her who had taken care of her all this time. She stared at me an instant as if she would avoid an answer, and then, dropping her eyes, gave way to tears, and sobbed out a hysterical "nobody." And I found it to be a true statement of the case. She had been three long weeks sick, in a little attic room, with no care, and with no food except the little unpalatable biscuit which the baker's boy brought up for six cents a day as he had done when she was well. During the latter part of her illness she received fifty cents from the wife of a prominent clergyman, and a promise of fifty cents per week thereafter. She, however, owed for the rent of her attic the sum of two dollars, and had been notified to pay the next day or give it up. She was in deep distress, and asked for work. She said that she could not beg, and must earn whatever she received. I promised her a piece of work, for which I paid in advance that she might pay her rent, and then took her to a lady whose benevolence had been heralded far and wide. Here I told her story and asked assistance. But the old lady refused to take a gift, as she was not a beggar, but an applicant for work. This offended the lady, and we were sent away without assistance merely because the old lady wished to live one grade above the beggar. Not only this, but the offended one sent a note to the clergyman's wife, and caused her to withdraw the promised fifty cents a week, leaving the poor old lady utterly destitute. Then it was, when she was abandoned by all, and left to face starvation alone, that she rose above her station and showed the natural majesty of her soul. She seized her basket, and, smiling cheerfully, pointed upward with a significant gesture, and trudged away with the air of one who, though in darkness, sees light ahead and is determined to wait not by the way. It was not many times that the landlord called for rent, and but a short time to look back upon, before the old lady found a home in that free mansion prepared for such as her before the foundation of the world.[3]

4

It was said by the members of the Twenty-Fifth Massachusetts Regiment, in the fall of 1863, that Richard Rheim had deserted to the enemy. The circumstances connected with his disappearance were such that the captain of his company deemed it safe to report him on the pay-roll as "a deserter." O, how little did the captain know of the heroism displayed by Richard when he was captured by the enemy, or of the tortures he was enduring in a Georgia prison at the time the report was made! For verily he was a hero. Eighteen months of prison life, however, reduced him to a mere skeleton, and although he recovered sufficiently to be able to walk about, he never was strong enough to work at his trade again. For a short time after his return from the war he felt quite encouraged, and, believing that he would soon be strong again, he began a job of light work, and married one of the brightest graduates of the Boston public schools. But years passed, and his health gradually failed, until in 1869 his general debility turned into consumption. Then, without money or wages, the poor fellow was obliged to see his little wife work night and day with her needle to support him and the two little children. Both were well educated, refined, and noble; and such a lot must have been hard indeed. For a while this brave little heroine supported the family well; paying the rent, buying the food and fuel, as well as caring with wonderful neatness and skill for all her household duties. She had a way of turning, patching, and mending which made old garments look as fresh and wear as well as new, and the little girl and the baby were thought by visitors to be the prettiest children in the neighborhood. Soon, however, the doctor's bills, the delicacies, and extra fire for her invalid husband made a greater demand on her purse than it could supply, and she began, in spite of the closest economy and the greatest frugality, to fall behind. Soon her rent was overdue, and the landlord became insolent; the grocer was not paid, and he refused to supply her with more bread; and at last, when she had not taken food for two days and her children were crying for something to eat, she determined to go into the marts of trade and ask for assistance. Her husband was confined to his bed, the doctor would not come, and they must move or pay their rent at once. She had never begged, and did not know what to say or to whom to apply. But she knew that the richest men of Boston assembled on State Street, and to that place she went with a heart full of hope. She did not see how men with plenty of money could refuse her truthful and heartfelt appeal, or turn a deaf ear to her touching story.

But they did. From one broker's office to another, from bank to warehouse, and to all classes of men this woman applied for aid. Not one cent did she get; while many cursed her and thrust her rudely aside. At last she determined to make one more effort, and, going into a broker's office, tremblingly told her story. Imagine, if you can, her consternation when coldly informed that she was not *very* poor as long as she had her virtue to sell, and he—the wretch!—would give her a fifty-dollar bill for that.

She fled from him as from a viper, and dared not look back until she had turned the corner; and then the broken-hearted little woman sat down in a door-way and wept the bitter tears of despair. Then it was—as if the cup of her sorrow was not yet full—that another man spoke kindly to her, and, after drying her tears with comforting assurances, made another vile proposition, and offered her in exchange for her purity money without stint. O the vile monster! How *can* there be a God of justice when such hellish fiends are permitted to prosper! The little sufferer was too stricken to be indignant at the second blow, and exclaiming "I cannot! I cannot!" tried to break away from him. He was attracting the attention of passers-by, so he permitted her to go; but not before he told her where she could find him if she should conclude to accept his offer. O, who can tell the torture of mind which the conflict of the most powerful of human emotions inflicted upon her! Her home was cold and cheerless when she arrived; there was no wood for a fire, no medicine for the dying one, no food for the pleading children. What a temptation it was to accept the wicked offer of the libertine! But she held out until the sight of her watch and chain reminded her of a pawn-shop, and at an early hour on the following day she paid her rent by pledging the valued gift of a deceased mother. Then with her clothing, furniture, and little jewelry which she pawned she gained a respite of another month. But the time came when she had lost irretrievably all she had pawned, and had nothing left to pledge except the blankets of her husband's bed. Could she take them? No. She had thus far studiously kept the invalid ignorant of their poverty, and often tried to excuse the "neglect" of which he sometimes complained by saying that she "must go away sometimes to get work." Could she pawn the blanket? Should she take that comfort from him, and bear the blame which his ignorance of the true state of affairs would make him ascribe to her; or should she sell herself to the cursed tempter? Hard question for a poor hungry woman to decide; but she finally took the blanket. O ye that have not known poverty, and over whose heads is a comfortable home, think how that hungry and shivering woman must have felt when at midnight of an unexpectedly frosty night, as she was crouching in the corner over her children to keep them warm, she heard her husband feebly calling from the other room, *"Mary! Mary! I am cold! Please bring me another blanket."*

She tried to shape an excuse, but she could think of none. Her tongue could not tell *him* a deliberate falsehood, and after trying to strip her own dress off to place on his bed, she broke completely down; and in a burst of anguish told him the whole painful story. Ah! how he must have chafed at the insult offered to his wife, and how his manly heart swelled as the truth broke upon him! That night of heroic misery should have been enough to blast forever the prosperity of every banker that refused her assistance. He thought of the State aid for soldiers, and the next day she applied for it. But he was entered on the rolls as a deserter, and, although there was sufficient proof of his capture, she must wait for the rolls to be corrected at Washington. Another fortnight crept along, during which time this wife worked until midnight upon the pants she made, and began again every morning at four o'clock. The appearance of a light so late and so early attracted the attention of the neighbors, and the story of her poverty began to gain circulation. Then a soldier of the State Surgeon-General's staff heard the tale and extended a generous hand to the family; providing for their necessities, and promising the stricken husband, who shortly after died in his arms, that the heroic wife should have a protector.

This in the city of Boston, where genius, patience, and merit are supposed to be always rewarded!

5

A few years ago a poor tailoress, whose earnings would scarcely support her when used in the closest manner, had so large a heart and such executive ability that she conceived the idea of organizing a "sewing-society" among her poorer acquaintances, and, by giving to each person the part of the work for which she was the best fitted, making the aggregate earnings larger than they would be if the party worked independently of each other. Among other women whom she assisted in this way was an old lady eighty years of age, who was addicted to drink, but who, when in a sober state, was as sociable and nimble as many women at forty. The influence of the tailoress upon the old lady was such that the latter wholly reformed, and became a pleasant and agreeable companion. Soon, however, her eyesight failed, and she could not work with the others. The tailoress then, to whom the old lady was no relation, and only a short time even an acquaintance, undertook to work more hours, and more steadily during hours, in order that she might support this old blind woman. It did not occur to her that it was possible to get assistance from the city authorities, and for a whole year she labored on in her work of love, caring for and nursing the aged invalid as if she were the tailoress's own mother. One day the old lady told "a secret," and said that she had a son, a rich banker in Boston; and the tailoress proceeded immediately to find him. She succeeded after a whole day's search, and found him in one of the largest banking-houses in the city, and learned that he was worth over three hundred thousand dollars. To her petition for an interview he sent the impudent reply that he did not receive *shop-girls* in his counting-room. But she persisted in her request, and, after a direct refusal, marched into his private office, and there, face to face, told him of his aged mother. The merchant cursed the old lady and all her associates, refused to pay anything toward her support, and, acknowledging the woman to be his mother, rudely thrust the tailoress out of the door. For years thereafter that poor tailoress divided her little wages with the old lady, and was at last the only mourner at the disowned mother's secluded grave. The tailoress has since died, and another of the noble poor added to the roll that has been called in a never-ending eternity.

6

A gentleman was passing the magnificently decorated windows of a city toy-shop, when his attention was called to a lady who was dressed in mourning, and who led a little boy about five years old. He was evidently his mother's only son, and, as her husband was deceased, her only love. The little boy saw a plaster-cast in the window representing two little kittens, giggling and grinning together in a most comical way; and, as it was near Christmas, he wished his mother to purchase it for him. But the lady turned aside with a sigh, and, wiping away a tear, said, "Not now, Freddie; *we are poor*." The little boy appeared disappointed for a moment and glanced wistfully back at the window, while his mother tried to call his attention to the passing teams. But when he happened to look up, and noticed that his mother was crying, he suddenly assumed a most cheerful look, and, seizing his mother's hand, danced about her, calling out in a conciliatory way, "We are *poor*, ain't we, mamma? O yes, we *are* poor. But *we* don't mind it, do we, mamma? Freddie *don't want* no kittens nor presents, *does* he, mamma? No, Freddie *won't* have a Christmas present, 'cause he don't *want* any, for he and mamma are *poor*! *We won't cry over it; will we, mamma?*"

There was nobility in that little body, even though his father was an oysterman.

7

Two sailors, who had been together for years, and upon whose heads had descended many a storm, came on shore at the port of Boston for the first time in three years. One was a liberal, open-hearted spendthrift; while the other, having some pet purpose, placed what money he could in the savings-bank. In an hour of temptation the spendthrift stole his companion's bank-book, and, forging the signature, drew out the money. It was only three hundred dollars, but to those toil-worn sailors it looked like a very large sum indeed. I saw the culprit in the police-court docks, and I believe that when he said "I'm sorry," he said it out of regard for his old friend rather than in fear of the law.

It was forgery, and the case was postponed until the next term of the Superior Court. After the prisoner was taken to the jail, his companion obtained permission to visit him, and, going to the cell door, spoke nearly as follows: "Tom, I did not suppose that they would shut you up like this, as I only wanted my money, which wouldn't do you any good. If I could get you out, I would do it now, for old love's sake, Tom. But I cannot; so don't feel bad, you'll get out some time. Here is my last dollar until the Judge pays back that which you had, and I don't know where I can get any more, but what I do get I will divide with you. You are a prisoner and I am free, so I'll take care of you. Don't be sad, Tom. I won't leave you. I'll cruise about and heave-to in front of this cell every day to see if you are in distress. Don't mind your quarters, Tom, *but think of good old times when you and I were afore the mast.*"

How many instances of noble generosity, as well as of refinement and ability, I might relate to prove that nature is not impartial, I cannot now say. The very thought brings to mind so many cases that I am almost ready to declare that man has, by some strange interposition, reversed the true order and thrown aside the fittest material for the construction of human society. Only one grade above the beggars are found industrious, ingenious, economical, stout, and generous-hearted men and women, whose proper mission would seem to be that of elevating and ennobling the race, instead of the life of nonentity which, as far as human progress is concerned, they now lead.

8

One warm day in the summer of 1869 I was called upon by a lady who stated that she needed assistance, and wished me to recommend her to some of the charitable institutions of the State or city. She was rather small in stature, having dark hair, blue eyes, with a girlish face, indicative of a loving and trusting disposition. Her sweet, musical voice was sufficient proof that no false words could be coined from it, and her sunken cheeks and worn dress "were confirmations strong as Holy Writ."[4] She was evidently in the deepest distress, and I listened with great eagerness to the story which she had to tell. She was a soldier's widow; or, rather, she thought she was,—for in 1865 she received a locket and chain with her little girl's ambrotype and a partially destroyed letter, said to have belonged to her husband, and found by a comrade on the person of a rebel.[5] Whether her husband was dead or not she could never positively ascertain, although she entertained no doubt of it, and these keepsakes sent her by a member of his company were of the greatest value to her. Since the war she had been at work upon white skirts, for which she received sixty-two cents a day, and, being fortunately possessed of a sewing-machine, she was able to do the work and attend to her other duties.

But her little girl was taken sick, and she could not then work all the time, neither could she keep her expenses within her income. She tried to live upon old crusts of bread and cold Indian pudding, but her child grew worse upon it, while she became so weakened that she was almost insane.[6] At the time when she applied to me she wore her only dress, and she was so nearly famished that her mind wandered, and her memory seemed to fail her altogether. But when the generous hand of General Dale, the Surgeon-General of the State of Massachusetts, had opened, as it had so generously to hundreds of others, and together with the great assistance given by the Superintendent of the Boston Soldiers' Messenger Corps, had placed her and her child beyond the reach of starvation, and redeemed from the pawnbroker's the locket and other gifts which she valued highly, her failing mental faculties came back in full vigor, while the child, having proper food, soon became robust and healthy.

One day, while conversing with her about her husband, I suggested the idea that he might have returned and never have taken the pains to find her, or that he might have abandoned her to live with another woman. I shall never forget her look of pain as she held up her hands protestingly, and exclaimed, "O don't, don't say that!" But an investigation which was soon after instituted in her behalf proved that my supposition was the true state of the case, and that, instead of being killed or captured, the wretch had come home to Vermont with his regiment, and had gone off with another woman. It was hard to break the news to her when the truth was known, and she withered under it like a leaf. O, it was sufficiently heart-rending to think of him as dead and buried in an unknown grave; but that was a pleasure to the pangs which this devoted heart felt when told that he lived and had deserted her! What bitter tears she wept!

It was then, when her sorrow culminated in the darkest despair, that the nobility of her character, which had shone so brightly through all her trials, gleamed still brighter than ever before. Without saying a word to the parties concerned, she went and pawned again the piece of jewelry and her clothes, and, managing, by reducing herself to entire destitution, to get the amount of money which she had received from General Dale and Captain Balcom, she went to return it, saying, "I cannot keep the money you gave me; for, instead of being a soldier's widow, *I am a deserted wife.*" They told her that she must keep that which she had, and promised to give her larger amounts, saying that she needed it all the more if she was deserted. Reluctantly she accepted the money "for her child's sake," and she now comes often to thank her benefactors, and tell them about her child, in language which establishes her unsued claim to natural superiority.

CHAPTER 4

Crime and Nobility

Able Criminals.—Fall of Companions.—Wellie's Fate.—Martha the Actress.—The Able Gambler.—Loss of Caste.—A Writer in the House of Correction.—She Is Not Worth Saving.—"The Prisoner's Friend."—Who Is Responsible for Crime.

1

It does seem to me that there are times when, notwithstanding the scripture, it is eminently wise to "thank God that we are not as other men";[1] and when the wisdom of that celebrated divine who never saw a thief, drunkard, or murderer without saying to himself, "It *might* have been me," is fully confirmed.[2] The thieves, robbers, swindlers, libertines, and murderers are usually taken from the most intelligent part of the community, as far as natural talent is concerned; and the causes which served to make them what they are have come from a faulty education, or the circumstances arising from an unnatural state of society. Lives of prisoners and public statistics prove the ability and intellectual power of this class of human beings; while examples are not wanting in the history of any day to prove the generosity, the honor, and the ingenuity of many men and women whom the law justly calls criminals. It is not my purpose to discuss in this chapter all the reasons why such talent is prostituted to such base purposes, nor to suggest the remedy. For the *facts* I relate seem to point out their own remedy in a clearer and more forcible manner than any writer, however gifted, could do.

I would remark, however, that, as society is responsible for crime, each individual is also responsible as far as he aids, or stands by without opposing, the institutions and laws which contribute toward these evils; and that, if there is any reckoning for the deeds done here in the body, the wickedness of sinning by masses will be as severely punished as that of sinning separately and alone.

2

It is a delicate as well as painful subject which I am here obliged to introduce in justice to the readers of this book, and I touch upon it with hesitation and fear. Its nature, as well as its enormity, cautions us to speak of it in whispers, and to hide our faces as we hint at the evils which we dare not describe.

Tears will flow, and my heart will wildly throb, when I think of some of the dear, dear friends whom I once knew and loved, whose lives were so full of sorrow, and ended in so much shame. Bosom companions, who once confided to me all their little plans, all their griefs and hopes, all their purposes and desires, and whose walks were so upright and thoughts so pure, have appeared again to me in after years haggard and wrinkled, liveried in vice and crime, and filled with everything that was disgusting and bad. O, what a wreck woman can be if perchance she fall!

3

One sweet face comes back to me now, and seems to cheer me on in my chosen work, although it is years since that sunny countenance disappeared from my companionship. Dear Wellie, how I loved you! How your bright eyes won me when first I saw you, and what a halo of holy light seemed to surround you wherever you went! How well I remember your kindness, your charity, your cheerfulness and industry! We were "shop-girls" then, Wellie, and yet we were as happy as the proudest queens. We thought that it would always last, and that you and I would always love each other and be ever boon companions.

They told me that it was you, Wellie, whom I saw yesterday so coarse and ungainly; but I do not believe them. It may be that it was your body, but it cannot have been your *soul*. You used to walk nimbly and uprightly, but that creature was clumsy and stooping. Your face was as bright as the sunlight; that woman, whom they now call by your name, wore a countenance dark as night. I remember your clear musical tones, and the purity and innocence of every word and thought. Yesterday that woman (O, it could not have been you!) was coarse, hoarse, vulgar, and even profane. O Wellie, my nearest, dearest friend, how can I tell them your story! Yet I must tell them, for it may serve to prevent the transformation of some other woman's friend; and, besides, you will not mind it, I know, for the curses you gave me when I entreated you to return to the ways of virtue are strong evidence that you are beyond the reach of human counsel, and that there is no modesty or sense of shame remaining.

Wellie Wallace was once an ornament to society, and her character was noble, high-minded, generous, and pure. Her life was as full of hope as that of the fairest maid that breathes. But to her heroism (strange as it may seem) is due the great change in her moral, mental, and physical condition. She loved a navy officer, and toward him her whole soul went out in the purest and most confiding admiration. He loved her truly and sincerely, as I firmly believe, and intended to make her his wife as soon as she had finished the education for which he supplied the means. She studied hard, and was deserving of all his praise for her astonishing progress. She loved refined and educated company, and the librarians all knew her face and bowed when she approached. But, alas! it seemed as if she had been lifted to this great height only that she might sink the deeper when the fall came.

Her lover had a hard-faced, aristocratic mother, who regarded her own family as a higher order of beings than the world usually saw, and she could not bear the thought of a marriage in which her son would unite with a person once a "shop-girl." So she opposed the marriage in every annoying way. But, notwithstanding all her threats, the young man was true to Wellie and his promise. At last the old widow conceived the idea of attacking the other party, and, without consulting her son, took her fine carriage and was driven to the residence where Wellie lived. Poor Wellie! She was taken by surprise, and she lost the battle almost without a show of resistance.

For the old lady said that her son was dissipated, in debt, and unable to live on his salary; and that if he married Wellie, all his family would disown him and leave him penniless. She knew that if he was disowned he would lose his place in the navy, and nothing but a life of drunken poverty would follow, and perhaps an unnatural death; while, if Wellie would release him, she, his mother, would settle a fortune upon him, and he could marry an heiress and become the great man that she had always expected him to be. A decision was demanded at once, for on that very day the fortune was to be made or lost. What could Wellie do but follow the promptings of a noble, disinterested love? and although it was crushing her soul into nothingness, she consented in tears to let him go. She wrote the letter at the old lady's dictation, bidding him never to come again, and with desperation signed her name in that cold way, without prefix or affix, and gave it to his mother. The old woman was overjoyed at her success, and, caring little for that heart whose joy had forever fled, she hurried to her son, and, taking him away, tried to win his affection from Wellie. She knew the arts and temptations which would lure him from his old love,[3] and finally he married the heiress whom his mother had selected for him, and people declared in their ignorance that it was a "lucky match."

From that day when Wellie came and told me her great sorrow and wildly called for death, I saw no more of her until yesterday; although I had heard that *he* had written her, and offered to fly with her and leave his luxurious home; and that Wellie refused to so punish his innocent wife. Yesterday she was—But I will not describe her now, it is too shocking. I love to think of her only as she was when I knew her and loved her *so much*.

4

Many of my readers will remember Martha Varley, who rose like a meteor and like a meteor fell. It seems as if it were only yesterday that she came to me and told me that she had, through influential friends, secured an opportunity to go upon the stage. She had a passion for literature, and her life seemed to exist in books. The works of Pope, Dryden, Byron, Shelley, Mrs. Hemans, Moore, Tennyson, and Longfellow lay upon her table, with those of Carlyle, Addison, Victor Hugo, Schlegel, Franklin, Scott, and Dickens,—nearly all the gifts of friends, and were dotted and crossed, from title-page to *finis*, with marks of censure or approval.[4] Her wages had been exceedingly small, seldom over one dollar a day, and she was an orphan. Yet she managed to purchase many books, and so wonderful was her memory that she could repeat Macbeth and Hamlet by heart.

So she went on the stage. I tried to dissuade her, and spoke of its dangers; for stage lovers, like good musicians have finer feelings, and are more easily tempted than any other class. But she drew for me so graphically the scenes she loved, and spoke so earnestly of the joy it would give her to earn sufficient wages to purchase all the books she desired, at the same time promising so resolutely and touchingly that she would certainly avoid the pits into which so many others had fallen, that I at last consented.

Her first appearance was advertised for a succeeding night, and I went to the theatre, that she might have the encouragement which she said the presence of her friends would give her. She was not given a leading part, because the managers were afraid that she lacked confidence in herself; but they promised that she should have such a place on the following week, provided they were pleased with her first attempt.

The play had passed into the second act before she appeared, and as it was awkwardly put upon the stage and many of the players were bunglers, the audience were getting quite tired. Some left the house in the midst of the best scenes, and the occupants of the galleries began to hiss and whistle. I cannot describe my feelings as the time drew nearer for Martha's appearance, and the dissatisfaction grew more and more evident. What should I do? I could neither go nor stay, and I became so excited that my escort inquired if I were ill. I wanted to go and warn her to abandon the attempt until another night. But so conflicting were my emotions that the scene changed and Martha appeared while I was in my seat. The audience were laughing and talking aloud; and many were throwing bits of paper about the hall, while others were showing their displeasure by shrill hissing and hooting. I expected that Martha would hesitate and tremble, and I did not think that in the face of those obstacles she could open her mouth to speak. But she came on as naturally and unconcernedly as the oldest actors, and with a calm, deferential manner undertook her part. She was a beautiful woman at any time, but in the rich stage dress, decorated with tinsel and sparkling beads, she did appear to me like an angel. The audience recognized her beauty, while they seemed to cower into silence before her pure and intellectual face. She had not spoken a word before the audience were wrapped in attention, and at the first sentence the applause began. On went the scene, and Martha glided in and out, and so much *heart* did she put into her words that she held the closest attention of the audience until she tripped from the stage amid almost deafening applause. She saved the reputation of the company; and the appreciative managers, in response to the united demand of audience and press, gave her a leading part on the following Monday evening.

The house was crowded in every part for many weeks, and she was made the "star actress" of a long and prosperous season, after which she visited several of the largest cities of America.

Soon she became so noted, and received such a large income, that she had a well-furnished house of her own, with a library of her own selection. People said that she was rich, and I thought so too, as she began gradually to withdraw from her old friends and to prefer the society of flatterers and gay people of the world. Soon she was too exalted to feel at home in my society, and our companionship entirely ceased. That was more than twelve years ago, during which time I had lost all trace of my old confidante, and seldom thought of her otherwise than as gifted, rich, and happy.

On the evening of the 27th of October, 1869, as I was coming from a poor family to whose assistance I had been called, and who lived in the lowest and dirtiest part of Boston, I met upon the sidewalk a ragged, besotted woman, whose bloated face, bloodshot eyes, and unsteady step indicated the presence of that demon of drunkenness, and whose uncombed hair and filthy apparel showed the absence of all shame or neatness. When she was about to pass me, I stepped off the sidewalk to give her room, and scrutinized her features. She did not look up as she passed, but there was something about the features which seemed familiar, and almost before I was aware of my own conclusion, I shudderingly gave a whispered exclamation, and the word "*Martha?*" escaped my lips. The woman started as if she had been dealt a furious blow, darted a frightened glance at me, and then began to run. But, stopping only a few paces farther away, she again turned toward me, and, clenching her hands above her head and turning her red eyes heavenward, exclaimed, "O Jennie, can it be that I am discovered by you? O my God, could not I have died without this torture? Jennie, for old friends' sake, O don't, don't think it is me! It is n't me! it is n't me!" Then, pausing for a moment, as if to recall the past, she struck her breast a heavy blow, saying,—

"No, it is *not* me. Your old friend Martha died years ago. I'm only the moving skeleton."

And before I could reply she turned again, and, like a frightened doe, sped down the street and around a corner; and doubtless passed from my sight forever.

5

In 1867 there was called up in the dock of the Philadelphia police-court a large man, whose high forehead and bright eyes attracted the attention of every one in court. As he stood up in answer to his name, the crowd gazed upon him with silent astonishment, and seemed to feel that a great soul lived within the prisoner,—too great to be accused of crime. It was "Willard the gambler." He was one of the finest classical scholars of the time, and Latin, Greek, and Hebrew were as familiar to him as to the most learned professors, and he could converse with Frenchmen, Germans, and Italians with astonishing fluency. He was a first-class literary critic, and a far-seeing politician, whose interest in passing events was so great that there was scarcely a periodical in the United States to which he was not a subscriber. Yet he was the greatest gambler in Philadelphia.

When the little judge, who seemed to be smaller in the presence of this majestic form, asked the gambler what he had to say for himself, his reply was, "Nothing."

"But," said the Judge, "have you nothing to say when a man of your talent and education is brought up as a common gambler?"

"May it please your Honor," exclaimed the gambler, excitedly, "I said that I had nothing to say, because my actions are all the justification I have to plead. Blackstone, Chitty, and Choate have declared, as your Honor well knows, that law is for the protection of society against *its enemies*.[5] My actions show that I am not an enemy to society. It is well known that I play with none but wealthy men, while the sums I win are given to the poor, or used in educating such young men as have genius but no money. If you condemn me to confinement, fifty boys must be taken from school, and a hundred mouths in this city will go unfed. I am not a gambler from choice, but from necessity. And my games are not antagonistic to society. Its present structure is such that I must game that others may be honest and noble, while to be arrested and fined or imprisoned is a sacrifice I gladly make to sustain the dignity of the law, which I shall be obliged, however, to break as soon as I am released."

6

Twenty years ago, in the town of Somerville, Massachusetts, there lived an aristocratic man and wife whom the world said were well worthy of their riches and position. They were both generous, gifted, and active, full of good works, and never lacking in sympathy for those whose scale of being was socially below them. They were reported to possess fabulous riches because they were so generous with their money and never turned a deserving suppliant away empty. They were also proud, and looked upon their position in society as on something deserving of praise. But their riches were not fabulous; neither was their income sufficient to feed all the poor of Massachusetts, and consequently their means began to fail. They, however, worked diligently with mind and hands to sustain their position and fortune. The wife, with commendable industry, obtained sewing, and the sewing-machine for the time took the place of the piano. The husband worked early and late in his store, and but for a sudden and unforeseen reverse by which he lost his whole stock in trade, he would doubtless have repaired their fortune.

With his reverses and disappointments came recklessness and despair, and in a darker hour than he usually saw he forged a note in hope of recovering himself without disgrace, and believing that he could pay the note before the party concerned should know of it. Of course he failed, was arrested, and sentenced to fifteen years' servitude in the State prison. Even Rufus Choate's eloquence could not save him. His wife, in her anxiety to save her husband from such disgrace, sold her jewelry, furniture, dresses, and everything to raise the money, which the party whose name was forged would not take in lieu of her husband's release. Soon after he died in prison.

Then she fell into recklessness and sin, and became but a wreck of the high-minded creature she once was. At last, arrested for common drunkenness, she was sentenced to three years' confinement in the house of correction. There, away from liquor and vile associates, the natural greatness of her soul began again to show itself, and in her leisure time she wrote a poem so full of deep and tender emotion, so polished and thoughtful, that it was copied in nearly all of the best periodicals of the land, and received praises of which Tennyson might well be proud. The only lines which I now recall are these,—

"Would you know why I'm leagued with this Despair?—
Because hell is heaven if he is there."

She afterwards wrote an article entitled "The Affectionate Lowly," in which she gave a sketch of her life, and referred to the beggars and the needy whom her husband had fed, and told—O so touchingly!—how those outcast mendicants cared for her when she was reduced to their level. How they carried her home when intoxicated, took her part when she was assailed, and offered their last cent in the payment of her fine when she was arrested. "Verily," says she, "even the thieves and beggars have a generous friendship which I never knew in the days of high life."

7

"She is not worth saving," said a police-officer one night, in Chicago, when, as he was dragging a drunken child of shame along toward the station-house, he was accosted by a woman with the words, "Why not try to reform and save her?"

She is not worth saving! ah, how concisely did that officer express the sentiment of human society toward the unfortunate women. Man may fall again and again, may dwell in the gutter for years, and become a loathsome, diseased, besotted wretch, and yet it is never said of him, "He is not worth saving." On the contrary, the people seem to think that a man who has been a libertine and a drunkard has done some noble thing, and it is all to his credit if, after his reform, he should even run for public office, or become a public lecturer. Ay! if he falls several times after having once reformed, it adds to his dignity, and increases his influence. What audience would gather to listen to a reformed woman? or what office opens its doors to her? None. Once an outcast she seems in the eyes of society to be an outcast forever. Not worth saving! O that I could for once force open that barrier to progress, the mock modesty of society, and feel at liberty to tell without curses or hisses the plain, simple *facts* which have been forced into my pathway as I have tried to aid the unfortunate. Not worth saving! Bright little children I know, as innocent as the blush of morning, whose widowed mothers are leading a life of social crime to support those children as they need to be supported. Aged parents I know, living in happy ease, little dreaming that their dear daughter earns the money which supports them in an unlawful manner, or that they might starve if she was pure and honest. More than this. *Husbands* I know, and I see their pale faces often now, whose wives have failed to get bread and medicine for them in a legitimate way, and in their despair have become awful criminals for very love's sake. You who doubt my word—and such there may be—have only to go to the criminals in the docks, and confess yourself a friend of the wretched and unfortunate, to be convinced beyond a doubt. Hundreds are criminals for food, others from despair. Few indeed are the women that are in the way of vice from choice. Thousands would reform if they could, but at every attempt the heartless hand of society thrusts them indignantly back. "There is a light in the window for thee, *brother*";[6] but no one ever heard of one there for his sister.

Not that I would censure the efforts made to reform fallen men. For God knows that I rejoice at the salvation of every human being, and while my heart gladdens at what is done for man, it only makes a darker picture of what is *not* done for woman. To save every being to whom the Almighty has given a human soul would seem to be the true theory. But discussion finds place better perhaps in subsequent chapters, and as it is *facts* that I am now giving, I will relate one more, and for the present pass over a topic about which, if the world would receive it, a thousand volumes could be written.

8

It has been but a few months since I visited the "Prisoner's Friend," at Pawtucket, Rhode Island, whose generosity toward the prisoners, as well as his eccentric manners, have made him somewhat notorious in the New England States.[7] He has given the convicts many Christmas dinners, and supplied many a suffering man with money while working out a sentence for crime. He has devoted his whole life to the alleviation of suffering within the prison walls. Hundreds of men are the recipients of his favors who never saw him or heard of him, until the present came which he prepared with his own hands. His cabinet is full of keepsakes, souvenirs and relics of prison life; and with each there is connected a story, most thrilling when told in his simple, affectionate way.

Having a long chain of gold pieces combined in a most curious manner, I inquired what it was for. In his characteristically queer way he spoke of the chain which was placed upon the neck of the Prodigal Son, and said that this chain was made by himself for a prisoner who was serving out a sentence of sixteen years' servitude for the murder of a young man who seduced the prisoner's betrothed.[8] The prisoner, he said, was an honest, innocent farmer's boy, while the seducer was rich and aristocratic, profligate and drunken; and such a nobleness of character had the prisoner displayed in prison that the chain was prepared with which to welcome his return. From this circumstance conversation passed to others, and instance after instance was cited where men had become criminals through injustice, cruelty, or unkindness. Murderers, robbers, thieves, and swindlers came before me, as, in his fascinating way, he moved the curtain of his conversational panorama, and I felt even more forcibly than ever before how many criminals are such from necessity, and how much wickedness the individuals of our States and communities have to answer for, which in this present time is loaded upon the shoulders of their instruments in prison.

CHAPTER 5

Newsboys and Bootblacks

*Success in Life.—Their Genius and Education.
—Newsboys' "Home."—Dividing the Profits.—You
May Borrow, but You Shall Never Pay.*

1

It is not my purpose to give in this chapter the many cases where bootblacks and newsboys have become wealthy and influential men; for many whose names I find in the "scrap-book" would object to the publication of their lives. A correspondent of the Boston Traveller, writing in 1857, stated that there were then "ten leading editors of New York who were once newsboys,—four in Boston, twelve in Philadelphia, and fifteen in Chicago." The newsboys, however, oftener seek other employments, and a far greater number of them are now among the merchants, army officers, politicians, and representatives of our country, than in the editorial fraternity; while men who once blacked boots on the corners or in the hotels are to be found now in nearly every community as manufacturers, merchants, aldermen, mayors, and congressmen; and even governors and senators have started, when boys, in the same humble trade. The reason why so many boys in this profession have succeeded so well in life is because the natural qualifications which fit them for bootblacks and newsboys are elements of success in the higher branches of labor and trade. A successful newsboy or an accomplished shoeblack will make as shrewd a trade as a Jew, and will weigh all its advantages and disadvantages with the wisdom of a banker. This is owing, no doubt, partially to his street education.

But to argue that he is indebted to that for all his talent would be to prove that boys in higher circles, who do not have that hard training, are always *unfit* to conduct the business which the newsboy seems to understand so well. If there were not many thousand people succeeding in life who never had this training, then we might think that successful bootblacks owed their wealth and position to the discipline which their early trade gave them. Culture and refinement are excellent helpmeets for a natural genius, and none appreciate the advantages of an education more than he does. But neither study nor "accomplishments" ever made a successful man of a person in whose construction Nature omitted the gift of genius; while the world is full of men and women whose natural endowments, without educational additions such as society now esteems, have made them leaders in the greatest and worthiest undertakings of their age. As a class in the community, the bootblacks and newsboys are *naturally* the brightest, the shrewdest, and the wittiest.

2

Several laudable attempts have been made in the larger cities of America and Europe to establish "Homes" for these boys, where they could get a good bed and palatable meals at the lowest cost price. Several of these institutions are now in operation, and, according to the reports of superintendents, are doing a great deal of good. It is said that boys who slept in door-ways and on the wharves before measures were taken to give them a better place now sleep in nice beds, and learn to comb their hair, wash their faces, and behave like little gentlemen. It is said, too, that the little laborers are taught to place their money in the bank, and to provide for themselves with economy and care. All of which is doubtless true, and reflects great credit upon the generosity of the projectors and supporters of those institutions. But, for reasons which will hereafter be explained, it seems to me as if all these "Homes," as well as every place of the kind secured for the purpose of charitably assisting the industrious poor, had much better be abandoned, and the money expended in missionary work among the wealthy. To give the bootblack a "Home" which he could not provide for himself takes away his independence and educates him into the habit of leaning upon other people, while the system which made and kept him poor is as much in force as ever; and the closing of a "Home" leaves the bootblacks who come into the field afterward no better chance for a livelihood than their predecessors had before the "Home" was established. "It may prolong life, but it does not cure the disease."

3

A gentleman was walking down one of the principal thoroughfares of Boston late one night in winter, during a heavy storm of sleet and snow, when he heard the newsboy's cry of "Herald! only *one* cent." The tone of voice was so plaintive, and the streets so deserted, that the gentleman was touched with pity, and stopped at a corner to listen for its repetition. Again it came, so subdued and sorrowful, "Herald, only *one* cent!" "Ah!" said the gentleman to himself, as he muffled closer in his great-coat, "that poor little fellow has lost money to-day, and is now hoping to save himself from total loss by reducing the price of the paper. I'll call to him and buy all that he has left." Soon the cry was again heard nearer than before, and, calling the nimble little tradesman to him, the gentleman purchased seven papers, and, giving the boy twenty-five cents, refused any change. The astonished boy took the piece of money, but, fearing that it might be a counterfeit, he rushed to the street-lamp to examine it. Doing so, he exhibited to the eyes of the astonished donor his little blue feet, the only covering of which was a pair of tattered cloth shoes, his benumbed and gloveless fingers, and his scarfless neck. Having satisfied himself of the genuineness of the coin, he asked the gentleman if he was not "strange,"* after which he walked away with a hearty "thank you." The gentleman, however, had not proceeded far on his way before he heard the newsboy calling out for a companion; and, curious to know what would become of them, the gentleman turned back to listen to their conversation. He approached close to the boys, unnoticed, just as they met under the lamplight, and heard the following colloquy:—

---

strange: Newsboys' phrase, meaning insane.

Bob. "Look o' here, Bill, I've jest seen a chap what's *cracked*, I'll bet. For he guv me a quarter of a dollar for seven papers, and said he didn't want any change; just as if that was the price of 'em."

Bill. "Say, can't we catch him and get him to buy mine, too?"

Bob. "Maybe! but then I *would n't*, Bill, 'cause why, it looks ter me like ridin' a free hoss to death. But I tell you what *I'll* do. Now the regular price of my papers would have been fourteen cents, and as I've got eleven cents more'n I'd orter hev, and you hain't sold your papers, I'll give you the extra eleven cents, and we'll get suthin' to eat somewhar and divide the expenses."

Bill. "No, Bob, I won't take nothin' unless I can *borrer* it, for I ain't goin' ter allers be so unfortinit as I've been ter-day. I'll borrer and pay again to-morrow or the day arter."

Bob. "Wal, Bill, I'll lend it to yer, 'cause we're cold and have nothin' ter eat, on the sacred promise *thet yer never try ter pay it back again.*"

Here the gentleman interrupted the dialogue, and giving them a dollar, left the little shivering brothers to secure their coveted supper and lodgings, if the poor things were so fortunate as to find any.

CHAPTER 6

Shop-Girls

Who Are Shop-Girls.—Their Condition.—The Little "Cash-Girl."—Female Clerks.—Their Trials.— What Society Owes Them.—The Tailor-Shops.—Acts of Kindness.—Ability of the Shop Hands

1

There is probably no class of persons in New England who are so necessary to its prosperity, and at the same time so little noticed or cared for, as the shop-girls. They are to be found in every department of trade, in nearly every workshop and manufactory; and every business man or woman is brought in constant contact with them. Behind the counter, at the book-keeper's desk, in the packing-room, at the sewing-machine and needle in the tailors' shops, and in all the positions that require light hands and quick thought they are seen successfully toiling day after day and year after year. Yet, with the exception of a few millinery and fancy-goods stores, they have no interest in the welfare of the companies, and no incentive but that of wages. Although there are forty thousand women in Massachusetts alone, who can never marry unless they go out of the State for husbands, and who must of necessity make the same preparation for their future sustenance which a young man makes for his prospective business life, yet it is not deemed necessary to hold out to the girls any inducement to make them diligent and honest. No promotion of any worth, no future partnership, no prospective wealth, shows its glittering castles ahead to inspire their zeal; and the wages which they receive to-day they may generally expect to get ten years from to-day. Just that and nothing more. They are always serving, and never being served; caring for immense sums of money which they can never own, making fine clothes they can never wear, handling delicacies of which they can never taste; and, like Tantalus, thirsty and surrounded by seas of water, they can never drink.[1] These are the "shop-girls" as distinguished from those who are employed in the large factories; and on them as much depends the mercantile business of Massachusetts as the manufactures of the same State do upon the factory-girls.

2

Behind the counter of a fancy-goods store and toy-shop into which the author has often been there was once a little light-haired, sunny-faced girl, about eight years old, who acted as "cash" girl and general waiter. Visitors often noticed her as she ran back and forth between clerk and cashier for change, or between clerk and customer with bundles. She was so cheerful and nimble that she soon became, as the clerks said, "a fixture," and the occupants felt as if "a part of the store had vanished" when little Viola was absent. She was an orphan, and had been taken from a Little Wanderers' Home as an act of charity. She was merely clothed and fed, without being adopted or receiving any pay. When she first came she asked a clerk for something which he could not give, and he told her that the "goods were for customers, not for clerks or servants." From that time she never asked for anything, and to all appearance was wholly satisfied with her lot.

She saw thousands of little girls about her age whose mammas came with them to purchase nice new dresses, new fancy shoes, little hats, picture-books, nice dolls, puzzles, carriages, and a hundred toys of which little girls are so fond, and she carried them from the clerk to the wrapping-desk, and, seeing them carefully folded in clean paper, delivered them to the customers. She saw the pleased recipients as they ran joyfully away with their presents, and wondered, no doubt, why everybody else had a mamma while she had none. Subsequent events have shown that she was constantly thinking how nice it would be if she could have a doll, or a ball, or a carriage, although I am told that she said nothing about it to any one. She saw all those desirable toys and dresses hanging and lying all about her, the possession of which would have made her little heart so happy, yet she was not permitted to touch one unless to give it to some more fortunate child, who was blessed with a kind mother.

One day Viola was taken sick, whether from hard work or her own indiscretion I do not know; but she was so ill that the matron of the house in which she boarded, after consultation with her employer, called a physician. The man of medicine said that she could not live, and advised little Viola to make up her mind to die. She knew, however, nothing about death or a hereafter, and the matron called a city missionary, who lived but a short distance away, and asked him to talk with Viola. This the good man did, and tried to impress upon Viola's mind the necessity of being prepared, and dwelt especially on the beauties and comforts to be found in heaven. Shortly after it was said that she was dying, and the physician, missionary, and several boarders gathered sorrowfully around the little girl's bed to await the dissolution. She had been for an hour in a deep stupor; but, a few moments before she died, she suddenly opened her eyes, and, stretching her thin hands toward the missionary, said,—

"Are you sure that I shall have a mamma in heaven?"

"Yes, darling," said he, "she will be there."

"O then," said she, smiling, "*I know that I shall have a doll and be dressed like other girls.*"

3

The most harassing position in which a woman can be placed is, without doubt, behind the counter in a dry-goods' or milliner's store, especially if, as is usually the case, her wages are so small that she cannot dress herself in what she considers a neat and becoming manner.[2] It is sufficiently annoying to be obliged to appear in a horse-car or omnibus with a number of ladies who are dressed better than one's self, and to one who has a cultivated taste for the beautiful it is a serious misfortune to be unable to gratify it in the preparation of her apparel;[3] but when one is obliged to face hundreds of ladies every day, every one of whom is more richly and perhaps more tastily dressed, and be questioned about the best styles or the most becoming cut, while measuring silks, satins, ribbons, or lace, is something which no sensitive mind can withstand without pain. "How would you do if this silk dress was yours?" "Would you take this one-hundred-dollar bonnet or the one at one hundred and fifty?" "Do you think that this color is suitable for one of my complexion?" "I can't judge by your dress, for shop-girls never dress decent." "Who is the best dressmaker in town?" "Have you ever had a skirt like this or that?" "If you had a husband to buy you everything you wanted, what dress or bonnet would you select?" These, and myriads of questions like them, are asked of the lady clerks every day, keeping their thoughts on dress and the things which they would like to possess, and creating an intense desire for dress and ornament, all of which they see and handle, but can never own. They stand on their feet until their bones ache, and measure silks until their fingers are numb, puzzle their heads through ten hours of constant mathematical calculation, and go home at night tired and disheartened, having earned just enough, perhaps, to pay their board. They live in a world of plenty, and yet have nothing; see money flowing from the hands of their sex as free as water, while they have none; and often receive large sums for goods which they know are squandered in frivolities that the buyers are better off without. They see many purchasing things they do not need, and investing money in gew-gaws they cannot use, while she who waits upon them has not enough for the common comforts of the body.

I say that it is a painful position for one who is endowed with an appreciation of the beautiful, a taste for decoration, and a sense of justice. This, however, does not apply to *all* the female clerks who are found at the counters of our mercantile houses. Some are not only satisfied and happy in their position, but show unmistakable signs of their fitness for the place. They have reached their level; and, with the exception of two very simple acts of justice, society owes them nothing. But to the more intellectually endowed, to whom the unseen agents of Nature keep saying, "You have a great work to do, why stand ye here idle?" the counter is a prison to the gates of which come few of the minds they esteem, and within which there is no light, no joy, no satisfaction. Many have stopped at the desk, in their course of life, who should be found in much more useful circles, doing the work which Nature demands of them. For such I enter my plea. Society cannot afford to lose their services; let it open the gates to such as would be free.

4

Needlewomen and machine-girls doubtless form the largest class of working-women now employed in America;[4] and, although this occupation does not require much natural genius or great skill, yet there are many minds now confined to it which are much better fitted for higher and more influential avocations. It is, however, when conducted upon the system usually adopted in our large cities, the most wearisome toil for both mind and body in which women, as a class, can at present engage.

It being an honorable employment and more independent than that of a servant in the household, it is sought by the most intelligent class of women, and is kept by many through all the toilsome years of life because they cannot see in all that time a single opportunity for bettering their condition. In no place can there be seen such mental variety as in the tailor-shops where girls are employed in the manufacture of clothing. Of those obscure persons who, perhaps in rags, perhaps in silk, come for their bundles of work in the morning and happen in with them at night, I can say but little. Some are, without doubt, poor women whose families would go unfed if they did not get this employment, while others are women in easy circumstances and perhaps in wealth, who will earn enough with their machine in a few hours to pay for the entire day's work of Martha in the kitchen. The latter class do their work at home, where they can enjoy the society of their families, and be cognizant of everything that is transpiring in the busy world without; and although their earnings could not supply one half their wants, yet with other means of support this employment makes them very comfortable. They are competitors with the shop-girls, whose only income is from the work of their own hands. While the daughter of the well-to-do farmer or the wife of the tradesman are taking work from the counter of the tailoring establishments and doing it for a very small compensation in order to occupy their leisure time and earn a little "pin money," they are decreasing the wages of those who must depend entirely upon this work for food and raiment, but who can exist on so small pay only by privation and suffering. It may be surprising to many of my readers to learn that the price now given for the making of sale clothing is only *one dollar and twenty-five cents a suit*, i. e. fifty cents for making the coat, fifty cents for making the pants, and only twenty-five cents for the vest. Linen coats are made for seventeen cents apiece, and shirts for *fifty cents a dozen*. Even ladies' morning-dresses, which are now included in sale work, are cut and made for *thirty cents each*. These are the ruling prices, while in some swindling cases, suits of woollen clothes are made for eighty-seven cents, and shirts for thirty-five cents per dozen.

It cannot be expected of employers that they will voluntarily pay one person more money for doing a certain piece of work than they give to another, nor can they be induced to pay a shop-girl "living wages" for making a suit of clothes which they can get manufactured elsewhere for one sixth of the sum. But whether they get more or less the shop-girls must work, and are, notwithstanding the boasted independence of the trade, the slaves of the manufacturer. He may or may not be a hard master, according to his natural fitness for his position; but in either case there is but little independence, as they *must* work at this trade and can have no control of their wages.

In those large establishments in New England where such immense quantities of clothing are manufactured for the "ready-made" market, there are sometimes several hundred girls employed in the same building; but in no department, from the journeyman tailors to the "bushel-women" and baste-girls, can it be said that the employment is in any way a measure of capacity.[5] They are fixtures. Before them there is no financial prospect but that of a reduction of wages when country competition is increased; and never can they see a partnership, or an interest in the profits of their labor, as the result of a few years' faithful service.

In the city of Boston there are eighteen thousand tailoresses, the greater number of whom are employed in the manufacture of men's clothing. As a class they are moral, intellectual, and refined in their literary tastes. They support lecturers and ministers, give to charitable enterprises, love the fine arts, and form a most important and intelligent portion of the community. Many of them are graduates of the high and normal schools of the State, and not a few are excellent writers, readers, and public speakers.[6]

Whenever this subject presents itself, I involuntarily recall the scenes in a large clothing establishment of Boston which for many personal reasons are still fresh in my memory. Some of these recollections are pleasant and others are painful, but I cannot say now that I wish to cross out any of them. It has never been my lot to witness a more pleasant scene than that of the sewing-room when, at an early hour in the morning, a hundred fresh and cheerful faces flocked into the door-way and with laughing playfulness took their stations at the bench or machine. There were friendships formed in those hours of toil that will never be forgotten, and acts of kindness and charity performed which will not soon cease to give satisfaction to the giver as well as to the receiver. There were exhibitions of affection, of integrity, of ability, and of honor, the memory of which makes life more valuable and lends a charm to humanity which I have not found in such potency elsewhere. It was a little separate community, in which each member not only provided for herself, but kept a careful eye upon the interests of the others; and, if in the race of toil there were any behind when the day closed, the most prosperous ones united in the assistance of the less fortunate. A happy family, in which could be found every shade of human temperament, and every grade of ability and character; but in which there never came discord unless for very weighty reasons. In that family were several remarkable characters, the mention of which will contribute toward the object for which this book is written.

5

Annie Masdon loved flowers. Any observer would have known this by the cast of her features. She loved them because Nature had made her like them. They were her fit companions; and she could see beauties in the delicately shaded leaf, the glossy petals, the variegated corollas, and the modest buds which others could not see. They bloomed just the same where the world did not see them; and so did Annie. They freshened the desert air with the same divine sweetness that they shed in the windows of the palace; and Annie was likewise as genial and obliging to the lowest and poorest as to the highest and richest. They were delicate in their construction, and mentally so was she. They drew all their beauty and life directly from nature and its God; so did she. She was born a flower; and her sweet disposition, delicate feelings, fine discernment and mental liveliness were a part of her constitutional nature. She was good, kind, sympathetic, and active because the combined machinery of her body and soul would not work in any other direction. Like the flowers, she ever looked upward, and from her humble position saw more of heaven than did thousands who could look down upon her. Nimble were her fingers, and the work which came swiftly from her hands was as smooth and perfect as the greatest skill could make it; but none of the less talented or less skilful ever envied Annie. When her work was done, and often it was early in the day, they would not permit Annie to assist them, as she many times wished to do, for they knew that she had a nobler work to perform among the suffering and destitute without. They seldom questioned her, and yet they knew, when she took her hat and shawl before the others had completed their tasks, that some poor family, some little homeless or parentless ones, were waiting for her coming. She loved children as well as flowers, and although she was near-sighted, yet it was seldom indeed that either escaped her notice. Her regular employment was no more than sufficient to pay her board and clothe her in a tasty manner; but by overwork and by little jobs which she secured for evening work, she earned considerable sums, every farthing of which was employed in clothing the ragged little urchins whom she found upon the street, and in furnishing juvenile reading for the poverty-stricken little ones who came to her mission sabbath-school.[7] There was a magnetic influence about her person that convinced the sinful of guilt, awed the criminal, and cheered the innocent. She never flattered, never condemned, but often praised, and in her frequented paths the vile slunk away into the corners, the poor said "God bless her," and the children cried to go with her. She seemed satisfied with her lot; feared no evil, and none seemed to come. She was always happy, and her presence made everything cheerful about her. In short, she was a model of female purity, innocence, and generosity.

For many years she has labored, devoting her spare hours and her Sundays to works of charity; and to-day she can be seen with her bouquet of flowers and flock of children, making her visits to the sabbath school, the attics, and the cellars, to comfort the suffering, to educate the ignorant, and to recall the fallen to the ways of virtue and peace. Men will say that she has done nobly, and speak of her with the same words of praise which they bestow upon every one "who does the best his circumstance allows."[8]

It may be that she does not appreciate her own power, and is contented to do her work in the small way and with the small means which her circumstances permit. But with those who have watched her movements there is a conviction that she is not doing one half the work which she might perform were she freed from the hours of toil which she is now obliged to devote to work, or were she paid sufficient wages to support herself as her intelligence demands. It is not her fault that the ten talents which God has given her are not used in the most profitable manner; for the use she has made of *one* shows that the spirit is willing.[9] Whose fault is it?

6

The measure of a generous act is the sacrifice which is necessary to do it. And often the gift of a million of dollars toward some charitable enterprise may not be really as generous an act as the giving of three cents by another and poorer person to the passing beggar.[10] Provided that a man never gave for the *name* of being generous, the gift of a million would, to some men, be a smaller hardship than that of fifty dollars to others. Hence, when I say that the shop-girls are generous, I do not mean to convey the idea that they give very large amounts, but that, in consideration of the number of stitches that must be taken for every cent that is earned, and their general poverty, the shop-girls are the most generous class of any in the community. They are always giving, and the thought of doing good or of making others happy seems to buoy them up and make their heavy tasks seem lighter. I remember an awkward boy by the name of Nat, who was employed in the shop already mentioned to sweep, carry bundles, and be a general waiter. He was so accommodating and good-natured that the girls respected him, and so poor and ragged that they pitied him. Their interest was much increased by learning that on his poor wages of three dollars and a half per week he was trying to support an invalid mother. A few days before the 4th of July Nat had been heard to remark that he must stay at home, as he had no clothes fit to wear on that anniversary. Then the girls with great unanimity contributed from their wages sufficient to purchase a complete outfit, which they intended to present to Nat on the evening before the celebration. In obtaining this contribution, none of the managers would take any money from such girls as were not in comfortable circumstances, or whose wages were insufficient to provide needed comforts for themselves. When the suit was made,—the hat, cap, shoes, shirt, coat, vest, and pants,—the girls were too considerate of Nat's bashfulness to present the gift in the presence of all the employees, and too kindly disposed toward the girls who could not contribute anything to let Nat know who did give, and so, after handing the suit to the foreman, they nearly all left the shop for their meals, leaving the foreman to present the clothing privately. This the foreman did, after making the remark that, as the girls were pleased with him, they had taken this method of showing their friendship. Nat was taken by surprise. He looked at the foreman, then at the clothes, and then around to see if anybody was looking at him, and finally, when he tried to say something, he utterly broke down, and cried like a child. He found five dollars in one of the pockets, and, taking that home to his mother, he donned the suit, and the next day appeared at the halls and entertainments with the other boys. That first new suit caused him to look upon himself, for the first time, as the equal of other boys, and from that time there was a marked change in Nat's behavior. He lost none of his good nature or kindness of heart, but he acquired a sense of self-consequence, without which no boy will ever succeed in life; and the day is not distant when Nat will look back upon that proud day in his first *new* suit of clothes, and regard it as the starting-point in a prosperous life.

7

Those girls would never permit a kind act to go unrewarded if they could by any means prevent it, and beggars and objects of general charity always found willing and generous contributors among them. They made presents to the foreman, that is, until they found that those who gave most were always discharged first, owing to his dislike of those to whom he felt under any obligation,—they surprised one another with gifts, and gave liberally toward fairs, lectures, and entertainments instituted for charitable purposes; but in no direction did their sympathies tend so strongly as toward the unfortunate and maimed veterans of battle. Without exception they were patriotic; and during the great civil war which devastated our land from the year 1861 to 1865, they were most earnest supporters of the government. Far into the night of many a weary day these tailoresses worked in the preparation of those little comforts which the Sanitary and Christian Commissions distributed, and which saved many a soldier's life. When the Soldiers' Homes were established in Boston, they received the constant attention of these working-women, whose efforts were unceasing in behalf of the inmates. One day the girls made up their minds to give a dinner to the wounded soldiers at the "Home," and selected the 17th of June as an appropriate time, because on that day everybody else would be enjoying themselves, while those poor cripples could not move from the house. For this purpose a large sum was raised, many giving away the wages of a whole week's work. It was all contributed from hard-earned wages, every cent of which had a value in the sight of those who earned it. Many of the wealthy men of that great city might have given ten times the amount contributed by all those girls without missing it in their business, or curtailing any personal comforts; but these givers were obliged to make a sacrifice, and to do without some needed garment, some book, some teaching, and perhaps some food, in order to give a substantial proof of their patriotism.

It was a pleasant occasion indeed, when that "surprise party" of ladies took possession of the Home. They arranged the tables, loaded them with food, set out the dishes of strawberries and of ice-cream, and in a short time after their arrival invited the maimed patriots to a feast that would have done honor to a banquet-hall in Fifth Avenue. With cheerful faces and willing hands the girls served at that table, and carried dishes to such as could not leave their cots, leaving nothing undone to cheer the desponding hearts of the ambitionless soldiers. Fine music enlivened the feast; and with speeches, kind farewells, and good wishes the girls went, as they came, quickly, modestly, gracefully.

The next day there appeared in the Boston Daily Transcript a card from the soldiers, in which were these words: "It is indeed pleasant to be remembered, and a New England soldier can appreciate such kindness, though it comes not from the lap of luxury. It shows that it can come from our working-women, and that their hearts and hands are with us. It makes us happy to know that the toiling and industrious women of Boston are with us, and appreciate the sacrifices which soldiers have made for our beloved country."

As it is my present purpose only to show that the working-women are generous, sympathetic, and patriotic, I shall not dwell upon the many other incidents which have occurred that might illustrate further the noble traits of their character in those respects.

8

As is the case in other occupations, there are sometimes found in the tailors' shops persons of such marked natural ability that no obstacle can prevent their becoming influential and wealthy. Thousands have more than the average ability who succeed no better than those to whom Nature has given less, because, in the present economy of the world, the way to success is so barred by prejudice and custom that it requires a giant to break through; and they who have *almost* enough strength to break the bars fare no better than they who are impotent and weak. There was one person in the tailoring establishment already mentioned, who, when a baste-girl, a needlewoman, or machine-operator, showed such talent for business and for overseeing that almost by common consent she took upon herself the care and annoyance of assisting and advising all the girls in her room. Soon she was made a forewoman, and paid well for doing that for which she was so well adapted. She was a generous woman, too unlettered to appear at advantage in society, or to be a good companion in high social circles; yet she was shrewd enough to see that the proprietors were making a very large percentage upon all the work which was done under her eye, and she determined to start in business for herself. This she did; at first in a small way, gradually increasing the number of her machines and employees, until she found herself at the head of one of the largest manufacturing establishments in Boston. She took care to employ none but able hands, and those she paid promptly and well. No sewing-girl ever complained to her of the wages, and none that were faithful were discharged, although hundreds applied every week for the places, and offered to work for less sums. The girls loved her as a mother, and although she was sometimes harsh in her demeanor, yet they never quarrelled with her. It was like a family. The proprietress had so much confidence in the honesty and honor of her employees that she permitted their accounts of work to supersede her own in case of a difference in which the employee claimed more than her account stated. Men may think that such concession indicated a lack of business ability, but the result showed its wisdom; for the woman became quite wealthy, and had the safest and most profitable business of the kind in the city.

So great was her prosperity that it began to attract attention, and in one year ten different men entered into the business in competition with her. They hired their girls at the lowest rates, often cheated them out of their lawful wages, and worked them over hours in order to do work cheaper than their lady predecessor and competitor.

The result was that the manufacture of clothing became unprofitable to everybody but to dealers and to the contractors for custom work. Then the lady closed her shop, and entered into a partnership with a large firm, who dealt in furnishing goods and clothing; and she is to-day a principal partner in a leading mercantile house of Boston,—an honored, industrious, generous, and popular woman.

9

It has been so often said that the "women are the most unkind to their own sex," and that no one is such an enemy to her own elevation as woman herself, that I cannot avoid a reference to the fact that the tailoresses of Boston are exceedingly charitable toward those of their own sex who, through ill usage, misfortune, or deceit, are led astray. It does often happen, for reasons mentioned in a previous chapter, that working-girls fall. But there are no curses for them in the circles they leave. No! when such a sad occurrence happens there is weeping in the shops as if their old associate were dead, and they mention her in whispers and tears, as if it was a calamity too awful to find a full-toned expression. Many efforts do they put forth to save and reform their wayward sisters, and many times those efforts are successful. The workshop is *not* an immoral place. Its social influences, as far as the employees are concerned, tend to a life of virtue and morality, and it is due to the fact that so many make the shop a last resort for help, in time of suffering, and, failing to find adequate relief in the wages which they get, strive no more against temptation, that the fallen are so often found within its walls. It is not the result of other association than the demon of poverty.

CHAPTER 7

Journeymen Tailors

The Troubles of a Tailor.—How Custom Coats Are Made.-Too Much Work, or Too Much Leisure.—Their Pay.—Intellectual Ability.—Oppressive Foremen.—Piece-Makers.—How They Grind the Face of the Poor.[1]

1

There is no class of workingmen so subject to annoyance as that of the journeymen tailors. They are either overrun with work, or have none at all. To-day they earn ten dollars and tomorrow will earn nothing. During this week, perhaps, they must work all day and nearly all night to fulfil the contracts made by their employer, and next week they will be seen loafing about the shop or street corners without employment. At some seasons of the year they have plenty of work, and can purchase every needed comfort; at another, they earn nothing for many weeks. Their tasks are usually those which require the closest application of mind and body, and which will soon exhaust the strongest physical or mental constitution. The strain upon their eyesight often makes them blind before they are forty years of age; the constant use of their right hand induces paralysis of the right side; their cramped position on the bench makes them rheumatic and gouty; while their irregular hours and nervous exhaustion create an unquenchable desire for stimulating drink. Receiving great pay for an uncertain period and then for many weeks little or no income, they find themselves subject to a cross-fire of temptation, coming from too great prosperity on one side and from compulsory idleness upon the other, either of which is likely to destroy the most cautious. If they are not as a class more intemperate, more immoral, more subject to poverty than other men, it is not because they have not had hardships and temptations sufficient to make them so.

During the "strikes" which have occurred among the journeymen tailors within a few years in Philadelphia, New York, St. Louis, and Boston, there has been a great outcry from the general public, and the tailors have been accused of many mean acts; and have been partially defeated in some of their attempts to get better wages by the united public, who feared a rise in the price of clothing. This would never have been the case had the sufferings of the workmen been known to those who opposed the "strike."

It often happens that a wealthy customer enters a clothing house, and gives an order for a coat, to be completed before a certain day on which he intends to wear it. It is possible that there is but one day and one night intervening, and although the proprietors are aware how arduous the task must be, the contract is made to deliver at the time requested, rather than lose the trade of the rich customer. The measure is taken, the cloth cut with all despatch, and the bundle hurried up to the coat room, where sit the journeymen tailors, perhaps crowded with other jobs for which there is the same haste, or perhaps waiting for a coat to come. "Here," says the person bringing the bundle, "is a fine broadcloth coat to be made and pressed before day after to-morrow morning without fail. Mr.——, the rich banker, wants it to wear on an excursion, and it must be one of your best jobs."

The "jour." examines it, and finds that it is one of the very best pieces of broadcloth in the market, and that the cut is in a style that will require the greatest care and skill to give it a tasty appearance.[2] He knows that at least three days' time ought to be devoted to it, and conceives of no way in which it can be completed unless he works through the entire night. Then begins a day and a night of toil, such as no one but he that has undertaken it can appreciate. Swift fly his fingers, flashing to the end of the thread and back again thousands and thousands of times; and at the end of each needleful of thread he seizes another needle ready threaded by an assistant, and proceeds as before. Hours wear on, piece after piece is fitted, stretched, ironed, sewed, until, far into the night, it begins to assume the appearance of a coat. Then he leaps to and fro between the bench and the press-board, plying the needle or tugging at the heavy iron goose, while his eyes run water, his back and arm ache, his head is dizzy, and his stomach empty.[3] The morning comes, and he has had no rest, and the coat is not done. He wets his head hurriedly in cold water, and as he must have *stimulus* and has no time to take food, he swallows a glass of brandy. Then comes the pressing, stretching, shrinking, which is necessary to make the coat "a perfect fit." The collar must have just such a neat roll, the cloth must wear a finished gloss, the sleeves must be round, and the lining smooth; and the workman stands pressing over the hot iron until the perspiration pours from his face, his head whirls, and sickening sensations run through his whole frame. Perhaps the hour comes when the coat is to be delivered, and the customer with his gold-headed cane walks into the store to try on his coat. Then the proprietor scolds the foreman, and the foreman curses the journeyman, and threatens to discharge him at once. Soon the coat is all complete. But if another customer has meantime arrived under the same circumstances as the former, another bundle is given him, with the request that he "pay more attention to his work"; and another body-and-mind-straining job is begun. So on perhaps for weeks, until he is wholly exhausted, and loses his place because he cannot perform human impossibilities. Or it may be that the trade is so dull, or the busy season is so near over, when his strength fails that he will have a chance to rest without losing his situation, and perchance "when the rush is over," he will be out of work for two or three months. He has, however, acquired a thirst for brandy, and this, together with the expectation of more work, soon makes him reckless, improvident, and perhaps dissolute. He spends his earnings thoughtlessly, and perhaps before another "busy season" he and his family are suffering for food. Even should he save his money and apply it economically, he would find a hard lot in life. For notwithstanding his great pay while he works, his aggregate yearly wages do not equal the wages of many laboring men who now appear to begrudge him his pay. When the Trades Union of the United States established a scale of prices for journeymen tailors, it was the intention of that body simply to equalize or average the wages so that this class of workmen should receive as much in proportion as do other classes; and when a "strike" was made to compel the dealers to accede to their wishes, this was all they asked. The justice of their demands was recognized at once by every person who examined into the matter, and living wages was given them. I say *living* wages; not meaning that they receive a fair compensation for the strength, health, and life which they give to the employer.

This is the general rule, as I personally know; but of course there are exceptions. Some few have constant work, are not driven, and make excellent wages; but so *very* few are they that no mention need be made of them here.

Intellectually the journeymen tailors are witty and thoughtful. They are ever discussing among themselves questions of local and national politics, points of law, philosophy, physics, and religion; and display in these controversies talents worthy of much better educated members of society. Many have a generous, frank, and cheerful disposition, and seem wonderfully like each other in natural character. Often have these men left the bench for a partnership, and sometimes for offices under the government; and in both situations they have shown great ability. Where a journeyman tailor has succeeded in *promoting himself*, the public may expect executive ability and industry; for the greater portion of them live and die in the same position, having perhaps no natural tastes for a higher life, or having been defeated, when attempting to climb, in that conflict between the unflinching rules of society and their sensitive consciences.

2

It sometimes happens that journeymen tailors, or men who, as cutters or assistants, have acquired a knowledge of the trade, are promoted by capitalists because they exhibit an unnatural taste for tyranny and abuse. This is one of the instances in which artful man defeats the aims of nature. And while the great body of tailors, and especially the high-minded, impartial, and unselfish, are killing themselves at the bench in some musty back-shop, the exceptions, such as the selfish, dishonest, and mean, are advanced into the position of overseers and foremen, in order that they may "look out for their employers' interest." The capitalist invests his money in the clothing business, and intends to make all the profits he can. Perhaps he purposes to do a strictly honest and honorable business. In any case he wishes to be sure that his interests will receive the first attention, and he hires such a foreman or piece-maker as will not be moved by appeals or shop-made friendships. Such I have seen; and the use which they made of their power has so connected the words "characters," "foreman," and "piece-maker" with injustice and cruelty, that I shudder when I speak them.

The foremen generally receive large salaries, and feel that they must in some way save to their employers sufficient to make themselves profitable; while many attempt to raise their own salary by cutting down the wages and oppressing those under their charge. Such men usually consider tailoresses as so many *things*, to use when profitable and to throw away when not needed; there being such a large surplus of female population in those New England States where clothing is manufactured, that it is easy to fill the places of such as may be discharged. These girls are not hired by the week or month, but always *by the piece*, so that the tailoress is supposed to receive such wages as she earns. But this is very far from the case. One generally works as hard as another and as many hours, but, allowing for a few skilled exceptions, they are paid in proportion to the value of the work upon which the foreman puts them. Two girls working side by side, and with equal skill, will seldom receive equal wages. One may earn ten dollars a week, and the other only four dollars. One has been given "good work," and the other "poor work,"—the former being work for which passable wages are paid, and the other such as must be done, but is neither profitable to dealer nor maker. Under such circumstances there is a great power in the foreman's hands; and if he chooses to make unreasonable rules of behavior, show favoritism, refuse to "accept" work when he is ill-natured, or to cut down the pay of such as displease him, he can do so without restraint. And I regret to say that this is very often the case. The girls cannot lose the place without great risk of suffering, and, knowing that many stand ready to take their positions, they weep and obey.

Although a situation under such a foreman is sufficiently irritating, yet there are conditions which are far worse. Here there is a hope of appeal to the proprietors for the girls, and a fear of censure for the foreman, provided he commits any very flagrant acts of injustice; but in the piece-maker's shop there is no such hope and no such restraint. A piece-maker is a person who takes clothing after it has been cut, and contracts to make it for a certain sum per piece.

When a journeyman tailor is induced, by the offers of several dealers, to start in business for himself, he hires a room in some upper story, and, perhaps running in debt for every article of furniture, hires a number of girls to assist him. He then contracts with the dealers to make all of their vests, coats, or pants, and without a cent of capital begins to compete with other shops of a like character. It is for the piece-maker's interest to pay very small wages, and he is usually selfish enough to take advantage of the necessities which crowd the working-women of his locality. In many cases he seems to be without heart or conscience. He keeps cutting down the wages week after week, as the girls are obliged to stay, until his employees exist from day to day on the very verge of starvation. He receives for making a nice coat the sum of ten dollars, but to a girl who has spent two or three years in acquiring her skill, and who does all the work, he gives only three or four dollars. If a girl offends him he refuses to pay her, or annoys her by making her do over again jobs that are well done; and in one case which came to my notice, some girls, coming from a distance, who reached the shop an hour late, were refused admittance until the next day. If he finds that by grinding still harder upon his victims, and increasing the amount of work, he can underbid those dealers who hire their own girls and do their own work, he undertakes it at once. If he succeeds, the wages of the girls in the shops of the dealers are reduced to compete with him; while if he does not succeed, he discharges his girls and "fails up to make money," frequently deeply indebted to his employees.[4] Thus year after year the poor women are drawn into the piece-shops, oppressed and starved into vice and shame, and finally left to occupy a grave in the potter's field;[5] while the hard-hearted tailors succeed one another in the diabolical task of oppressing and cheating the unprotected, and of "failing in business" in order to pay their gambling, whiskey, and debauchery bills.

Stand by the door-way of a piece-shop at the hour of closing, all ye doubting ones, and observe the thin frames, the swollen eyes, the tattered dresses, the unsteady steps, and the hands that press the foreheads, if you would be satisfied of the truth of my words. I dare not tell one half the truth, for few indeed who have not taken the pains to examine would believe me.

CHAPTER 8

Servant-Girls

*Why American Girls Prefer the Shops and Factories.
—Their Taste and Refinement.—Incidents in
Kitchen Life.—The Old Cook.—The Nurse.—
The Waiter.—Anecdotes, &c.*

1

When the cry of the working-women of New England finds lodgement in the ears of the wealthy housewives, the first question which they put is always this, "*Why do they not go out as house-servants?*" and the question is asked in that decided manner which indicates that the speaker declines to do anything for them as long as that field is open.[1] There is a great demand for housekeepers and servant-girls even in New England, and the greatest annoyance which a wealthy mistress now has is in the finding of suitable servants and retaining their services when once engaged. Hence it is very natural that the subject of these perplexities should excuse her lack of interest in the poor working-women by saying that "there is work enough for them in the kitchen." "Every class complains," said an English writer, "but the housekeepers. The factory operatives, the needle and machine women, the female printers and clerks, the school-teachers and accountants, are all discontented, and this land of women (Massachusetts) has found that there is no joy for woman in any occupation but housekeeping." Now that writer was right as far as his statements with regard to the discontent are concerned, but his conclusion that there is "no joy for woman in any occupation but housekeeping" is very far from the truth. I do not doubt that, as a class, the married women are the happiest; and the possession of a nice home, bright children, kind friends, and plenty of money ought to make them so. But there are found many women in other stations in life who are as happy as human beings can well be, and who would not leave the school, the hospital, the life of business, for the pleasantest mansion in America. Woman is discontented as a laborer for wages because she does not receive a just compensation for her work, and because she is unreasonably restricted in her choice of occupations. She is discontented in any position where she comes in contact with wrong which she cannot remedy, suffering which she cannot relieve, and degraded humanity which she cannot elevate. She would be equally discontented as a "housekeeper," did not those who assume that title have a right to their own time and all the opportunities for relieving their own distress and doing good to others that they desire.

A kitchen-maid, or a chambermaid, is not a "housekeeper" in the sense which the writer above quoted intended to convey. "Housekeepers," in the best sense of the word, are the mistresses of houses or mansions; and without doubt they, as a class, are happy. Although they cannot protect themselves, yet they are supposed to have a protector in the form of a husband, father, or male friend; and in many cases, no doubt, are happier in their blissful ignorance than they would be if cumbered with the responsibility of protecting their own moral, social, and political rights. The servant-girls are not only without protectors, but without the commonest means of shielding themselves; and in this fact may be found the reason why so many fly to the shops for sustenance rather than to the kitchen.

In the first place, it is looked upon by all classes in American society as a disgrace to be a servant in a family, or even to have a relative who is one. I will not dwell now upon the reasons why this is so, as it is a fact so patent that it needs no arguments to establish its truth.

American girls are naturally sensitive. The hereditary refinement of their natures, combined with the educational and social advantages which are fortunately or unfortunately offered to young girls, gives them finer feelings and more delicate organizations than characterized their great-grandmothers or marks the immigrating women of our own time. Hence the respectability of an occupation would affect their choice much more than it would the choice of the coarse and vulgar. They will make greater sacrifices to retain their good name than would the uneducated, unrefined masses of Europe. To make a sacrifice for one's name is an indication of natural nobility which is honored everywhere, unless, perchance, the laboring American girls be an exception.

A second and greater reason for the antipathy of the American girls to the "kitchens" is the loss of their native independence. In "free America" there is no shade of character more cultivated and applauded than independence. The child is taught it at its mother's knee,—or at the knee of its mother's nurse-girl,—and has that idea instilled into its mind in almost every circumstance in life thereafter. Be independent! is heard from the lips of every philosopher and statesman, and the American girls have unavoidably inherited some of that noble spirit. They cannot at present be wholly independent, but they adopt the next best course, and be as independent as they can. The store, the tailor's shop, the factory, the printing-office, and binderies are, as I have already shown, very far indeed from being independent situations; yet those places permit a far greater latitude in mental and physical action than do the kitchens or chambers of a modern mansion. In the former the girl is supposed to be paid for what she performs, and it depends upon her ability or disposition whether she earn more or less; in the latter she works always for a stipulated sum per week, and is well aware that the employer intends to get all the labors he can for that sum. Again, in the shop, no one is placed over her as an overseer or master who is not fully qualified to tell her how to do her work, in case she is unacquainted with it; while in the kitchen it would be a rare thing for her to find a place where the mistress of the house—who controls everything about it—was able to tell her how to cook, or wash, or mend. There is not as much slavery in being obliged to follow the directions of one you know to be better qualified to judge for you than you are for yourself as there is in being driven about by one who knows not what would be either for her good or for yours; so that, as far as respectability and independence of character are concerned, the New England girls are in better circumstances as shop-girls than they would be as kitchen or chamber maids, were they physically capable of doing the work. There is, however, a very good argument in favor of the positions as house-servants, viz. they are *sure* of sufficient food to sustain life while they remain in their situation; which cannot always be said of the shop-girls. But this, with the uncertainty regarding its duration, would not affect the decision of those descendants of that race whose first motto was "Give me liberty, or give me death."[2] If you call this foolish pride, then you condemn the spirit of the nation which preferred hardship, dangers, bloodshed, and slaughter to a life of servility.

But this is by no means all; there are hardships and even sufferings among the house-servants which are as great a disgrace to the employers as they are a grief to the victims. Cooks sometimes are without proper food, chamber-maids are often over-worked, ladies' maids are many times cruelly tortured, and nurse-girls are often most grievously oppressed. I say *often*; not *always*, for fortunately there are some hearts that are soft, some employers that are considerate, and some positions that are what they all should be, viz. *homes*. A few incidents occurring within the limited circle of my acquaintance, all the parties to which are personally known to me, may not be inappropriate as illustrating the general treatment of servant-girls to-day in New England, and showing why the worn and destitute shop-girls do not turn their attention to housework.

2

In the spring of the year 1869 a sewing-girl of my acquaintance, who had been abused by the overseer and could not earn sufficient money to clothe herself properly, determined to leave the shop and seek employment as a servant-girl. She was intelligent, easy to learn, and very nimble. She was acquainted with the details of housework, and her friends predicted that she would succeed much better in that branch of industry than she had done in the piece-shop.

Her first trial was in the family of an officer on Governor Andrew's staff, who was reputed to be one of the most fearless advocates of abolitionism to be found in Massachusetts.³ She was engaged as a nurse for two little children; and she supposed, when she accepted the terms, that her only labor would be in waiting upon those children. She was undeceived, however, at once upon entering the mansion, for she was told by the haughty mistress of the house that she was not only to take care of the children, see that they were always cleanly attired, studious and polite, but was expected to go to bed after all the others at night, build the fires in the morning, sweep the whole house, assist about the breakfast, and do the washing and ironing for the children. The coal for the fires in the nursery and sitting-room must be brought up three flights of stairs, and she was expected to do that, although she was very slender. She attempted to perform the task set for her, and arose early, worked all day without an hour's rest, and oftentimes was obliged to leave some unfinished work at midnight, in order to get a little rest and sleep. If there was dust in the halls or on the stairways; if the children cried, or in her absence fell and hurt themselves; if the fires burned low, or a certain favorite dress was not ready for the children when required, the mistress would call her down to the dining-room, and, after cautioning her to "stand erect with her hands beside her when in the presence of the mistress of the house," would pour upon her such a volume of abuse and apply such vile epithets, that the poor girl would go back to her work crying and most piteously lamenting her sad fate.

She did not remain many days, and ran away because she dare not meet the mistress and tell of her intention.

She then attempted to obtain work again in the shop, but before she succeeded she learned that the wife of the leading labor-reformer of Boston was in need of help, and, thinking that in the family of such a great philanthropist she could not fail in being well treated, she applied for the situation. Mrs.—— wanted a waiter-girl to "show callers into the parlor," assist her about her "small work" and do "such little errands about the house" as the mistress could not well do for herself. This appeared to be a good place, as she was to be in the house of one who was supposed, above all others, to appreciate and reward the laborer. The first day she was given the job of cleaning the ceilings and scouring the kitchen floor. The second day she was instructed to take up the carpets in the parlor and dining-room and renovate those apartments. The third day the chambers were to be cleaned, and all the furniture carried out and, after washing, returned. All this the girl did cheerfully, thinking that after the whole house was cleansed, her work would be lighter. But on the fourth day, after the rooms had been thoroughly renovated, and the lame and exhausted girl thought she saw the end of such hard work, the mistress called her to the sitting-room, paid her for one half a week's work, and, saying that she had no fault of any kind to find with the girl, discharged her because the mistress "did not need her services any longer." The girl asked permission to leave her trunk until she could find another place, but this was granted only for *one day*, as "it lumbered up the house so." The girl put on her bonnet and shawl, and with a heavy heart and moistened eyes was about leaving the house when the mistress called out to her,—

"Mary! Mary! *Won't you come in and bid me good by, now that you are going to leave me?*"

When the girl returned and Mrs.—— saw that the servant was crying, she inquired the cause.

"I am an orphan," said the girl. "I have no home and no friends."

"Then go to the Young Woman's Home," said the mistress.

"But," replied the girl, "I have not sufficient money to pay for my board even there, for I have been very unfortunate."

"Well," said the hard-hearted consort of a great man, "I don't want you any longer, for all the work is done that I wanted you for, and you may as well go along without more crying."

3

The persevering servant-girl was not wholly discouraged upon the second failure, and after watching the "wants" in the daily papers, and inquiring of all her acquaintances, she found a situation as kitchen-maid in the mansion of a very prominent philanthropist of Boston, who had given, besides many private donations, one hundred thousand dollars to the Methodist Church. The generosity and benevolence of the man were famed everywhere; and this friendless girl, who had not entirely lost her faith in human nature, hoped to find kind faces and considerate treatment in the home of such a man as he. It so happened that, in anticipation of her coming, the washerwoman who usually visited the house on Mondays was discharged, and consequently a large amount of fine clothing awaited the girl's arrival. The mistress, who had discharged the washerwoman in order to save seventy-five cents, and who had hired the girl with the understanding that the washing should be done by other parties, directed her to wash the clothes and iron them at the earliest possible moment. The astonished girl undertook the hard task, and had so far completed it as to be ironing the fine shirts, when the mistress rushed in and demanded why she had not "completed that ironing two hours ago." The girl was nearly exhausted with the lifting and pressing which is necessary to finish starched linen, and to that unkind attack she could only reply in tears. The mistress was not touched by the girl's distress; but, having in view the almighty fifty cents, told her that she (the mistress) *could not afford* to hire a girl who was so slow; and, giving the girl the exact wages which she had earned,—reckoning the washing and ironing days as two sevenths of a week,—she discharged her without further ceremony.

He could give a hundred thousand dollars to a wealthy church, but his wife could not afford to keep a girl, and pay her two dollars a week, who was not able to do the work which usually requires four persons to perform.

The servant-girl, having failed for the third time in the homes of the most philanthropic, abandoned housework in despair, and accepted a position in a clothing establishment, where she sewed upon thick leather cap-visors. There were four long stitches in each visor, and she must take nine hundred of those stitches for twenty-five cents, yet with all the toil and diminutiveness of the wages, she was much happier and much more American as a shop-girl than as a house-servant.

4

Now there is a class of old families in the cities who pride themselves upon belonging to the "old school." This is not so much the case in the West where everything is new, as in the established communities of the older States. These families claim to treat their servants better than the new or modern school, and many of them pride themselves upon retaining a tried servant for a number of consecutive years. The "new school" is understood to be a hard place for servants, as the masters and mistresses never presume to hold any social intercourse with "menials." In their households a girl must expect to suffer slight and insult, privation and the severest toil, without a murmur. This, however, is not *supposed to be* the case in the "old school." But, to show that the position of a maid-servant is not as inviting even in those families as has generally been supposed, as well as to show that Nature slights not the servants in the disposition of her favors, I will mention one case which came to my notice ten or twelve years ago.

A maid-servant having retired from one of the "old-school" families, a girl fresh from the country was employed to fill her place. Everything seemed to go smoothly, and the work to be done satisfactorily, for a considerable time. But there came a season when, without any apparent cause, the mistress of the house became dissatisfied with the servant-girl, and was overheard to say that "unless things went better" another girl would be engaged and the first one discharged. On consulting with the cook the perplexed servant learned that the mistress had several times taken up the door-mat and, rubbing her fingers on the carpet beneath, had applied them to her handkerchief and found them dusty. The cook believed that this was the sole cause of the dissatisfaction. Taking the precaution afterward to sponge as well as sweep the carpet and mat, so that no dust should adhere to the fingers of the fastidious mistress, the old feeling of mutual confidence between mistress and servant was restored.

About six months after, another cause of dissatisfaction arose as inexplicable to the maid as the first. But after uniting with the kitchen "colonel," for whom she entertained an *especial* friendship, and who devoted all his energies to the discovery of the secret, she ascertained that the cause lay in her negligent manner of sweeping the parlor. The windows of that apartment were double, with sandbags on the casements, and thick curtain folds within, so that it was an impossibility for dust to drift in, yet the rules demanded that it should be swept every week, and the kitchen-maid and "colonel" were detailed, and given one half a day to perform that task. One very large piece of furniture required their united strength to move it, and for several weeks it had not been done. They never found dust there when the room had not been used; and under such circumstances they presumed to omit the removal of so cumbersome a piece of furniture. On moving it, however, at a time when the blinds had been thrown open to admit the light, they found a number of little apple-seeds behind it, which the mistress had thrown there for the purpose of detecting the girl if she were remiss in this part of her duty. The cabinet was ever after removed, the seeds swept away, and the smile of the mistress resumed its accustomed sway. After that day the maid and "colonel" many times entered the parlor, and while one picked up the seeds, raisin-stems, &c. which the mistress had slyly strewn around in the corners, the other took the books from the shelves and read aloud; and sometimes I fear that they sat in that closed parlor discussing more touching topics than the Waverley novels or Pope's poems;[4] for, a few years after they were married, and, inspired, as he says, by the ideas which he read and heard in that tidy parlor in those stolen hours, the "colonel" began a business for himself which has made him one of the richest merchants of Boston, with servants, liveries, and parlors of his own.

5

There is a science in housekeeping as in every other occupation that requires system and skill; and to one who thoroughly understands the theory, and loves the practice, it is as aggravating to see the housework awkwardly conducted as it would be for a sensitive architect to be forced into the construction of a zigzag, irregular stone fence. There are servant-girls who are thoroughly acquainted with all the best methods of housekeeping, and who are mentally and physically fitted for that kind of work. They can sweep a carpet, make a bed, cook a pudding, arrange a dinner, or iron a ruffle with equal skill; and whatever they do is well done, and, at the same time, with an astonishingly small outlay of strength and time. One of these girls was Allie Fenbush. All her work was like the mechanism of a clock, smooth, prompt, exact. She could do more work in a given time, do it better, and exhaust herself less than any other whom I ever saw. But it so happened that she was employed in a family where the mistress was not only ignorant of household duties, but unrefined in all her ways and tastes. She was arrogant and disagreeable, quick-tempered and vain. She wished to oversee everything that was done in the house, and was incapable of doing the least thing herself. So she began to give her orders, saying, Do this, do that, do the other, and interfered with everything that was done, replacing system by disorder, neatness by slovenliness, and ease by arduous toil. To a nature like Allie's, this lack of system, and perpetual, unnecessary annoyance, was a greater hardship than the arrogance of a mistress or the toil unnecessarily introduced. The confusion troubled her so much that she became very nervous. Having no certain place for any article, she must burden her memory with the place where it was last dropped; and without any regulation or system, she was sometimes driven beyond her strength, and sometimes idle, until it became so excruciating that Allie abandoned the place where she received good pay and plenty of food for a place in the shop, where, notwithstanding that her income was less, her liberty to systematize and economize was unrestricted.

6

It may seem inconsistent to some persons that there should be anything great or noble about a life in the kitchen. And a few may smile because I give so much space to housekeeping details, and will doubtless laugh outright when they hear that human greatness may be found in the cook-room or laundry, as well as in the halls of legislation. There is one woman now in my mind, who, although the greater part of her long life was confined to the kitchen and dining-halls, was just as great in her sphere and in all that makes true human greatness as were those men of the age just passed who conducted the ship of state over such dangerous shoals.

Her name was Mattie, and she was an only child. Her father died when she was quite young, and consequently her mother humored and "spoiled" her in those youthful days with too much love. Mattie was active and intelligent, but was little inclined to study; and her over-indulgent mother never urged her to undertake anything that she disliked. Thus Mattie grew to womanhood, poorly educated in everything but good manners, and with no capital but her handsome features. The latter won a seaman by the name of Parboly for a husband,—whose character, however, was unknown to her until too late,—who, when her little girl was a year old, left her to the mercies of a world concerning which she knew so little. Then, when she was left destitute, with no living relative or near friend to whom she might apply, with no trade and but little education, she was obliged to find some employment to supply the necessities of herself and child. There was nothing that offered itself but the position of a kitchen-maid, and, although she knew nothing about the duties, she entered into the work with earnestness and a determination to make it a life-work. Forty years ago, when she entered the kitchen, it was a far different place from those apartments now answering to the same name. Then a servant was a member of the household, entitled to privileges which are now laughed at, and considered the equal of those she served. It is my belief that any person as wonderfully endowed by nature as Mattie seems to have been should be accepted even now as the equal of the richest and best-educated women of the day. She seemed to get her knowledge by instinct; and could cook a pie, arrange a dinner, or talk politics when she first began with the same readiness that she did after years of experience. She preferred cooking, however, to any other work, and her skill in that direction made the house where she lived noted in all the aristocratic circles for its fine roasts, puddings, pies, and edible delicacies. Meantime she paid the board of her child in a refined family, where she placed it, in order that it might be brought up and educated as a lady. There was only one stipulation, however, between the mother and the guardians, and that provided for the discipline of the child without a blow. For that child she strained every muscle and nerve; and provided it with all the fine dresses, books, toys, &c. which the wealthy family purchased for their children. She was never idle, and whenever she saw a spare moment in her duties as a cook, she applied herself to embroidery and fine stitching, which, before the introduction of that great invention the sewing-machine, was all done by hand. She was as skilful in that as in everything else, and the aristocratic ladies of that time often came into the kitchen to persuade her to accept their assistance for a while as a consideration for some fine work which they wished her to make for them. When her skill became noised abroad, ladies came to see her work, and always carried away a report about that "wonderful woman." The family of her employer belonged to the very highest circle of Boston society, and, as was sometimes the practice then, she was induced by them to go out and cook dinners for other families on certain great occasions. Soon she became an indispensable accompaniment to every public dinner, and the question was always asked, "When can we get Mrs. Parboly?" before the day was set or the funds raised. So great a favorite was she that carriages were sent for her, and servants appointed to wait upon her while a dinner was in preparation. Her employer obtained for her a divorce from her husband, and, seeing that she could make much more money as an independent cook, advised her to make it her sole work. This she did, and for many years she was the only popular caterer in Boston. She prepared all the state dinners of Daniel Webster, Edward Everett, and their contemporaries, and had entire charge of the cooking department at the dinners given to Lafayette, to General Jackson, to President Fillmore and Lord Elgin, when they visited Boston.[5] It is said of her that at one of Daniel Webster's great dinner-parties, at which she was always present, i. e. in the kitchen, she sent out one of her best puddings with the brandy-flame flickering over it. The shape of the pudding and its composition caused it to be recognized at once as the work of her hands, and the whole assembly, among whom were many of the greatest men of that day, arose and gave three deafening cheers for Mrs. Parboly.

During these years her daughter grew to womanhood, having obtained a finished education and, at the same time, ripened into a most beautiful lady. A young man from the wealthy circles wooed and won her, and with the cheerful consent of Mrs. Parboly they were married with great pomp.

Her son-in-law soon began to feel that it was a disgrace to be so closely related to a cook, and he induced her to leave her chosen calling and take up her abode with him. This she did; although she felt much more comfortable in the kitchen than in the mansion. Her son-in-law proved to be too generous, and in a few years ran through all his property. The beginning of the Mexican war found him penniless and despairing, and entering the service as an army officer he went to Mexico. Then Mrs. Parboly again entered the kitchens and officiated at dinners, earning sufficient sums to support herself, her daughter, and the two grandchildren that had now been added to the family. At the close of the war the son returned; but his health was so shattered that he was a confirmed invalid. Mrs. Parboly then undertook to support him with the rest, and for the two years which he lived she kept him and his family in comfortable circumstances, paid for medicines, doctors, &c., and devoted a considerable time to a personal supervision of their household affairs.

After his death—at which time he asked Mrs. Parboly to keep his children from the shop, and wished, if it ever became necessary for them to work, that they should be placed in the kitchen where, as he claimed, she had learned such generosity and kindness—his wife became insane and was taken to the hospital, while the two girls were left to the care of their grandmother. As true and as kind as she was intelligent, and as cheerful, lively, and nimble as ever, the lady, now far advanced in life, undertook the care of those two girls. She clothed and boarded them, kept them in school and in church, anticipated all their wants, and by wearing herself out gave them luxury and ease. Soon the daughter died, and the grandchildren were nominally—as they had *really* been before—dependent orphans. But they never knew care or trouble; for this little gray-haired woman, who could dance, sing, joke, discuss questions affecting society or the nation, always supplied their wishes and necessities, and they grew into womanhood without a full sense of the devotion which made them what they were.

Mrs. Parboly was a patriot and an abolitionist. She would make great sacrifices either for the nation or for the slave.

When Daniel Webster sent for her to cook a dinner for him, shortly after his great 7th of March speech, she refused to go, and when questioned by him she defiantly assured him that she should not cook another dinner for him as long as he lived,—and she never did.[6]

When the great civil war began, with slavery upon one side and freedom upon the other, she was as regular a subscriber for the newspaper and as devoted a patriot as any in the land.

During the war, and while she was keeping a boarding-house, her granddaughters were married. One entered a comfortable home near Boston, while the other married an army officer. To the Major Mrs. Parboly was particularly devoted, as she admired his manhood and honored his fervent patriotism. But, as if her sorrow were not yet enough, this idol was torn from her at the time when it was the dearest, and the wife became insane. He was killed when leading his regiment into battle, and the sorrow-stricken wife, losing her reason, followed her mother to the confines of the lunatic asylum, leaving her little boy, a great-grandchild, to the care of this noble woman, then nearly ninety years of age.

Her fame has departed with the generation to whose tastes she catered; her little body refuses to obey the behests of her will; the friends whom she once knew, the successful business-men whose prosperity is due to her efforts years ago, the children she once fondled, now perhaps gray-haired and wrinkled, all have become as strangers to her. There in her little cottage, unassisted by the government pension which is paid for the wife and son of the patriot one, seldom leaving the little country town to visit the old scenes, she awaits the end, cheered by the loving caresses, cheerful smiles, and undisguised love of a little orphan great-grandchild. Surely she was a princess in the royal line of nature! and how much better would it be for the people if such as she were seated in power, in the place of the pretenders and usurpers who now throw out their banners as the rulers of the world! Her *acts* proved her nobility, and they show a much better title than money or descent.

CHAPTER 9

Then and Now of Factory Life

Spirit of the Age.—Why Servants Are Impudent.—The First Manufacturers.—Treatment of Operatives. —The Factory-Girls.—The Boarding-Houses.—The Golden Age of Factory Life.—The First Factories in New England.—Growth of the System.—Incorporation.— The Factories of England.—The Ten-Hour Bill. —John Bright.—Americans Descending and the English Ascending.—The Operatives Now in American Employ.—History of a Factory Which Prospered with the "Old School" and Failed with the "New."

1

This is an age of bargains and contracts. Those good old days of generous hospitality, of friendly assistance, and of mutual good-will have passed into history as a thing that existed once, but can never come again. Everything that is performed to-day seems to be done under a contract, in which each gesture, step, and thought is entered in the specifications. Once, when a laborer was employed, there were many things "understood" that were not expressed in the contract. The laborer was to give a fair return for his wages, and if it could not be done in one way it was to be done in another. The employer, when he contracted to pay a certain sum for a stated amount of labor, was understood to include friendly treatment and reasonable assistance. Then the servant-girl was not only paid her weekly wages, but made a member of the family, and cared for with a friendly interest. Now she contracts to do a specified amount of certain kinds of work, and cannot be induced to do anything more without an increase of pay. When the annoyed mistress gets angry at the applicant for a situation who asks how many shirts there are to wash, how many beds to be cared for, how many persons in the family and how many servants, how many spare hours the servants are allowed each week, and, perhaps, if the mistress permits the waiters to use the library or parlor, she forgets that it is the fault of mistresses themselves. Now there is nothing whatever *understood* between the parties, as the mistress expects to do as she promises and nothing more. She is not nowadays supposed to treat a girl as an equal, make the house into a home for servants, or give them any sympathy, unless she *contracts* to do so. The girl gets nothing but money, and she intends to render such service as will earn just that and no more. Once servants were under obligations to interest themselves in the prosperity of the house, and have a friendly eye to the comfort of the inmates, because they received, besides their wages, sympathy, kindness, respect, and even love; either of which is of as much value as the wages.

To be able to drive a sharp trade or overreach a competitor seems to be the *summum bonum* of modern ambition.[1] No regard is had for the value of an article, either to the seller or the purchaser; but the life of trade consists in getting as much and giving as little as possible. A hundred years ago there was a man in New Haven who hired a neighbor to come and sit on the fence while the employer picked up the stones in the garden-patch. His reason was that, although he could do the *work* "sorter well enough" himself, yet "the *lonesomeness* did n't go so well alone."* The idea of hiring a person "to keep company," or paying for sociability or kindness, is not so ridiculous after all; yet to the money-worshippers of this day such a proposition would be hooted with contempt. There is no value in anything but exchangeable representatives of gold and silver. Even public and private parties, balls, receptions, dinners, and celebrations are patronized only just so far as they will *pay* in dollars and

---

*Yalensia Magazine.

cents; and the first question usually asked of a friend after marriage is with reference to the financial standing of the other party. It is not my intention to say that affection, sociability, and respect are unknown, or that everybody has drowned his moral self in avarice; but that the spirit of the age tends most astonishingly toward this result.

This tendency is exhibited in its strongest light in connection with the factory system of New England, which has fallen very far from the "high estate" that it once occupied.

2

When the first factories of New England began their existence, they were owned by men who had made their money in honest industry, and who started those enterprises because they felt themselves naturally fitted for such a work. They were truly models of natural genius, and subsequent events proved them to be the greatest men of our land. Under their guidance the factory system of New England was everything that the most philanthropic could claim for it. They not only made themselves millionnaires, but they made all their employees happy by providing them with ample wages, good homes, and with friendly assistance in every time of need. In those halcyon days an operative was an equal with the owner and agent, and was treated as if entitled to all the privileges which the employer enjoyed, having of course a regard for the relative occupations. One was a shopman, and in the shop was expected to do a shopman's work. The owners were overseers, and were respected in that station. The whole system was like a community in which every person was equally privileged, but where each cheerfully undertook the work best fitted for his natural talent. Owner, agent, overseer, and day-laborers visited each in the other's family, and discussed politics, or chatted together, out of work hours, without presumption or restraint. Then the owner was generous enough to give the working men and women wages in a measure proportionate to their profits. When he prospered he made them presents, and in times of unsuccessful trade he did not visit his misfortune upon them. They were his friends; and on anniversary days and occasions of unusual interest he would consult with the employees about closing the factory, and, if desired by a large majority, the wheel was stopped, and all joined in whatever exercises the day demanded.

3

The factory buildings in those days were large in proportion to the number of operatives, and were constructed in the most stable manner. They were clean and tidy, convenient and cheerful. The yards were sodded, and adorned with evergreens and flower-beds; while bath-houses, and even libraries, were attached to several. There were persons employed whose entire business consisted in sweeping and cleaning the factory, and who understood well the arts of neatness and convenience.

The employees were selected from the healthiest and most buoyant farmers' girls, and from the ranks of genial, honest men. They were the most intelligent class of New England society, and have since filled many of the highest offices and most influential positions in the nation. Many of them were school-girls, and spent their vacations in the factory; others belonged to wealthy families, and wished to show their independence of character by earning their own living; while the men were, many of them, students paying their way by factory work, or heads of families who wished for employment near their homes. The girls usually went home during the summer, to assist at the farming or attend the academy; and when they returned to the factory, blooming with health, they were welcomed by such as remained or had previously returned, with affectionate demonstrations of joy. They were never overworked, as there were a large number of "spare hands," always ready to take the place of one who was ill or exhausted, and their wages were such that they were satisfied with the care of one or two machines. Their work was really play. For in no place did they enjoy themselves so well as in the factory; and often there were found wealthy men's daughters crying for a chance "to go into the shop." It was industrious recreation; and in it no person was idle. Tatting, edging, fine stitching, embroidery, crochet, and braiding were produced by the thousand yards from the nimble hands of the loom-tenders or "spare hands." At every interval when the loom required no attention, or when waiting for "supplies," those happy, light-hearted girls plied their needle or wrought their threadwork with untiring industry and with astonishing natural skill. They were endowed with literary taste; and some of them wrote articles for magazines and first-class periodicals, while others read and criticised the latest books, or employed their spare hours in arranging Shakespeare's plays for the stage of private theatricals, and rehearsing them on the packing-boxes. Books were then seen on nearly every window-sill, lying open or containing embroidered "marks," which, like everything valuable that the girls brought into the factory, were never liable to injury or theft.

The boarding-houses, where operatives were provided with board for $1.25 per week, were provided with all the comforts of a rural home; and the keepers were always kind old ladies, who were acquainted with all classes of cooking, knew how to arrange a house, and loved young people. Many a girl formed an attachment for the cheerful, kind-hearted boarding-house mistresses which was as tender and nearly as strong as that which they entertained for their own mothers. Those evenings when sewing, reading, games, and jokes entertained the company were the happiest of many a girl's life; while those quiet Sabbaths, when the church-bell was the only breaker of the holy silence, were the sweetest and dearest Sundays of life. Ah, happy days! when in youthful vigor the innocent and guileless daughters of old New England were able, without disgrace or contamination, to earn their own livelihood and rest in the sweet satisfaction of being dependent upon no one! No coarse jokes, no drunken suitors, no vile gossip, no jealousy, no care, and no fear. That was the "golden age" of factory life, and many hearts will sigh for "the days gone by" when this reminder of the past comes to their notice.[2] They will recall with pleasure even the days of illness, when, with the factory physician, the owners' wives, and the detailed operatives, who cared for them, they were happier than they have been since when in health and strength. They will remember the kind face of the agent who made them a present, and paid them for the lost time when they had recovered. They cannot suppress a tear as they recount the kind reception, the congratulations, and good wishes of their associates, when they joyfully took their places at the soul-stirring and fascinating loom, to listen again to the magic click of the flyers, the tingling "cracks" of the drop-wire and shuttle, and be lulled into a waking repose by the monotonous roar of the mighty machinery in the rooms below.

4

The growth of the factory system in the United States, and especially in New England, furnishes an excellent field for thoughtful research. But a lengthy discussion of the subject cannot find place in this book.

The first cotton-factory ever built in this country was constructed in the town of Beverly, Massachusetts, in the year 1787, and the machinery was propelled by horse-power. Between that date and the year 1800 several factories—rude, of course, in their construction, and able only to weave the thickest and roughest fabrics—were established in Rhode Island and Connecticut. But the year 1793 is the date which the cotton manufacturers of the United States have adopted as the "birthday" of the cotton manufacturing system of the country. That year Samuel Slater, the "father of cotton manufacture," opened his mill at Pawtucket, Rhode Island, and for the first time tried the experiment of manufacturing cotton with water-power.[3] There was but little encouragement, however, for American manufacturers during the twenty years that followed, owing to the cheapness of labor in England and the other vastly superior advantages which the English possessed for the manufacture and improvement of machinery. But in the war of 1812, which stopped the importation of all English goods and sent the prices of such fabrics into fabulous figures, the necessity of being able to make our own clothing and of assuming a greater independence of England was recognized, and measures were adopted for the increase of our manufacturing facilities. In 1813 the first factory in Lowell was erected on the site which is covered at present by the great factories of the Middlesex Manufacturing Company. That building was constructed almost entirely of wood, and drew its water supplies from a dam of very small proportions, if compared with the mighty dikes and butments of the present day. In 1814 the first power-loom was started in a small factory at Waltham, Massachusetts, and was soon after introduced in Dover, New Hampshire; Lowell, Massachusetts; Pawtucket, Rhode Island; and in several places in Connecticut.

In 1820 calico print-works were established on a flourishing basis, and the manufacturing system was declared to be in every way a success. Each succeeding year saw new buildings, new dams, new companies, an increased demand for laborers, until, after adding untold millions to the wealth of the nation, and giving us real national independence, we find, to-day, in New England one hundred and eighty thousand operatives employed in that single branch of American industry.

When it was proposed to charter a great corporation, and give to that body certain privileges and rights which individuals did not enjoy, there was great opposition in the Massachusetts Legislature. It was said that corporations were prejudicial to the liberties of individuals, and that as moneyed monopolies they could defeat any attempt to compete with them on the part of private parties. It was feared by the statesmen of that early day, that although the men then applying for a charter were no doubt honest, honorable, and capable men, yet they might have successors in whose hands such corporations would be a dangerous power. They hesitated for a long time, and there is no doubt that this jealousy of all encroachments on private liberty would have defeated the first attempt at manufacturing incorporation, had it not been for the argument that in no other way could we compete with England. It was thought that the superior intelligence of our operatives would balance the *quantity* of labor in England, and that our great water-powers would give us sufficient advantage over the costly steam-power of England to meet the expense of crowding our fabrics into the markets where only English manufactures had been known. So confident was one of the proprietors of a Waltham factory who had visited England that by incorporation we could compete with England, he declared it to be his belief that the day would soon come when, instead of receiving thirty-three cents per yard, which in 1816 was the price of cotton cloth, the manufacturer would be able to make money by disposing of his cotton productions at eight cents a yard. Few believed him then, though the result more than fulfilled his prophecy. These arguments overcame the objections, and, thinking that it would be better to trust our own citizens with a "dangerous power" than to be so dependent upon such an enemy as England, the legislators withdrew their objections, and a precedent was established which would be followed in all applications for similar establishments. By this act of incorporation several men were permitted to form a stock company, construct buildings, hire laborers, and make their own by-laws. The enforcement of the rules and by-laws was also placed in the hands of the corporations; so that within their own precincts they were the sole legislators and executors. But so generous were the corporators, and so democratic were the officers, that the factory system was everywhere hailed with delight; and the thoughts of oppression, wrong, and cruelty were as far from the minds of the operatives as they were from the hearts of the proprietors. No moneyed enterprise was ever started under the guidance of better men or with purer motives; nor was there ever employed such a number of educated, able, honest, and industrious men and women in any country, at any time, as were the employees in our cotton "factory system," during the first half-century of its existence.

5

The English factory-system with which American manufacturers were obliged to compete was just the reverse of the American system. Ours began by employing the best class of the community, and by paying them ample wages; while the English capitalists hired the very lowest classes, and paid the smallest wages possible. The competition was wholly between our intelligent few and their ignorant many, with high wages on one side and small pay upon the other. In the contest, America had the disadvantage of being without skilled laborers, of having no ready-made market, and of having none but small capitalists. Yet the advantages which *intelligent and well-paid labor* gave us over the English cheap *brute-force* counterbalanced the great disadvantages, and America was able soon not only to compete in the same fair field, but to *underbid* England in the sale of her best staples.** Then, as now, and as ever has been, and ever will be, well-paid labor was the most profitable to the employer. It may be that the generous and prosperous example set by America awakened the statesmen of England to a just sense of their duty; for it was at the beginning of our factory enterprises (1818) that Sir Robert Peel called the attention of the British Parliament to the tyranny and cruelty practised in the large manufacturing towns of England.[4] At that time the condition of the operatives—the greatest portion of whom were children—was most deplorable. The old English plan of apprentice-slavery was abolished, so that "cheap labor" could not be secured under the cover of that device, and when the introduction of machinery led the proprietors to think that the employment of skilled labor was unnecessary, those short-sighted and stony-hearted men sought out all the little ignorant children in the lowest and poorest parts of the great cities, and, with threats and even lashings, made them tend upon the machinery of the cotton-factories. Under relentless overseers, these poor children, in rags and dirt, were made to work fourteen or sixteen hours a day, and given the most slovenly quarters and the most unpalatable food. As disease or exhaustion carried them off, others were found to take the vacant places, and a worse slavery instituted, under the very shadow of Britannia's Parliament, than any which that body had been so long opposing in the Colonies.

Notwithstanding Sir Robert's earnest appeals, and his evidence showing the outrageous treatment of the girls and all classes of employees, that dull body, which at times seems, like corporations, to have "no soul," took no action, but, like so many bullfrogs, croaked one another into a fury, and adjourned without action. Then began that "thirty years' fight" which raged with such animosity nearly every year in the halls of British legislation, culminating, at last, in the passage of the Ten-Hour Bill, in 1848. Why it was necessary for Lord Ashley, Richard Oastler, Thomas M. Sadler, Sir Robert Peel, The Bishop of Oxford, Lord Macaulay, Earl Grey,[5] Philip Grant,***[6]

**In the American markets.
***Philip Grant: Charles Cheeryble, of Dickens's *Nicholas Nickleby*.

Lord Palmerston,[7] and other great men to prove and reprove, frame and amend, so many bills, make so many appeals and so much sacrifice, in order to convince that legislature of a crime that was patent to the eyes of the least observing, is now a wonder. Yet such men as Lord Brougham, John A. Roebuck, and John Bright would not be convinced, and through a period of thirty years—time enough to make old men and women of the abused operatives about whom the controversy first began—it found such able and influential opposers.[8]

There is no man who, taken in the light of subsequent history, would seem less likely to oppose oppression and advocate the claims of the suffering children than John Bright; yet he was one of their bitterest and most relentless foes. He frightened the House of Commons with threats that if they meddled with the cotton-factories, the manufacturers would remove their mills to Switzerland. He claimed that the children had better "work out than rust out," and he even accused the advocates of reform of hypocrisy, avarice, and a silly desire for cheap notoriety. He pandered to the aristocracy, was cheek-by-jowl with the capitalists and stockholders, and made for himself a dark record, which will require a few more years of patriotism and stronger words of repentance than he has yet spoken to convince the author that he is the "disinterested philanthropist" which he now claims to be. Notwithstanding his great speeches against the bill, and the opposition of "our most noble Queen," the right prevailed and the hours of labor were reduced to ten hours; the pay remaining unchanged or being raised, while the stockholders obtained greater dividends than ever before.

During all those years of fierce agitation the condition of the working-classes gradually improved, and, when the bill finally passed, the manufacturers had so far learned the necessity of paying some attention to the health of their employees that there was much less necessity for it than when the agitation began. Nevertheless it was needed, and had a great influence upon the social and moral condition of the working-men. As those natural and social noblemen who advocated the cause expected, it gave the laboring-classes courage, impressed upon their minds some sense of their own importance, and created a desire for education and social standing never before exhibited by them. So that for sixty years the operatives of England have been gradually ascending the scale of human progress, and are asserting their natural right to the same consideration which other men and women enjoy. Their condition to-day is not by any means an enviable one; and to the observer who sees them as they are, and knows not to what degradation they were once reduced, it may seem absurd to speak of their progress in the past. Even now, notwithstanding that they have been going up and American operatives have been going down in wages and social privileges, the English working-classes as a body are far below those of America. Charles Dickens saw this on the occasion of his first visit to America, and, speaking of the factories at Lowell, said****[9]: "I have carefully abstained from drawing a comparison between these factories and those of our own land. Many of the circumstances, whose strong influence has been at work for years in our manufacturing towns, have not arisen here; and there is no manufacturing population in Lowell, so to speak, for these girls (often the daughters of small farmers) come from other States, remain a few years in the mills, and then go home for good. The contrast would be a strong one, for it would be between the good and the evil, the living light and deepest shadow. I abstain from it because I deem it just to do so. But I only the more earnestly adjure all those whose eyes may rest on these pages to pause and reflect upon the difference between this town and those great haunts of desperate misery, to call to mind if they can, in the midst of party strife and squabble, the efforts that must be made to purge them of their suffering and danger, and, last and foremost, to remember how the precious time is rushing by."

Although Dickens made a pretty accurate estimate of the high character of the Lowell factory-girls, yet he saw their *life* necessarily through the mental lenses which his escort of stockholders gave him, and his exalted opinion of American factories was perhaps gained more by a contrast with those of England than by measuring them by any ideal standard of his own. Doubtless that Gener-

****American Notes.

al who marched through "files of beautifully attired factory-girls, miles long," thought them to be the happiest beings on earth; perhaps he would have thought differently had they worn hearts on their sleeves instead of the stockholders' frocks.[10]

But it may be that they were all happy then, as that was a long while ago, and perhaps they were comfortable when Dickens made his visit. But they were not as happy nor as comfortable when Dickens saw them as they were when the General saw them, neither are they as well situated today as they were when Dickens saw them. "*Getting much and giving little*," which marks the age, is raising the cost of living, reducing the wages and the value of money, and affecting them deeply, as it does all the other laborers in the land.

6

Within ten years the class of operatives in American factories has almost wholly changed. The great men, for whom nature did so much, and who valued mankind for their mental and physical qualities, have passed away one after another and left their places to be filled by others. Unfortunately their mantles have in many cases fallen upon the shoulders of men who, although they were heirs to the property, were not inheritors of their fathers' natural goodness or ability. Money, not nature, has made them aristocrats. In New England, where the manufacturing wealth was confined to so few, a select aristocracy was years ago established, and as each rich man wished his child to marry into a wealthy family, they were obliged to marry cousins. This defiance of nature brought upon the stage a race of half-witted, mental cripples,—if not idiots, at least possessing unevenly balanced minds. And to-day, as much as I dislike to own or record it, there is but little of that open-hearted enterprise and far-seeing sagacity which characterized the generation of factory-owners who have just gone to the grave. The present generation have but little confidence in themselves, and entertain the idea that everybody else is as unstable and unprincipled as they. Hence they never venture their money where its safe return depends upon human love, honesty, or honor. They reverse the law maxim, and think everybody guilty until proof has been entered in due form establishing innocence or honesty. Their fathers could see a fortune in the distance, and made others rejoice with them in the delightful prospect; but the stockholders of to-day hold the cent so near their eyes that a fortune farther away is not visible. They do not consider the good-will of the operatives of any consequence, and can see no more value in the man who cares carefully for their interests than they do in another who does just what he is told and nothing more. While such *natural* aristocrats as their fathers were would be raising the pay of the workmen, beautifying the factories and homes, educating the children, and at the same time filling their own coffers with untold riches, these usurping successors cut down the wages, take no care of the laborers, school none but their own, and wonder how it is that they cannot increase their riches as readily as did their fathers. They think that the "times" have changed; but individual examples which remain of nature's "old school" show that it is not the "times," but the "*men*," that have so much changed.

7

An apt illustration of the short-sightedness of descendants, whose only claim to position or notice lies in the fact that their fathers were what they are not, occurred a few years ago in connection with a cotton-mill with the history of which I happened to be well acquainted. When I first became familiar with the mill and its operatives, it was one of the most flourishing establishments of the kind in New England. The first generation of proprietors, who by their genius had raised themselves from poverty and obscurity to wealth and fame, understood well the detail of each department, and were practically, although not nominally, the overseers. They were still in active life when I first entered the town, and the marks of their enterprise were everywhere apparent. Each operative was known to some one of the proprietors, and their industry and good character was established before they were admitted to the mill. The boarding-houses were often visited by the owners of the mill, and the health, comfort, and recreation of the girls cared for in the kindest manner. If a keeper of a boarding-house was not obliging and lady-like in her deportment toward the employees, she was dismissed at once and another secured. Everything within the mill was kept as neat as a parlor; and as the overseers and owners took pains to praise those who showed great care in the appearance of their looms or apartments, all took the utmost pride in keeping everything about them clean and tidy. Every person in the shop wished the kind-hearted proprietors the greatest prosperity, and contributed much toward that end by being as careful as possible of the machinery, wasting no oil, no cotton, no yarn, or cloth. I do not think that money could have hired one of the girls to steal a yard of cloth or a "cut" of yarn, nor would the men be seen by each other idling or in any way wasting their time. The agent was a friend to whom all went for advice or favors, and he took nearly as much interest in their trials and joys as he would in those of his children. Although there were rules laid down by the stockholders, they were seldom spoken of and never transgressed. New-comers learned them, and were always too happy to do as the agent wished to think of breaking the by-laws. Wealth seemed to roll in like a river, and everybody was happy. Cheerful minds made healthy bodies, and glad hearts made nimble fingers, while the clear consciences of the owners gave a double value to the fortune which they made. In fine, it was the "true factory-system" of which America then had so much reason to be proud.

Fifteen years later I visited that factory again. But the changes had been so great that I hesitated before entering, lest I had made a mistake in the locality. The building was the only feature which had not entirely changed; and even that was marred, stained, and broken, with rags in the windows and patches on the doors. The yard was strewn with lumber and rubbish, with here and there small pools of stagnant water, while drum-wheels, gearing, old reeds, and refuse cotton almost choked the main entrance. The condition of the factory within was even worse than it was without. The stairs were unswept and dirty, daubing the skirts of the visitor with oil, verdigris, and lint at almost every step. The ceilings of the weaving-rooms were covered with dust and cobwebs, the floor was strewn with pieces of yarn, splinters, and broken bobbins, while the looms were black with grease, and bore the finger-prints of many a dirty hand upon the painted portions. The gearing was thick with sticky, dirt-mixed oil, and grated upon the ear like the filing of a saw.

The laborers completed the picture of carelessness and slovenliness, and were ragged, dirty, neglected, and ignorant. Dirty faces, torn dresses, uncombed hair, dull eyes, and expressionless mouths were to be seen everywhere. If threads broke in the warping-machine, the gearing was stopped because the operative lacked the intelligent skill to tie it while the machinery was in motion; if the shafting squeaked for oil, the attendant did not seem to care, or, if she did care, could not stop to oil it, owing to the constant attention which the management of so many looms required of her. She had no thought but of wages, and, if she would earn sufficient to meet her expenses, she must work with all her mind, strength, and time. There was no embroidery, no half-finished socks, no paper flowers, no books, no spare hands, no play, and no jokes but such as were coarse and pointless. When I left the weaving-room and followed the filthy crowd toward the door-way of the lower floor, I was surprised to see each operative called into a room adjoining the agent's office, from which they issued with a pass that they must show to the sentry at the door before they went out. I was only the more astonished when I learned that no operative was permitted to leave the building without having been *thoroughly searched*, and that the laborers were all of them "notorious thieves." On inquiry of the agent I ascertained that the plan of searching had succeeded in recovering property amounting to many thousand dollars, which the girls and the men had attempted to carry away under their clothing.

"They love to steal," said he, "and I have caught them carrying away old iron, oil, and even waste, which could be of no possible use to them. They have such a devilish desire to impoverish the company that they throw yarn, cloth, beams, bobbins, paint, and cotton out of the window into the river, and I believe that, did we not keep a most vigilant watch in every room, they would set the building on fire."

"How everything has changed since I was here!" said I.

"Yes, it has changed. Factory operatives are not what they used to be," said he.

"Could you not get a better class of laborers by paying more wages?" inquired I.

"Perhaps," answered he; "but the company cannot afford to pay more wages, for *they are losing money now!*"

So they were losing money, and about a year from that time failed, deeply indebted to the employees, and having so small an amount of property compared with their liabilities that they paid but twenty cents on a dollar, while other factories were making the owners rich. At the creditors' meeting the following facts came to light: the original owners had died, leaving the property to the care of their sons; and these new proprietors, having none of the liberal spirit which characterized their predecessors, undertook to introduce "cheap labor." They employed those persons—many were imported for that purpose—who could be hired at a low rate; which, of course, introduced such a vile class that it drove out all who laid claims to respectability.

Hoping to enrich themselves faster than their fathers had done, they killed the goose which laid the golden eggs, by discharging spare hands, paying no attention to the cleanliness of the building, neglecting the boarding-houses, and concentrating their entire energies on the present dollar, to the exclusion of the fortunes that lay but a short distance away.[11] No operative ever saw the proprietors in the factory; and as nobody took any interest in the working-people's affairs, they had no interest in the prosperity of other people. A mutual ill-will and a social warfare were the results, in which, as must ever be the case, the operatives were the victors; in a campaign, however, that brought them no honor, no pleasure, and no gain.

CHAPTER 10

How Cotton Is Manufactured.
—Factory Friendships

*Brotherly Affection.—The Destitute Wife.—
The Widow's Trial.—The Country Girl
and the Actress.—Drunken Pickard and Bob.*

1

In order that the reader may be able to understand the terms which I shall be obliged to use in the chapters that follow, a few words may be necessary in explanation of the processes through which the cotton passes while being manufactured into cloth. The cotton when taken from the bale is passed through a machine, usually placed in the basement of the factory, which picks and combs out the sticks, seeds, and hard lumps, leaving only the light, feathery cotton. This machine is called a "picker." Then the cotton passes into another apparatus near by, which draws it from the pile into a long straight roll, without twist or strength. This machine is called a "drawer." From the drawer the roll passes into the "speeder," when it is pressed into a smaller size and slightly twisted. The cotton is then called "roping," and is wound upon great spools, as it comes from the speeder. The spools of roping are taken to the spinning-room, where, by means of rollers to press and flyers to twist, it is reduced to thread. The thread which, as it comes from the spindles, is wound by machinery upon small spools called "bobbins," is very fine, and is known in the factories as "the warp." From a large number of these small spools, which are placed near together, in a large frame, the threads are wound upon a very large spool called a "warping-beam." The warping-beams, when full of thread, are taken to the "dressing-machine," where the threads, a great number at a time, pass from the warping-beam over a roller that turns in a trough of starch, then under a series of constantly moving brushes which equalize the starch and brush away lint or any foreign substance that may be adhering to the thread. From the brushes it passes over a large heated copper roller which dries the starch; and then is wound upon another enormous spool called a "web-beam." These great web-beams are then put upon a "drawing-in frame," where an operator draws every end—and there may be thousands—through a "reed," in which there is a little aperture for each thread. These reeds are parts of the "loom," and keep the threads separate when the machinery is in motion; and, together with the web-beams, are placed in the looms whenever they are required for weaving. From the looms in which the threads that wind from the web-beams through the reeds combine with the threads which braid in from the "shuttle," the "cloth" is taken, which, after inspection, is packed for market.

Should the manufacturer wish to make calico, the cloth is put through a chemical process called "bleaching," and taken to the print-works. Calico "printing" is done by passing the cloth under an engraved roller which is so ingeniously supplied with dyes that it prints all the different colors and figures at the same time. Until the recent invention of roller-printing it required the greatest skill to dye calico; and it was never sold for less than fifty cents per yard. Then there was a different stamp for every figure, and the workman was obliged to dip each stamp in the color and strike it with a mallet when placed on the cloth. Hence it was a slow and expensive process. Now it is so rapidly done by machinery that the cost is reduced a hundred-fold, while the only great skill required is in mixing the colors.

2

All the different processes of cotton manufacture have their divisions and subdivisions, each of which requires the attention of intelligent laborers; consequently there is in nearly every factory a number of persons employed in the same room who, as they are constantly in one another's society, become intimately acquainted with each other's manners and disposition. This leads to the formation of friendships and associations, many of which are as sincere and lasting as any of earth. The circumstances which surround their individual lives, and the hardships which they endure together, have a great effect upon these friendships. Like the soldiers in the field, the sailors on the sea, the travellers far from home and country, they are deeper and stronger in proportion to the danger and suffering which they see. So that out of oppression may spring some sweet fruits, and in the factories where the operatives have the least privileges and the lowest wages there may be a slight compensation in the attachments which are formed among the operatives for each other.

Again we will say that it is not the object of this book to sound the praises or advocate the cause of those who, like Burritt, Franklin, Lincoln, and Banks, have succeeded in obtaining the position for which nature designed them; nor to repeat the old stories of their friendships in low life and generosity in high life.[1] We speak for the defeated ones, about whom the world has heard but little and cared less. The factories of New England have teemed with philosophers and statesmen who have toiled year after year in obscurity, not that an "occasion never called for them," but because an opportunity was never given them. Somebody has said that "circumstances do not make men, but men make circumstances," and it is one of the truest sayings ever recorded;[2] but, unfortunately, it often happens that the men who make the circumstance are not the men to be affected by it. And the factory operative, however gifted and good, belongs to one of the classes for which other men make the circumstances. That they make the most of their opportunities is proved by the attachments they form and the ability they exhibit in the station to which they are confined.

As a person without enemies may be considered a nonentity or a fool, so a person with no friends may be counted as a very bad individual. But the true test of nobleness has ever been in the possession of a few friends and loving them with all the heart. Such has been the characteristics of all great heroes; and, applying that standard to the factory operatives, we find many who show themselves worthy of the title which I claim for them.

In 1854 there were two young men at work together in a factory at Chicopee, Massachusetts, between whom there was a most marked intimacy. Their work brought them often together during the day, and they occupied the same room at the boarding-house. They were seen so often together, and dressed so nearly alike, that the citizens of the town believed them to be brothers,—caring for each other when sick, one taking the work of both when the other was obliged to be absent. It happened that the youngest, whose name was Mortley, one day was adjusting a belt while his companion, Wesley, was standing near. The belt ran upon the pulley quicker than Mortley anticipated, and caught his hand under it as it started around the pulley. Wesley saw the danger, and, knowing that a moment's delay would draw Mortley's whole arm and perhaps his body into the gearing, leaped upon the pulley, and, thrusting his foot against the belt, threw it off before the pulley had half completed the first revolution. But neither escaped without injury, for the forefinger of Mortley's right hand was crushed, and Wesley's right ankle thrown out of joint. Neither ever completely recovered, and ever after the limp of the one and the crushed finger of the other were mutually considered to be "bonds of friendship." In 1855 they married sisters, and began keeping house in the same tenement. But soon after Wesley moved to Meriden, Connecticut, and Mortley took up his residence in Holyoke, Massachusetts. In 1861 Wesley died, leaving a wife and two children with no property but a little house in the suburbs of Meriden. The widow was in delicate health, and could do nothing toward the support of herself or children, and applied to the town authorities for assistance. Those officials refused to consider her as a pauper, or treat her as if entitled to any assistance so long as she owned a house; and the woman in her despair advertised her house to be for sale. A few days before the day set for the sale she received an anonymous letter, which said that "a poor debtor of her husband's" would try to pay off his debt in small instalments, to be found on the first of every month at a certain bank. The writer closed his letter, after bidding her to be of good cheer, with the remark that he "dare not tell how much" he owed Mr. Wesley, but it would "last her a long time." The widow, finding the first instalment already deposited, and unable to obtain from the bank the name of the depositor, did not sell her house, but managed to live comfortably upon the twenty dollars per month which the unknown debtor supplied. For seven years the money was always ready on the first day of the month, and the widow had begun to wonder how it was possible for a person to owe her husband so much, when she heard that Mortley had been killed by a boiler explosion at Rutland, Vermont. On going to the bank on the following pay-day she found no money, and, as the banker said that the giver was dead, she felt assured that Mortley had all that time been dividing his hard-earned wages equally between her and his own family. She subsequently learned from her sister that Mortley had adopted that plan because he feared she would not accept it if she knew who was the giver.

3

In the town of Holyoke, Massachusetts, there are two factory-girls, whose sisterly regard for each other has often been the subject of remark, and whose conduct in life has ever been the most exemplary. Having had my attention called to the fact, I made inquiries about them, to ascertain if there had been any particular cause for their affectionate behavior, and their sad history was related to me as follows: In 1862 they were boarding together, and were working side by side in the same room, when they were wooed and won in marriage by two young men who were equally intimate with each other. Both of the girls were married at the same time, their husbands enlisted in the same regiment, and were both killed in the same battle.* Meantime both of the girls bore a son, and during the days when they were obliged to enter the shop they hired the same nurse to care for both of the boys. Four years of hardship and the greatest suffering cemented their friendship, and increased their love for each other. But the trials which they had seen were light compared

---

*Holyoke Transcript.

with the one in store for them. When the boys were five years of age, they were counted as the brightest scholars in the beginners' class at school, were clothed in the neatest style, and made to attend the school exercises with the greatest regularity. It happened that one afternoon, when there was no school, the mothers were too busy in the mill to care for their little boys, so they sent them out into the yard to play, and directed them to keep within sight. This command the boys fully obeyed; and hour after hour passed with the children running, jumping, and ball-playing, while the proud mothers looked on and were happy. But when the boys had become tired of every other amusement, they placed a slab across a log which lay near the canal, for the purpose of playing "teter."[3] The mothers saw the preparations, and would have run down to the yard to prevent the trial of so dangerous an experiment, but the looms must not be stopped, and their presence was every moment necessary. Soon they saw the boys mount the slab, one upon each end, and attempt to balance each other. The slab was near the end of the log, and at the second attempt of the boys to "teter" it swung from the pivot, and both were instantly thrown into the canal. The mothers rushed down the four flights of stairs with their utmost speed, but when they arrived at the spot both of the little boys were dead.

4

Malinda had been an actress, and had been the recipient of praises, *encores*, and bouquets while playing with Booth, Cushman, Costar, and many other notables in the theatrical world.[4] But she became too corpulent to appear at advantage in any part but that of "heavy old woman," and after a while lost that by contracting very intemperate habits. She had no relatives, no friends, and was in a destitute condition, when, after several utter failures, she abandoned the hope of ever going upon the stage again. Too proud to beg or apply for public charity, she attempted to find some kind of employment, and at last found her way into the Pemberton Mill at Lawrence.[5] She was unacquainted with any kind of work. Her fingers, that had been trained for throwing kisses and holding the gauze of a dance-dress, were too soft for the loom, and her tiny feet, which had been shaped and trained for the footlights, were unable to hold up her heavy body for six long hours, with little or no change of position. But it happened that a little girl by the name of Ann had charge of the looms next to those which the actress had been hired to superintend, and she noticed the awkwardness and the disconsolate expression which accompanied the actress in everything she undertook. The little lady, regardless of the bad reputation of the actress, undertook to teach and assist her in the management of the looms.** It had been so long since a kind word had been spoken to her or a kind act done for her that the actress formed at once a most sincere attachment for the innocent country-girl, who so generously came to her assistance. They would converse together through the evenings,—Ann telling about the rural attractions of her country home, and the actress in turn describing the stage, the players, the music, the scenery, and the whims of the audiences. Thus a year passed away, and the actress, who entered the mill a coarse, vulgar, and reckless woman, had become, under the influence of little Ann, an affectionate, quiet, well-behaved lady. Upon Ann the actress poured out her whole soul. Ann was all the friend whom she had, and to her she clung with the most ardent fondness; while the actress was to Ann a subject of pity for her misfortunes and of respect for her great experience.

On the morning of the 11th of January, 1860, Ann and the actress entered the mill together.[6] At the door-way they paused a few moments to watch the crowd of operatives as they came toward the mill. The actress was quite dejected because Ann had declared her intention of taking a vacation, and, perhaps, of leaving the mill altogether. The former was remonstrating with Ann, and as they turned to ascend the stairway, caught her arm and said, "Ann, I don't feel like working to-day, and if you go away I shall never feel like it again."

"I'm of no consequence," said Ann, laughing; "you will do just as well without me."

"I tell you, dear Ann," exclaimed the excited actress, "if you leave

---

**Every new hand must have a "teacher."

this mill, we part; and parting with you, the only being I have to love or care for, means *death*."

Ann laughed, and said she thought the actress was getting "tragical."

"So I am," said the disconsolate one,—"so I am; and I tell you that this river, which has floated so many, may float another if you leave me."

As they entered the hall leading to the weaving apartments three girls passed them, laughing, joking, and pulling each other.

"Do you suppose," said the actress, "that those girls, who think so much of each other's society, really *love* as you and I have loved?"

"O yes," said Ann; "and perhaps better; we cannot tell about others' friendship or love, you know."

The bell began its toll; the steam began to hiss, and the water to swash in the basement; the belts began to move, and the flyers to rattle; while picker, drawer, speeder, spinner, warper, and loom began at the same instant to pick the cotton, make the rolls, twist the roping, spin the thread, and weave the cloth for another day's production.

Noon came, with the clamoring bells, the usual crowd, the hurried meal, and the hasty return; and many hearts thanked God that they were on the last half of another wearisome day. Three o'clock came,—the afternoon was one half spent,—and the anxious operatives noted the hour and minute hands, and said, "Only three hours more."

Four o'clock came; the voices of the girls were still; they were now too tired for conversation, and even the overseer gave his orders in a low tone, for he, too, was getting exhausted. But the great, restless, and exhaustless machinery rattled over the head of the actress, roared in the stories below her, while the whole building trembled and waved beneath its ponderous load of lifelike mechanism. She was thinking of Ann, and wondering if the time ever would come when they must part, and had stopped her loom to mend the thread, when the great building seemed to be seized with a sudden tremor. The windows rattled, the floor creaked, the walls cracked, the great looms rocked to and fro, and a wild shriek, mingled with dull, jarring thumps, echoed through and through the writhing building. One glance,—and only one,—which showed the girls flying wildly in every direction,—some out at the windows, hundreds toward the stairway, and others for the elevator,—while the shafting fell from its bearings, the belts flew from the pulleys, the great piles of web-beams came tumbling down, the landscape through the windows seemed swinging, sliding, and falling with a dizzy, sickening motion; and with one awful crash, that echoed through the streets, and re-echoed from the distant hills, the great five-story Pemberton Mill, with all its freight of life, crumbled and *crashed* into a distorted heap of ruins. O that terrible, terrible scene! Who can ever efface it from memory that looked, though but an instant, upon that sickening mass? Great timbers broken and splintered, piles of shattered brick and mortar, crooked pieces of shafting, ponderous wheels, and under, in, over, and through all were writhing, maimed, shattered, and bleeding human beings. The great chimneys, which stood as grim spectators, looked coldly down upon that pile where heads, arms, and legs were protruding, and through which the streams of human gore gurgled and bubbled, drowning some that had not perished by the fall, and changing the color of the water far below the ruin.

And the cries! How it appalled the stoutest, and chilled the most hardened! The air was resonant with human misery, and carried a dull sense of the fearful disaster to the hearts of men for miles around, long before they knew what had occurred, or learned by human testimony that anything unusual had happened. The great city, together with all who were within hearing distance, seemed palsied with fear, and when the earth had ceased to tremble, and the reverberations died away, men whispered one to the other, with pale faces, "Something awful has happened."

Then came the crowd of mothers, fathers, sisters, brothers, relatives, and friends, to join in the chorus of shrieks, groans, cries, and choking sobs that came unceasingly from the unseemly heap. Men, women, and children, inspired with supernatural strength, tugged away at timbers, shafting, and rubbish, searching and calling for loved ones. Some few of the victims lay near the surface, held only by an arm, a foot, or a finger, and from them were the timbers quickly lifted, and one after another they came bleeding from the wreck. Night came quickly on, but it saw no cessation in the work; neither were the awful cries abated. Then, with a great bonfire that shimmered on the great canal and cast a lurid gleam over the gory pile, the workmen worked nobly on. Lifting a great timber to release a man who was crying for help, four mangled and dripping bodies were discovered, which were carried through the shuddering crowds to the hall. As the hours fled the number of workmen increased. Extra trains brought in the firemen and volunteers from other cities; the alarm-bells called in the farmers, and the long ruin, which covered an acre of ground, was teeming with zealous workmen. Headless, armless, crushed, torn, and dissevered bodies, soaking in blood, were drawn out to get at the living, whose cries could be heard far, far down beneath the rubbish. Fainting ones, slashed and mangled ones, living and dying ones, came swiftly by on the shoulders of stout men, while the wild and frenzied assembly of relatives shouldered, crowded, and fought for a glimpse of each bleeding mass, to know if it were the body of their beloved.

Among the great throng of workers, whose disregard of danger and contempt for arduous undertakings was marvellous, could be seen the actress, flying hither and thither, treading upon uncertain timbers, leaping over grim chasms, and lifting weights that would in calmer times have defied a person possessing double her strength; crying in the bitterness of her woe for her companion and friend.

Though she stayed and worked until daylight, ay, until noon came, and night again, yet no answer came to her cries, no word from Ann's familiar lips. The three girls whose friendship she had doubted were found dead in each other's arms, but they were so interlocked with the timbers that they could not be extricated. "Truly," thought she, "they were friends in life, and in death they were not divided."

Fire! Fire! How I shudder now when I recall the terrible import of those words, as the cry went up and the ascending smoke convinced the horror-struck spectators that the ruin was in flames. The heart stopped its beating at the sound, and soul-breaking despair took the place of awe and sorrow. A pile of human beings burning alive, and so near that their voices could be distinctly heard, while some were within easy reach. Some had been given food and drink, and led to hope for speedy deliverance. But the appearance of that flame dashed all hope. Some of the victims far down in the wreck, thinking that they must burn, cut their throats or stabbed themselves, others yelled and writhed in their despair. One party who seemed to have fallen together and to have some little room faced the fate that awaited them, and with Christian resignation began, amid groans and shrieks, to sing that well-known hymn:—

"My Father's house is built on high,
Far, far above the starry sky;
When from this earthly prison free,
That heavenly mansion mine shall be.
   I'm going home, I'm going home,
   I'm going home, to die no more.'"

At last the lifeless form of poor Ann was exhumed from the ruins, and the actress, frantic with grief, moaned over it, and called on her to come back with most touching appeals to the unheeding body.

Meantime the fire spread on in the ruins, lapping up the dead and alive alike, while the fire-department poured on water and dug at the pile with superhuman endeavors; and after two days and two nights of toil the thousands of laborers were obliged to give way before the fire, and such as still remained in the mountainous ruin were consumed to ashes. The cries which had been growing weaker and weaker were at last drowned by the hissing and roaring of the terrible fire; and a cragged, blackened wreck of iron and brick was all that remained of the great cotton-factory which, by the adoption of a criminally short-sighted policy, was lightly and weakly constructed *by cheap labor*.

The actress, whose life had been so much cheered and elevated in little Ann's society, sank at once into melancholy, and after a short and aimless existence followed her little friend to the grave, giving a striking example of the elevation of a fallen one by factory associations, and of the maxim that "none love truly who act not nobly."

The general opinion in the non-manufacturing communities seems to be that factory associations are degrading, and that it is dangerous to trust a woman within the walls of such an establishment. It may be more so now than it used to be, because so few can live respectably if dependent entirely upon the wages they receive. Yet I not only claim that, with the exception of those traitorous establishments which import their help, there is little or no cause for the present opinion with regard to the class of working-women; but that very many more are raised from fallen wretches into true womanhood by the elevating friendships which they form than fall into wickedness from the same cause.

5

One of the most remarkable cases that ever came to my notice where a factory friendship called out the best traits of human character, occurred in Pawtucket, Rhode Island. An old man, who had never been married, and whose friends had all forsaken him on account of his excessive intemperance, was employed in the warping-room to lift the large heavy beams of yarn as they were filled from the bobbins, and carry them to the elevator. He had been there many years, and as he was an excellent shop-hand when sober, the overseers secured some one to fill his place when he was intoxicated, who gave it up without question when the drunkard returned. The old man prided himself in the name of "Drunken Pickard," and was usually addressed by that name whenever his roommates or associates wished to speak with him. In 1858 there came a boy about fifteen years old, who was engaged as a "bobbin-boy," and who, like Drunken Pickard, had no living relatives who would recognize him. He was an orphan; and found his way into the factory from a country poorhouse. He was soon known among the operatives as "little Bob," and by his sprightly and graceful manners won the respect of all who knew him. Drunken Pickard became especially attached to him after hearing that he had no friends and no home; for, to one in Pickard's circumstances, those were just the characteristics to call out sympathy and love.

Drunken Pickard and little Bob became fast friends; although Pickard was over thirty years older than Bob. Pickard told Bob all about his "sprees," and Bob told Pickard about his life in the poorhouse. Each was the other's companion when occasion required, and several times Bob was rather roughly used by some of Pickard's intoxicated companions while trying to help him home at night.

One day there was a political meeting at Pawtucket, and Pickard happened to be present when the speeches were made. He did not seem to be favorably impressed with the eloquence displayed on that occasion, and when, according to his usual custom, he related what he had seen and heard to Bob, he remarked that he would be ashamed of Bob if he "could not on occasion make a better speech than that." Bob said that he wished he were a public speaker, and told Pickard about a little piece of poetry which he was taught to declaim when quite small. Pickard suggested the idea of Bob's attempting to make a speech, but Bob pleaded that none but educated people could make political speeches. The conversation led from one idea to another, until Pickard proposed that Bob should attend school, and "edicate" himself for a public speaker, while Pickard should work in the factory, and "pay the bills."

"I'm gettin' old," said Pickard, "and can't last very long. But now I can earn enough to support us both; so you get your larnin', and by that time you can earn money like all the big-bugs, and you can turn around then and take care o' me."

Bob fell in with the proposition, and, having purchased an outfit from his own earnings, took the advice of a resident pastor, who wished him to attend school in Middletown, Connecticut. Three years passed away, during which time Bob was well supplied with funds, paid close attention to his studies, and had shown a most astonishing proficiency. So great was his improvement that, notwithstanding the defects in his early education, he was nearly equal, in the common branches of education, to other young men of his age. But he enlisted in a Connecticut regiment, in 1863, and went to the war, having first obtained the consent of Pickard. He was wounded in a skirmish on the Potomac, and, being discharged in 1864 for disability, resumed his studies again at Middletown. He did not attempt to take a complete college course, but went, in 1867, to New Haven, where he entered the Law School.

Meanwhile Pickard became so industrious and sober that he could no longer lay claim to the title of "Drunken Pickard," and his whole life was devoted to Bob's welfare. To send the greater part of his wages to Bob, and to get the letters which the latter wrote regularly to him, were the two greatest joys of his life. He could not afford the money for a drink, so he never got drunk; while his desire to increase his wages—which was often gratified—was so great that he paid his undivided attention to it, and performed whatever extra work was given him with promptitude and care.

Bob graduated, and has begun the practice of law as a junior partner in an old New York firm, and declares that after this year "Uncle Pickard" shall not do another day's work; while the old man, somewhat bowed with excessive labor, but the healthier for his temperate habits, declares himself perfectly satisfied with that "good old-fashioned way of *changing works*."[8]

CHAPTER 11

Among the "Strikers"

*Character of "Strikers."—Homes of Workmen.—
Life of a Factory Girl.—Of Factory Men.—
Tailors' and Telegraph Strikes.—The "Dover Strike."
—Incidents of Factory Life, &c.*

1

If it needed any argument to prove what is already patent to the most careless observer, namely, that the working-classes are naturally intelligent and able, nothing would be more forcible than a reference to the "strikes" which have occurred among the operatives in New England within the last ten years. It may be thought that because the Chinese, the Jews, the Romans, and the Gauls "struck" in the early ages of the world, and because these organized attempts of laborers to raise their wages have been frequent in modern times, that it is a very simple and easy thing to do. But it is something more than simply refusing to work; and in these days, when the political economy of the world is so regulated that the laborers of one locality are financially interested in those of every other, it requires courage, perseverance, honesty, and fidelity,—courage to face starvation, for the sake of justice; perseverance to hold out until the loss of money—often the only avenue to a capitalist's heart—compels the factory princes to do justly; honesty in the desire to obtain what is their due and nothing more; fidelity to each other, in order that the traitorous behavior of a few shall not defeat the purpose of the many.[1]

That the operatives have often shown all those characteristics which distinguish the highest type of manhood and womanhood is easily proved. Thousands of the working-people are in the lowest state of poverty, and living a domestic life not one grade above the hogs that wallow about their hovels. I know of no better evidence with which to convince my readers than the published public reports of State officials in Massachusetts, New Hampshire, Rhode Island, and Connecticut. General H. K. Oliver, of Massachusetts, whose interest in the welfare of the working-men has been one of the leading traits of his noble character, says that: "Here will be found, in the labyrinthal slums of cities, in narrow courts, dark lanes, and nasty alleys, wretched tenements, with small rooms, dismal, dark, unventilated, into which the sun, God's free gift, never sends a shimmering ray; packed full of men, women, and children, as thick as smoked herrings in a grocer's box. Here they breed, here they live (!), and here they die, with their half-starved, ill-clad children,—death's daily dish, with typhus and scarlet fever and cholera for his butchers; and these festering stys, owned by gentlemen of fortune, 'who live at home at ease,' and whose gold is of the sweat of their tenants' brow, in a rental of fifteen to twenty per cent, *paid in advance!* In such dens, if a horse were kept, the society for the suppression of cruelty to animals should look after his owner."[*]

Speaking of the tenements in which the working-people of Boston live, he states that on the occasion of a recent visit to one locality he found fifty-four families occupying fifty-six rooms. "These families comprised whites, English, and Irish, mostly the latter, blacks, mulattoes, and Indians,—men, women, and children. From the testimony of the lessee and others, there had been as many as 450 occupants at one time, an average of seven persons to a room, each room being 17 x 15 feet and 7 feet high, or, say, 226 cubic feet to each person. The rooms are smoky, damp, unpainted, and mostly unwhitewashed, and are sitting-room, kitchen, wood-room, and living-room all united in one, with no solar ray ever entering them, excepting at the uppermost floor. A few plants in some of the rooms had died, and no wonder. There was no transom-window over any door, and not a window in the house could be let down from the top

---

*Massachusetts Report of the Bureau of Statistics of Labor, p. 88.

for air, and no ventilation in any entry. There is no fire-escape of any sort anywhere about the building, and no banisters to many of the stairs, so that, in case of fire, it would not be possible for the tenants to escape without loss of life. The cellars were very damp, and only lighted by what light could get into them through the interstices between the wooden bars nailed on in the place of windows. There was but one solitary sink in any room, and that was in a room occupied by a colored woman."[3]

Now when a man can afford only such a tenement as this, and has employment sufficient to pay the rent, it will require no small amount of courage to enable him to "strike" and risk his very existence and that of his family on the result. For the loss of a single day's wages would insure suffering, while a month or a week might result in a dreadful death. Yet many have faced the terrible possibility, fully conscious of their risks, with the hope of bettering themselves, or of assisting others. Some idea can be formed of the risk which "strikers" run by those who are acquainted with the "code of honor" that has been adopted by manufacturers, and which obliges the agent of each factory to deny work to every working man or woman who has ever joined in an unsuccessful strike! This makes the strikes in many cases the mere choice between starvation and an increase of wages; and no man or woman would place himself or herself in such a position, or hold out against a powerful corporation for a single day, who had not a large endowment of moral courage. We see, however, that thousands of intelligent laborers do place themselves in this hazardous position, and hold it through privation and pain until justice is given them. More than this; there are many who, in the face of almost certain discharge, have boldly petitioned the corporations to investigate and prevent the future recurrence of the grievances recounted. Many times have these martyrs to a cause which had not only themselves but many others in view been persecuted and hunted for daring to ask for right. It is no exaggeration to say that there are hundreds of operatives now out of employment in New England and living in abject poverty, who would still have been in the factories, had they not obeyed the personal call of State and national committees who asked for information upon the treatment of laborers. Many have been discharged for *consenting* to communicate with public committees, and as all the manufactories exchange pay-rolls, the name of the discharged person is known and posted in every factory of New England.

2

It is not owing to the degeneration of the working-classes while employed in the shops that has made the difference between the operatives of today and those employed a half-century ago. It is the result of the introduction by the factory-owners of the very *lowest* classes to the exclusion of older and more moral employees. It may be that honest industry tends toward moral honesty, and that the acquirement of physical power gives mental and moral strength; for it seems to be a fact that very few ever leave the factory morally worse than when they entered it, while many develop there the noblest traits of human character. If under such circumstances, with no opportunity to pursue a course of education, little time for thought or discussion, they show a natural nobleness, what might they not be if given all the wages to which they would be entitled on the co-operative principle, and, with short hours of labor, allowed to cultivate and discipline their intellectual powers?

That it requires an effort to sustain a good character amid the influences of factory-life, and that the present good behavior of the operatives is due much more to their natural inherent virtue than to oppressive and unnecessary "regulation," can be seen at a glance.

The girls who work in a factory are never alone,—always in a crowd, always conversing or working, always in fear of observation; sleeping in crowded apartments, eating at a crowded table, entering the mills at a crowded door-way, and seeking recreation on streets which are crowded with their companions. In this concourse are persons of every grade and shade of character, all of whom are necessarily the associates of each person who enters the employ of the corporation. The girl who enters the factory as an operative is always called to the agent's desk and directed to sign the "regulation paper," by which she binds herself in contracts, the import of which is as unmeaning and mythical to her as are the army regulations to newly recruited soldiers. She may not, and in nearly every case does not, know that she binds herself to do whatever the agent demands, or pay a forfeit. But she is educated into her slavery by degrees, as accident or opportunity calls her attention to the long roll of by-laws and rules. She rises at an early hour in the morning at the imperative call of the "second bell," and, after dressing herself in the most hurried manner, and with scarcely time to brush her hair and to wash her face,—which is done in the general wash-room near the dining-room,—she rushes with the crowd to the table where the coffee has been poured out and the biscuit distributed for the hasty meal. She swallows the coffee in hurried draughts, snatches a few mouthfuls of bread, and with as little breakfast as she has appetite jumps from the table to don her hat and shawl. Then in the rushing, pushing, joking, shouting multitude she is carried along to the factory. Crushing up the stairway, dividing on the landings, spreading through the building, the mass of human machinery moves to its station, and she finds herself at the last stroke of the warning bell near the loom, the dresser, or the flyers. Slowly the belts begin to turn upon the pulleys, faintly sounds the roar of the wheels below, and faster, louder, stronger, move the dizzy wheels about her, until at last, with a rattle and a hum, the whole mechanism of the great factory bursts into eloquent activity. Then with lively steps and nimble fingers she applies herself to her arduous task. As the hours pass on her appetite comes, and she craves the breakfast which in her haste she did not eat. O, such hunger! as the slow, tantalizing minute-hand creeps around the face of the clock. Every minute is an age. The pangs of hunger become almost unbearable as the hand approaches "twelve," and her feet will hardly sustain her as she flies back and forth in her work. The clock strikes twelve. Instantly the speed begins to go down, the flyers, the spokes, the belt-knots, and shuttles gradually to show their outlines, and with a steady decadence the whole apparatus sighs and starts as if dying, then trembles, shrieks, and stops as if dead.

Seizing her bonnet and shawl, the operative joins in the general rush for the door-way, leaps down the stairs, hastens across the yard, and, with the smallest show of ceremony, seats herself at the table, which is prepared, as before, for a hasty meal. There can be but little table etiquette in such circumstances, and as the time is short and the hunger uncontrollable, she eats as every other being would eat which found itself in the same condition.

Then another rush for the mill, six more wearisome hours, and the day's work is done. There may or may not be a rush of the boarders for the supper-table, as that depends much upon the reputation of the house for plenty and impartiality. But the manners of the dinner-hour are likely to be repeated from force of habit. Then come a few spare hours in which the girl may sit in the parlor reserved for her and her lover, may walk upon the street, or busy herself in her room with reading or sewing. She is never idle, and often denies herself necessary exercise in order to read some favorite book, make some additions to her wearing apparel, or wash the extra clothing which the regulations do not allow in the "general washing."

It is a frequent practice among the girls to select one of the number to read aloud during the evenings while the others, seated around on the cots or trunks, do the reader's sewing or mending together with their own. Then the nine o'clock bell sounds its warning to the girls, and, as the lights must all be out at ten o'clock, they disrobe and lie down upon their hard couches, from which they often arise in the morning as weary as when they retired.

This dull life follows day after day with monotonous routine in the experience of the factory-girls, and one would think that the natural spirit of enterprise or ambition which they possess when they enter the mill would be wholly crushed out. But with a wonderful exhibition of recuperative energy, they retain their vivacity and spirit of independence (sometimes rendered *impudence*), and, with the very meagre opportunities given them, continue to improve their minds and hearts. The most oppressed class in factory communities, they are, nevertheless, the most independent-spirited, and the least patient when others are wronged. The frequent expressions of contempt for meanness, the undisguised dislike of arrogance or foppery, and the common phrase, "If I were only a man!" which comes to the lips when there is wrong to be righted, show a natural character which only needs culture and justice to mould into the highest form of nobility. This spirit they have ever shown in their "strikes."

3

What shall I say of the men? What *can* I say of them as factory operatives that will not be offensive, and at the same time strictly true? Here is a field for thought. With a few hundred bright exceptions the men are in a worse slavery than the girls,—worse because it holds both body and soul in bondage. Go to the mills and see how the mendicant workman kisses the rod that wounds him, praises the overseer that swindles him, bears curses and even kicks without a murmur, and then tell me if you can that his condition is a desirable one. Through years of toil and servility he has perchance obtained promotion, or he sees that by demeaning himself humbly he will be given such a position; and, knowing that a single word, act, or vote may cause his discharge, or the reduction of his pay, and of the consequent chances of promotion, he wholly enslaves himself. Perhaps, if his natural disposition is not too pure, he may so stunt his affection and sympathy as to become a fit tool for tyranny, and hence an "excellent overseer."

Such men can have but one ambition and one idea. If they are known to be thoughtful, reasonable men they will be discharged; and consequently they care nothing for education, principle, or enterprises of any kind. Mere automatons! The cotton-lords pull the string, and jumping-jack crooks his senseless legs.

To this rule, as to all others, there are exceptions, and the success of these exceptions in enriching the stockholders, elevating humanity, and making whole communities happier only serves to throw the great majority into a deeper and blacker shade. The exceptional factories have no "strikes" and run on full time.[4]

4

In 1858 and 1859 the shoe trade of New England reached enormous proportions, especially in the sale of the cheapest and least durable class of goods. Whole trains of cars were required to carry away from the town of Lynn, Massachusetts, the manufactures of a single day. Thousands of workmen were employed in putting—perhaps I should say, pasting—together a kind of shoes which, as they were intended for the negroes, the Indians, and the general "Western trade," were stuffed with old rags, "chips" of leather, and soled with pasteboard and other equally cheap material. At that time sufficient stock could be manufactured by working four months in a year; and although very good wages were paid the shoemakers during the busy season, yet, as many of them could not obtain other work for the remaining eight months of the year, they were reduced to abject poverty. The shoemakers of Lynn were looked upon by the people of surrounding cities as a vile and undesirable population. This opinion gained support, and doubtless was originated by the poverty-stricken appearance of the houses in which these workmen resided. Yet in those same years the shoe manufacturers increased their wealth at a most astonishing rate. Gold rolled in upon them like a flood, and men who in 1856 were the possessors of very moderate means found themselves money kings in 1859. Great was the contrast between the capitalist and workman; for while the man who earned the money was becoming poorer and poorer, if such a thing were possible, the man who did nothing but venture his money in an investment of the safety of which he was well assured, had so much money, so many houses, lands, and luxuries, that he hardly knew what to do with them.

It took the workmen a long time to awaken to a sense of the injustice which afflicted them. They could not understand how it was that, while they were suffering for food,—their wives taking washing, picking berries, or making articles of wearing apparel to supply the usual meals,—their employers, who a few years before were shopmen or retail store-keepers, now had their servants and livery, their palaces and banquets.

But the time came when, with the teachings and under the leadership of a few natural aristocrats who arose to dispute the claims of the moneyed aristocracy, the workmen of Lynn fully realized their situation, and claimed a greater share of the enormous profits. They asked for a small advance in their pay. It was not much when the profits were taken into consideration, but the capitalists would not grant it. They believed that they had the power to compel the shoemakers to work for the same wages, and they attempted to exercise it.

Then came a hard-fought battle, such as sometimes startle communities in time of peace, and in which there are more wounded and killed than there are in time of war. It was labor against capital; and was fought upon either side with the greatest determination. Capital was organized; labor was not. The manufacturers had a large supply laid up for future trade; but the laborers had nothing laid by against such a time of need. So for lack of discipline, organization, and supplies the laborers lost the battle. The capitalists held possession of the field, but the workmen were not captured.

After passing a hard winter, in which they suffered untold privations, and during which some died, others became permanently disabled with disease, and many adopted other callings, they scattered in the early spring,—some to the South, some to the West, and a few to the farms of Northern New England. Meanwhile the capitalists secured a partial supply of laborers from other parts of the United States, to whom they granted better terms, though not the exact wages which the strikers had demanded and on which as on a "point of honor" they remained firm. But the shoe business never resumed its former prosperity, for other towns and cities during the "strike" took the workmen and trade of Lynn, and retained a good proportion of it.

In 1861 the great Civil War began, and there was a call for troops. To this patriotic request the shoemakers were among the first to respond, and that same city of Lynn sent out two regiments, the greater portions of which were shoemakers. The remnants of the strikers from all over the land met again on the battle-fields of the South, and renewed the old friendships which existed when such adverse fortune drove them asunder. In those camps and garrisons, on the picket posts and parapets, these shoemakers told over and over again the story of the great "strike" and the incidents attending it. All this while the military campaigns failed or succeeded, the army was defeated or won victories from day to day, and each result taught its lesson to every common soldier engaged in the battles. The necessity for close organization, for discipline, union, and concentration, was apparent to the most casual spectator.

Why not apply army tactics and strategy to the battles which are fought in time of peace? Why not unite the shoemakers in a bond of sworn brotherhood, and hereafter make no demands which they did not feel that they possessed the power to enforce?

They were thoroughly schooled in the science of army organization, and saw that, however ill they might be treated in time of peace, they were of great importance to the nation when it was in danger. They saw a powerful organization, under the leadership of a single mind, overthrowing one system of slavery; and they discerned how, by the same means, another system might be destroyed.

The war closed; and these men, who had been four years planning and discussing, returned to their old labors in the shoe-shops of the country. Again the shoe trade began to flourish, the contractors gathered again the whole harvest of gold, as the laborers thought, and every week made more and more apparent the necessity for an organization strong enough to compete and, if necessary, fight with capital.

At this juncture Newell A. Daniels, one of that titled band for whose cause this book is written, appeared as the champion of the shoemakers.[5] Possessed of a mind as able as his heart was good; being earnest, practical, persevering, and industrious; having the enterprise which accompanies New England nativity, and the open-heartedness of a Western man, he founded the order of the "Knights of St. Crispin" (St. Crispin was a travelling monk, who made shoes for charitable purposes, and to supply himself with food). With the assistance of William J. McLaughlin, of Massachusetts, and several other able and honest men, the order was rapidly extended.[6] In 1870 it included nearly every male shoemaker in the United States, and a great many in the Canadas; all of whom united in a band of brotherhood, not for the purpose of warring on capital, not merely to raise their wages, but to secure their just rights, educate one another, and provide for the needy. In this they have succeeded. There have been "strikes" in Chicago, St. Louis, San Francisco, Rochester, N.Y., Worcester, and many other cities; but by taxing the whole order to provide for the strikers, and having been so successful in pledging to their cause all the best workmen, the capitalists in every instance were obliged to yield; and both labor and capital are receivers of their due returns.

In no case do the Crispins counsel violence, and their strikes, like their intentions, have been peaceful and unassuming. Even when the first load of Coolies were brought into Massachusetts for the avowed purpose of insulting and breaking up the organization, there was no riot and no disturbance of any kind.[7] They are brothers now in word and deed; and so long as they remain united upon the broad ground of justice and equality which they have now taken, and strand not upon the rocks of discord so apt to underlie a too calm sea of prosperity, they will be powerful agents in the elevation of the workingmen and in the support of national prosperity.

5

The women! how men run after them when there is money to be made, and how soon desert them when there is money to be lost! Even the Knights of St. Crispin, with all their strength and honesty of purpose, could not hope to be successful if the women did not second their efforts. The men might strike and strike till doomsday, for all the capitalists would care, when so many thousand women stood ready with able hands to do the work which the men refused. But the women are generous,—far too generous in some respects for the good of the race,—and, seeing the justice of the Crispins' demands, came at once to their relief by organizing the order of "The daughters of St. Crispin." The women knew that if they did not organize, the Knights of St. Crispin might be defeated; and a defeat of the men would really be a victory for the women, as in every strike the women would be given better places and better wages. But they entertained no such selfish, contemptible spirit as such motives would create, and they have ever stood ready to assist in maintaining every effort of the men which has right for its end.

Now, in perfect harmony, being careful to ask for nothing unreasonable, the Knights and Daughters of St. Crispin work together; and it needs but a glance at the neat homes, the tidy dress, the happy faces, the shelves of books and periodicals, which occupy the sites of former hovels, to convince the lover of humanity of the wisdom and goodness of those who founded these orders.

6

During the year ending October 1, 1870, there were twelve strikes in New England, and it so happened that I was present at a part of the meetings in six of the disturbed localities.

In October, 1869, the journeymen tailors of Boston struck for an increase of wages. Before taking the step, however, the Boston branch of the National Trades Union consulted with their brethren in other localities as to the expediency of the proposed measures, and when they were wholly prepared they submitted their new "bill of prices," giving the employers the choice between the new prices and no work. No arrogance, no force, no ill-will marked their movements, but every request was couched in respectful language, supported with unanswerable arguments, and pressed with a calm spirit of determination. There was a great bluster among the dealers and contractors, and much loud talk about "never submitting." But as they lacked an organization, and could not agree among themselves upon the best course to pursue, they concluded one after another to pay the demands and supply their impatient customers.

Yet they did not submit with a good grace, and muttered vengeance while they consented which boded no good to the tailors.

Since that time the dealers have turned their attention to the tailoresses, and finding among them many efficient persons who were as well able to make a coat as were the men, they quietly gave them the needed instruction and discharged the jours. The jours. took too little notice of the tailoresses to ask for a national organization of the women before the "strikes" began to protect them,[8] and to this cause more than to the introduction of foreign workmen is due the present unfortunate condition of the journeymen tailors of the country.

7

It will be many years before I shall forget that cold, blustering December day when I stepped from the train at Dover, New Hampshire, during the great strike of 1869. The Cocheco Cotton Manufacturing Company of that city, having in its employ about eight hundred operatives, gave them notice that from December 1, 1869, the pay of the employees would be reduced twelve per cent. To this reduction the operatives protested, saying, among other statements, that the company was as prosperous as it had ever been, which was shown by the facts that its stock was held at two hundred and fifty dollars premium on each share of five hundred dollars, and that its premiums had never been less than sixteen per cent. They also showed how the manufactures of that mill, owing to the superior work which its intelligent employees turned out, brought two cents more on a yard than the cloth of any other mill, with not one exception, in New England, while the employees were not paid as much as they were in many other mills to which reference was made. But their protest was of no avail because the agent had no authority "to disobey the commands of the directors," and they had decided "after due deliberation" that such a course would be "for their advantage." Consequently all the weavers—nearly four hundred—and the majority of the other employees left the factory, and refused to enter it again unless they could be guaranteed the same pay that they had been receiving.

When I arrived there were over eight hundred of the employees out of the factory, and hence out of any kind of business; and although the day was cold, the snow deep, and clouds overhead, the streets presented a lively and interesting appearance. All the people of Dover espoused the cause of the strikers, and the excitement called out all the citizens of the city and attracted many strangers from abroad. Great was the enthusiasm. The girls were confident of success because the justice of their cause was so apparent. No person thought that the corporation could hold out against such a strong current of public opinion, or that they would risk the reputation of the mill and the value of their stock in the market.

They had, however, determined to reduce the pay, and, make or lose, they *would* adhere to their resolution. But for this tyrannical resolve I should never have seen the beautiful and intelligent faces which stood upon the platform, nor have listened to their sweet voices in speech or song under the "starry canopy" of Exchange Hall. The voices, the day, the place, the songs, and even the words of welcome, may perhaps be forgotten, but the faces never will. They have become a part of my being, and wherever I go the bright faces, the dark faces, the happy faces, and the sad faces all gather around me urging on the battle which is only just begun. Never was there gathered an audience of eight hundred persons in which there were so many remarkable countenances. They all belong to old New Hampshire stock. There was but the slightest mixture of foreign blood, and nearly every person in the hall was born among the granite hills.[9] They knew their rights, "and knowing *dared* maintain," while their every act was indicative of natural sprightliness, independence of character, and a laudable amount of self-culture. It did not seem possible that the wishes of such an intelligent and considerate class should be ignored when they asked for bread. I remember one old lady who was introduced as "a soldier's widowed mother," who entered the mill twenty-six years ago. What changes she had seen! Once she had been a weaver in that same mill, having the charge of only two looms, with spare hands to spell her, and had received more wages in value than she now received after an apprenticeship of twenty-six years, and while attending upon *four* looms. Time after time the company had cut down the pay,—always reducing when the market was dull, and never raising when the goods were in active demand,—until now the new girls who had charge of six looms received the same pay that was once given for tending two. Meantime the board had advanced from $1.25 a week to $3 per week.

The strikers assembled every day in the hall, as they had no other place to go, and encouraged each other to hold out with speeches, anecdotes, and songs. I recollect a song now, which was rendered in an excellent manner by a boy, and which seemed to thrill every person present. It was entitled the "Sailor's Grave," and in it were the following words:—

"Death struck,—he gave no coward alarms,
For he smiled and died in his messmate's arms.
We proudly decked his funeral vest

With the stars and stripes upon his breast;
We gave him this as a badge of the brave,
And then he was fit for a sailor's grave.[10]"

Sitting near me at the time this plaintive song was sung was a beautiful young lady by the name of Cynthia Howe. I noticed that she showed much interest in the ballad during the rendition of the first verses; but when the singer came to the words above quoted, she burst into tears, and, laying her head upon the back of the seat, sobbed in a most piteous manner. After the boy had taken his seat, I asked her why she felt so grieved, and this is the story as she told it to me on that occasion.

Her only brother was an officer in the Gulf naval squadron, under the command of Admiral Farragut.[11] On him the hopes of the aged and indigent parents depended, and he was consequently the idol of parents and sister. But he was killed by a piece of a bomb-shell as he was walking the deck of his vessel in the attack on Mobile.[12] He died in "his messmate's arms" and was "decked" in the stars and stripes; and hence the power of the song on the only remaining child who was trying to cheer the declining years of her parents with the fruits of industrious toil.

This affecting incident led me to inquire further, and to my surprise I found that a very large number of the girls who "struck" were the widows, mothers, sisters, or daughters of soldiers who were killed in the war with the Rebellion. Many of these were the relatives of soldiers who disappeared in such circumstances that no trace or record of their death was found, and the families for that reason could get no assistance from the government. This was the case with the old lady who entered the mill twenty-six years ago.

Taking into consideration the great promises which were held out to those soldiers, and the moral agreement which the State made to provide for the destitute whom such men left behind, I cannot refrain from reproaching the people—the men—of New Hampshire with ingratitude and perfidy for permitting those women to be swindled in the way they were by a rich corporation, the members of which lived and carried the profits out of the State.

It was evident that some of the strikers must suffer for food unless an organized effort was made to provide for them. The citizens crowded themselves and boarded as many as they could accommodate, taking a lively interest in the operatives' welfare. A levee and festival was given at the City Hall, to which the people of the city and the Knights of St. Crispin contributed large amounts, the proceeds of which were devoted to the sustenance of the strikers. Contributions were received in money from other manufacturing towns.

Meanwhile the directors of the company, the stock of which had depreciated one hundred per cent, scoured the country as far as Canada, and brought in every woman, man, and child whom they could hire at any price. Nearly a week was employed in this way, during which time the mills were silent and dark. But after a sufficient number of hands had been secured to work a part of the machinery, although the company must lose much money through the awkwardness of "green hands" and the expense of running without a full supply of operatives, notice was given that the mills would start, and such persons as wished to resume work at the reduced wages could do so on the following Monday morning.

Great was the consternation among the strikers, for, until then, they had not deemed it possible that the company could be so "cruelly unjust." There was weeping in many a household, and a gloom was cast over the whole community. Sad faces everywhere. Many of the girls *must* work even at the reduction, if they could not get better terms, while others, seeing that their condition would be even worse than it had been, abandoned the mill, left Dover, and sought for other and more remunerative employment.

Then followed the New Hampshire election, and it was thought that the excitement resulting from the Dover strike would give a large vote to the labor reform party. Politicians who addressed the girls during the sessions of the mass meetings promised them justice through the polls. But, alas! the real sufferers, like those strikers who were promised the same thing thirty years before, could not vote;[13] while the great reduction of wages made it easy for capitalists to buy the votes of servile men, and defeat the advocates of justice. The smaller the wages paid a man the less value does he put upon his vote, while the employer has more money to expend for political purposes than he had before. It is said by many that the general rule now is to make the operatives pay for all improvements, for election expenses, for accidents, and for other losses, always by a reduction. So that the sight of a new wheel, new blinds, new buildings, improved machinery, a destructive fire, or the sickness of stockholders are only the forerunners of a reduction in the rate of wages.

So the Dover strike closed, and as noble an assembly of human beings as ever congregated under one roof were defeated, captured, and bound by their avaricious taskmasters, for no other reason than that the captives had none of the arms which political power supplies, and were consequently bare-handed, defenceless, and impotent.

One remarkable fact in connection with that strike will show the character of the parties who joined in the movement. During the week a working-woman's association was formed for the purpose of mutual aid and mutual instruction; and when the officers were chosen they were nearly all found to be graduates of the High Schools of Boston, and about nine out of ten of the members were the graduates of some institution of learning. To their intelligence alone was the corporation indebted for the premium at which its productions were held in the market over those of other manufactories.

8

The strike of the operators connected with the Western Union Telegraph Company in the winter of 1869–70 was one of the most remarkable events of the kind that ever occurred in the United States. At nearly the same hour the telegraph-operators in a thousand different offices, including almost every town and village on the line between Boston and San Francisco, left their desks and refused to return until an operator, who had been unjustly discharged in California, should be returned to his position. It was a small matter, the public said, about which to make so much disturbance; but it was just as important to the operators as it would have been had a thousand been discharged, or the wages of all decreased. It was an infringement of the rules laid down by the "Telegraphers' Union," and to those rules each member had been sacredly pledged. If they would strike under any circumstances, then they must strike for that cause. They did not hesitate or waver. There was nothing cowardly about them, and they showed marks of heroism when they risked their livelihood in defence of principle.

But the "greatest monopoly of the age" was not to be defeated by fair means; and, taking advantage of the careless neglect of organization in Maine, and availing itself of such woman's help as had not been considered of sufficient importance to organize, it began to do business again in an awkward, limping manner. The victory for the Telegraph Company was complete as far as the strikers were concerned; for their organization was broken up; their most skilled workmen changed their occupation, and the remnant went sorrowing back into such positions as the victors chose to give them. But the battle was not won without sacrifice on the side of the company; for, after they had lost many thousand dollars on unsent despatches and misused apparatus, and had so disturbed the commercial world as to give fresh life and great respectability to a rival company, they were obliged to increase their expenses in order to do the same work which the old operators had done so cheaply. Two such victories would be the death of any company that has not imperial power; and it is doubtful if the glory of that success will ever prompt that company again to defy the united strength of the operators in defence of a cause where

"'Tis sure defeat to win."

9

During the same winter there were strikes among the Crispins in several cities, but as they asked so little and succeeded so completely, I cannot give space to them here. In the month of June, 1870, however, there was a strike among the operatives in a small cotton-mill at Canton, Massachusetts. That town is one of the most beautiful villages in New England, and is remarkable for the advantages of its location, the picturesqueness of its scenery, and the general enterprise and ability of its people. The company in whose building these operatives had been employed was evidently determined at the outset to be very generous and considerate toward the operatives. They built nice little cottages for the families of the operatives, and spared no pains to give the grounds and houses a tasty and tidy aspect. They had every appearance of *homes*, and one would have thought, before family secrets were known, that the inmates of those cottages must be very happy. But as the subsequent action of the company seemed to indicate that the houses were "for effect" when Congressional committees, State boards, excursionists, and friends should visit them, the cottages answered that purpose and nothing more.

The company had been making preparations for a strike by inducing the operatives to work fifteen hours a day, and thus getting a sufficient supply ahead of the demand to fill orders during the suspension.

When a sufficient quantity of goods was manufactured, the company decided that the pay of the operatives should be reduced ten per cent, and directed the innocent agent to carry out the orders and "take all of the curses." He obeyed the orders and received the maximum number of curses.

The operatives in their protest stated that their wages at the old rate were less than they could live upon, and procure the comforts of life; that at a previous strike the proprietors had shown perfidy in acceding to the demand for an increase in the pay per "cut" or piece, and afterwards lengthening the pieces, so as to compel the operative to weave forty-six yards into each piece instead of thirty.

This had been repeatedly done in other factories. Once a "cut" was thirty yards, and the operative received twenty-five cents for weaving it; now it is forty-five or forty-six yards, and the weaver receives no more pay than she did when there were only thirty. The strikers also showed that the company were growing very wealthy, and could well afford to raise their wages twenty per cent instead of cutting them down ten. But the agent bore these blows with becoming meekness, "would see about it," "was sorry for them," &c., and probably said nothing to the directors about it, for fear that those avaricious hounds would pitch upon him and "take his head off." So the girls were "on the strike," and a jolly time they did have of it for a few days. Nearly all of them boarded with their own families, and were literally at home, and a few days of rest, with enough excitement to prevent monotony, was something to be appreciated by these weary working-women. A morsel of fresh air, a little recreation, time to think, and time to sleep were something precious to them; and when they secured it even by a strike, they were for the time carelessly happy. It happened (somehow, this *happens* often when the girls of any place are on a strike) that the machinery of the Iron Works broke down, and the employees of that company joined in the crowd of strikers, swelling it to very imposing proportions. Mass meetings were held on the bank of the river, in the public park, and wherever the assembly deemed it to be expedient speeches were made, and the usual demonstrations customary on such occasions.

After a week of idleness the mill was again put in running order, and the news circulated by the agent that the company had secured a sufficient number of hands to run the mills, and a notice was served on all the occupants of the company's cottages to vacate the premises at once, or resume work in the mill at the reduced rates.

Many of the twenty-six families who rented houses of the company believed the report about the supply of operatives, and felt that they must yield. Then came as great sorrow as there had been joy. There was a choice. They could stay out and leave their homes, or they could go into the mill and suffer. Either course led to privation and to grave dangers which they hesitated to face.

Addressing myself to one lady who seemed undecided as to the best course to pursue, I asked her why she did not make up her mind; and I received the following pointed reply: "There is but little choice,—it is *starve* if you go in, and *starve* if you stay out. Once when I had only two looms, and earned more than I can to-day, we had a petticoat overseer who assisted us, and took our places when we wished to rest, or were sick.[14] Now I run six looms, and have no assistance of any kind. Now I get twenty-five cents a "cut," and by working eleven hours I can earn on six looms one dollar a day. This leaves me only six dollars a month for clothing and other expenses, after paying my board and laying up nothing. If I take another loom, as I am urged to do, to earn my old wages, I cannot do my work well. Often when we have plenty of time, and only four looms to watch, the mildewed thread is so weak that it constantly breaks, and we are fined for doing poor work. Sometimes we are obliged to purchase the whole piece, and pay the rich owner out of our little wages for cloth which an angel could not make strong from such rotten material. On the reduction it is not possible to live.

"On the other hand, if I go out the owners will do by me as they have by others, taking the pains to get me discharged from any factory in which I might otherwise be employed. Considering then the pure air of the hills as compared with the tainted atmosphere in the unventilated mill, and the glorious freedom of out-door life, I have come near to the conclusion that it is better to stay out and starve in the sunshine than to work and famish in those musty shades."

Among the strikers were two young ladies of fine tastes, handsome personal appearance, and refined education, who had sought employment in the mill as a last resort, for the support of themselves, their widowed mother, and a little orphan cousin. They had a cultivated taste for music and the fine arts, and delighted me during my stay at their home with occasional musical performances. There was nothing more heroic about their toilsome life and the support of their mother than I had seen in many other places, although that was praiseworthy; but to see them dividing their earnings with the little orphan boy, when they had not plenty for themselves, was an uncommon and a most touching sight. The father of the boy had been a soldier, and after the war he did not recover the health which he lost in the South. In a fit of insanity he wandered off, and had never been heard from by his sister since his departure several years ago. She believed that he was dead, and she had taken the little boy as a member of the family. I pitied the little fellow, whose intellectual face saddened whenever anything happened to remind him of his father, or of his dependence upon his kind aunt and cousins. How kindly they cared for him, and how considerate they appeared to be of his feelings! They were happy, even in their privation, receiving the purest joy which comes to man as a reward for their benevolence and sympathy.

If the Canton strike gained the employees nothing financially, and if the manufacturers did not so far disgrace themselves as to depreciate the stock or value of their goods, there was, nevertheless, a profit to me as a spectator beyond anything which money can bring. I saw there the best side of human nature, and gained such fresh confidence in the human race by contemplating the faces and actions of that kind-hearted family, that I felt as if the world were more attractive and life more desirable than ever before.

There are many bright gems which the world has not seen, and a thousand joys in the hearts of the benevolent poor which the *avaricious* wealthy can never know.[15]

> "There are more things in heaven and earth, Horatio, Than are dreamt of in your philosophy."[16]

10

One evening in the summer of 1868 there were gathered in the largest hall of Fall River, Massachusetts, one of the most intelligent audiences that ever assembled in a manufacturing town. It was an occasion when the friends of the "Ten-Hour Movement" were to show their strength and explain the objects of the associations which were springing up in all parts of the Eastern States. There were lawyers, officials, factory proprietors, and wealthy merchants mingled with the assembly, while many accepted the invitation to come forward and occupy seats upon the platform. There seemed to be but one opinion. Rich and poor, employer and workman, were united upon the question of reducing the hours of labor. I remember the cheers and the eloquent words which came so spontaneously from the mouths of the assembly, and I felt, as the meeting closed, as if the factories would begin, if not on the morrow, certainly at no distant day, the experiment of ten hours of labor, and ten hours only. But when on the next day I visited some of the owners at their invitation, and asked them why they did not undertake the experiment at once, they said that it was a movement upon which it was necessary to have a union of the manufacturers before it could be put in practical operation. They knew that ten hours, and perhaps nine, would give them just as much work and less expense, while the laborer would have the extra time for mental and social improvement; but they said that it was a system which they could not introduce alone. It would spread discontent in other factories, the owners of which might not be believers in the ten-hour plan. These men, however, were willing to give their money and personal influence toward the institution of ten-hour associations.

In this they kept their word, and the factory-owners of Fall River were the most liberal supporters of that movement for a considerable time. They tried the plan of running ten hours a day for a year or more, but gave it up, as they claimed, because they could not compete with other factories. The union of manufacturers upon the ten-hour question has not yet come, although the National Congress and State Legislatures, through the influence of those associations, have made some wise provisions by statute. The manufacturers of modern times seem to think that man is a machine which will run as long as the power is applied, and be as efficient during the last hours as it is at the beginning of the day. One would suppose that with all their experience and boasted Yankee "sharpness," they would see the fallacy of that argument; especially since the astonishing results of the Ten-Hour Bill in England have shown so conclusively that men and women will do as much work in a year at ten hours a day as they will if required to toil twelve hours a day.**[17]

In July, 1870, the mule-spinners employed in one of the mills in Fall River struck, and left the factory because the proprietors wished to reduce their wages ten per cent.[18] Before doing this, however, the spinners attempted to make a compromise, and indicated their willingness to work on at a reduction of five per cent. But the haughty capitalists treated their communications with silent contempt. Consequently, twenty thousand working men and women were either voluntarily absent from their business, or compelled, from their dependence upon the spinners for supplies, to suspend their labor. Many people prophesied that such a large number of laborers would not remain long in peaceful idleness, and the whole

---

***History of the Ten-Hour Legislation,*—Richard Grant. *Workmen and Wages*—Ward.

city was more or less in fear of a riot. The exasperated factory officials were longing for a riot, or some other unlawful demonstration which would give them some legal hold upon the strikers, and, it is said, took a great deal of pains to advertise the time and place when a riot "would come off," in order that a crowd might gather and their wishes be fulfilled. The crowd gathered, but there was no riot. And that twenty thousand, exasperated by injustice, in a measure, coarse and crude, and insulted by the presence of police that were brought to awe them, and by companies of militia ordered out one day by the capitalists to make the public think there was great danger, did not commit a single act of violence, or damage a dollar's worth of property. There were some individual *mêlées*, and some threats by a few inconsiderate ones; but the great body discountenanced any violence, and were peaceful, well-behaved citizens. For two months the strike continued; furnishing a most exciting theme for New England gossip; and at last ended in the return of the operatives at the reduced prices, and under a pledge never to engage in another strike. The strikers were literally starved into submission, and after enduring the greatest hardships which men ever accept in defence of a principle, they cowed before the capital, and another page was added to the record of defeat which weakness and right suffer from strength and wrong.

Taking sides with the mill-owners on all occasions were to be found the ardent advocates of a "ten-hour system"; so inconsistently supporting a reduction which must sooner or later compel the employees to labor an additional hour a day in order to support themselves. Consistency may be a jewel, but it never ornaments the persons of such men. The fact is that "ten-hour systems," "labor reforms," or any other of the many hobbies that men now ride into popularity upon, are all worse than useless unless founded upon the one great principle of justice, and it was on that ground that the strikers of Fall River took their stand.[19]

The "factory system" or any other system that has the subject of labor and capital in view, is morally, and should be lawfully, nothing more nor less than a co-operative association. Philosophers claim to see in the future a new system in which the laborer shall be a partaker in the profits of the factory or farm. They would have the laborer receive a stipulated sum and the capitalist another stated amount, after which the profits shall be equally divided; or there is to be no wages, but a fair division of the profits instead,—either of which seems nothing more than simple justice. But that end could just as well be reached by an increase of the wages, until the laborer received in that way his just proportion of the profits, and when money was lost, a proportionate decrease. I do not believe that a strike ever occurred where the operatives knew, when the decrease was announced, that the stockholders were not then growing immensely rich out of the profits of the business or had not already received enough more than their just proportion of previous profits to carry the employees equitably over the "dull season" at their old wages. There is no equity or justice in giving to one man a million of dollars a year, while fifty thousand of his partners in the work receive only six or seven hundred. He may be, with his capital, entitled to a larger proportion than the workmen, but never to such a share as that or as great as one half of that amount would be.

That the laborers are naturally entitled to a position on an equal with the employer is shown by their equality in intellectual and physical endowments; and as such they have been recognized by every great statesman or lawgiver of the world. "The world is the Lord's," said an eminent German writer, "and we are his children. How then can it be that so many of us are born into the world with no landed inheritance?" He might also have asked, How can it be that fellow-men are permitted to curse the disinherited ones with a life of bondage, in which they earn much and get little, see plenty and have nothing?

CHAPTER 12

Charitable Institutions

*What Is Charity?—Wages According to the Profits.—
The Lawrence Calamity.—Charity and Small Wages.—
Cutting Down the Pay of Operatives to Make Great
Donations.—Temporary Relief Not a Permanent
Cure.—"Homes."—Their Uses and Abuses.—How a
"Soldiers' Home" Was Supported.—Incidents, &c.*

1

Charity!—how many conflicting reflections that word brings into the mind! Love, pride, vice, shame, benevolence, ambition, hate, righteousness, and sin seem so squeezed and mashed into one another in the idea it suggests, that an accurate definition would be impossible. The time was when it meant a simple, unostentatious act of the purest sympathy and love. But that day passed more than eighteen hundred years ago. To-day it is applied to anything and everything which a rich man may do to gain praise. It consists, not in doing justly, not in permanently assisting unfortunate mankind, or in such acts as prevent poverty or suffering, but is applied to the giver of presents. If a man is wealthy enough to give a million of dollars to a church, college, school, or hospital, without missing it, his action is emblazoned on the banners of worldly praise as charity.

The state of that society is sufficiently unfortunate and unnatural where charity, according to the Bible definition, is needed to prevent suffering; but it may be said to be in a very demoralized condition when both the acts of old-fashioned charity and new-fashioned benevolence cannot alleviate the pangs consequent upon compulsory poverty. It is dreadful to think that when a man gives back to his victims, in a provision for "an institution," a part of the sum of which he deliberately robbed them, he is to be lauded to the skies as an example of mortal perfection.

In a true and natural state of society there would be no paupers who deserved charity. Where there are equal privileges and equal remuneration, the people are never poverty-stricken, and never suffer for any of the comforts of life. A case of a person mentally and physically disqualified to earn his own living, and at the same time destitute of relatives able to help him, would be, indeed, a rare occurrence in such a community as that; while they who wilfully or lazily neglected the opportunities given them ought to suffer, and their poverty be held up as a warning to others. That we shall never see such perfection in human society as long as human nature undergoes no radical change is self-evident; but there is no reason why we should not attempt to come as near to perfection as we can. Though we may never expect to see the time when there are no deserving poor in our midst, still let us at least keep that number at the lowest possible figure.

Much can be done by increasing the wages of those classes who earn more than they get. This would be much more charitable than robbing them through a series of years, and then giving the money to which they are morally entitled to an asylum where they may be cared for when broken and crippled. Many a man who secured his money by grinding the poor and appropriating that which belonged to the laborer has, at his death, made "munificent bequests," and been lauded as a saint. I cannot say that these gifts and bequests are not of great use to the world, for I am aware that a great many institutions of learning and religion have been founded and perpetuated by these means. If man must be avaricious, and feels compelled to overreach his less talented or weaker brother on every occasion, then it is better to give it to charitable institutions than risk the poor man's earnings in the hands of reckless or profligate children. But how much better is it to do justly all one's life, and at death have no great riches, nor see the need of them for "charitable purposes"!

2

When the great disaster at Lawrence, Massachusetts, caused by the fall of the Pemberton Mill, to which reference has been made, became noised abroad, there was such a flood of contributions from every part of the United States that the committee on the distribution of funds did not know what to do with it. At first all kinds of provisions, medical stores, and personal comforts came in by the car-load. This was followed by gifts in money, and so frequent and liberal were the donations that a card was published, saying that the committee did not need any more money for the comfort or future welfare of the sufferers. The funds remaining on hand after the burial of the bodies, paying for medical attendance, and providing homes, were invested as a permanent fund, established for the benefit of the crippled ones, and after their decease to other unfortunate factory operatives. "What a charitable people!" says the reader; and I would echo the words of praise which naturally follow. But how much better it would have been had the proprietors shown a little charity for the laborers who built the mill, and given them such wages as would have insured its stable construction!

Again, the Lawrence disaster was not such an extraordinary occurrence after all. It seemed more terrible because the victims were all together, and their cries for help were united; yet there are nearly as many killed or maimed every year in the factories of the United States as were injured by the fall of that mill. Here a man is crushed in the gearing, there one has his arm or leg pulled off by the belting, while in another place some poor fellow has been mutilated by a saw, or had his ribs broken by a fall. Day after day, and year after year, we read of these cases, think nothing, care nothing, about them, and go our way pitying the sufferers at the "great calamity."

A few years ago a young man of my acquaintance was standing near a carding-machine, when he noticed that the supply of wool, in the absence of the female attendant, had run out.[1] He knew that in a moment the cards would clash, and the machine be damaged to the extent of several hundred dollars. He did not wait to discuss the probabilities of danger, or think of any reward for such an active interest in the owner's welfare, but sprang to the machine and attempted to push the belt from the pulley. He succeeded in his efforts to stop the machine, but before the belt was wholly off the drum of the pulley he slipped upon the soaped floor, and his hand was caught in the machinery in such a way as to draw in his right arm.

He had been an excellent hand about the factory, and was the most faithful servant that the corporation ever had. They expressed much regret at the loss of his services, and gave him verbal assurance of their sympathy, at the same time *thanking* him for saving the valuable machine. That was all. The arm was paralyzed for life; and the cripple often seen afterward around the mill with a basket of confectionery, trying in that way to earn a scanty living. No rich stockholder ever thought of giving him money, nor did he appear to be conscious of any indebtedness to him, yet those same men of money sent very liberal presents indeed to the sufferers at Lawrence.

3

It appears to be a singular fact that those parties who are the most charitable pay the smallest wages to persons in their employ. It often happens that while the mistress of a house is visiting the poor or attending the board meetings of some charitable institution, there are servant-girls at her home washing the clothes and ceilings, taking up carpets, or cooking the dinner, with whom she has had a long and exciting debate over the twenty-five cents per week which the servant wished to have added to her wages. Nine chances out of ten the mistress refused to pay the additional twenty-five cents to the servant, while she gave away ten dollars during the day to women who had been servant-girls once, and who would not have been the wrecks she saw had they received reasonable compensation for their work.

A woman who had purchased a new set of furniture for her parlor at the cost of two thousand dollars, sent for an upholsterer to lay the carpets, &c. On his telling her that, as he had spent years at his trade, he must have five dollars for the day's work, she dismissed him and sent for an upholsteress, whose price (as usual) was only half that of the man. With her the mistress discussed and pleaded until the upholsteress, rather than haggle longer, consented to do the work for twenty-five cents less than the ruling price. The furniture was heavy and the carpets thick, so that the woman had a most severe job, but this did not attract the attention of the mistress, who was all the while cogitating upon the appearance of the parlor, and who, after concluding that the covers for the chairs and sofas were not rich enough to suit her taste, sent without hesitation to the store and purchased another set at the cost of fifteen dollars.

The same day she sent a servant, whose pay was only $2.25 a week, to the florist's for a bouquet of flowers costing $5, so that she might see if flowers "increased the effect" of the new mantelpiece. Soon after this a board of private charities met in that same parlor, and the mistress of the house gave four hundred dollars toward the "charitable object" of providing a home for needy children.

A prominent factory-owner of Rhode Island was requested on the Sabbath to subscribe to the fund for the building of a "branch chapel" where the poor might receive the gospel. He cheerfully placed five thousand dollars against his name, and the very next day ordered a reduction in the wages of his employees in order to make his "accounts balance."

During the strike in Canton, Massachusetts, when so many girls were obliged to accept such wages as placed them within the reach of want and its attendant temptations, there were men in Boston who expressed great indignation that laborers should attempt to dictate to capital. "The employer has a perfect right to pay just such wages as he chooses, and if the girls do not like the terms they can turn their attention to something else," said one, without stopping to consider that, owing to the rules adopted by each factory and the unskilfulness of the girls in any other business, they could only turn their attention one way,—downward and hellward. Yet the very next day some of the members of that social circle went to the office of the Boston Chief of Police and urged him to accept money in aid of the projected movement toward the reformation of the one hundred nightwalkers arrested on the previous evening. "How very, very sad," said those philanthropists, "that so many beautiful and healthy women should be brought to the dock of a Boston court for crime!"

No one will doubt the benevolent intentions of those gentlemen, nor their desire to see the reformation of those unfortunate fallen women; but when we consider that the effect of their example in paying servant-girls, factory-girls, or shop-girls small wages had so reduced the income of these girls while in other men's employ, that they adopted this life to avoid more acute suffering, it seems a rather tardy charity after all. It may be that some of the girls were once the employees of these same philanthropists.

A manufacturer of ready-made clothing in Chicago gave eight thousand dollars toward the construction of a house of worship, and then cut down the price formerly paid for making garments. Fortunately for the shop-girls, there is a scarcity of their material in the West, and the larger part of the employees left the shop for other situations. But, according to the testimony before a coroner's jury, there were a few whose necessities were so pressing that they dared not risk the loss of employment, even for one day, and who, after working along for two or three months, abandoned their work,—eight seeking a house of ill-fame and two committing suicide.

A gentleman and lady quarrelled, one Sunday morning, with the milkman, who had to rise at midnight in order to supply his customers, and who prosecuted his labor with unfailing promptness in cold, rain, or heat. The cause of the trouble was a difference of eight cents between the account of the mistress and that of the milkman. The milkman lost the eight cents and went on his way, while the stingy couple prepared for church. That day contributions were requested for the education of the negroes, and this same couple threw each a ten-dollar bill into the treasury-box.

A gentleman of great literary talent and reputation wished for a copyist. I recommended to him a poor orphan-girl, who had succeeded in graduating at the Normal School. She was an excellent writer and very intelligent, and was without doubt a first-class copyist, while the gentleman's handwriting was so difficult to read that correspondents cut out the autographs from his letters and pasted them on the returning envelopes because they could not make out the name. He kept the girl at work copying his letters one day, and, finding that she had done all that he desired for the time, he gave her a one-dollar bill, and said that as he had no change and she was so poor she might keep the whole. (Wonderful generosity!) A few weeks after another lady, who was also an orphan, but a relative of an aristocratic family, was sent to him for work or assistance. He said that he had no work fitted for the hands of "such as she," but he would give her ten dollars, and promise to furnish more if she should need it. Both the applicants were equally needy. One, because she performed a hard day's work, obtained one dollar as her wages; while the other as a mendicant aristocrat received ten dollars as "a charity."

Ladies in New York, Philadelphia, and some of the other large cities have certain days on which they give charities, and some have as large a number as twenty to whom they give fifty or seventy-five cents per week. Perhaps the lady of the house knows of other parties living in the street who give other stipulated sums to the same beggars, so that the mendicants receive from two and a half to five dollars per week. Meanwhile the maid who works hard all day in the nursery or chambers, dresses the mistress for an evening party, and sits up until one o'clock to assist her to disrobe, receives $2.50 a week. The mistresses are so anxious that these maids shall earn their wages that they never leave the house without studying out some method for keeping the maids busy during their absence. These same ladies will pay two dollars a week for the board of a poodle-dog, and discharge a servant during the summer trip into the country because there is but "little for a servant to do for several weeks."

I remember a public dinner which was given in the "Cradle of Liberty" to the poor children of Boston.[2] Long draped tables, vases of bouquets, flags and mottoes, graced the hall, and a feast fit for a king was spread around the little ragged, dirty gamins of that city. Of course they enjoyed it, and were happy. They had never seen anything to compare with it in their short lives, and gave themselves into the hands of the benevolent ladies with gratitude and cheerfulness. I saw them file into the hall, and march down beside the tables. There were many bright faces, many a flashing eye, and many a high forehead. But, on the same plane of unnatural equality on which they dwelt without, those poor children stood side by side with the foolish and dull-headed denizens of their damp alleys; eating their turkey, pastry, fruit, and sweetmeats with awkward greediness.

Speeches were made to the children, urging them to be thankful for such a magnificent banquet, and filling their ears with professions of friendship. At the close of the feast each child was given a pair of shoes, or some other useful article of dress, and sent back to his musty and cheerless home, to be forgotten as soon as the press which lauded the benevolent projectors had distributed its last edition; yea, they were at once forgotten by all in the "upper" world except by the generous contributors, who rested in the proud satisfaction of having made two thousand children happy.

Thoughtful ones studied over the problem as from time to time they recalled the circumstances, and were not a little puzzled with the question, whether that dinner was a charity or in any way a kindness. It appears to me that anything which does not alleviate the condition of the poor, while it serves to make them very discontented with their lot, is a curse rather than a blessing. After partaking of such luxuries there would be but a small appetite for the cold, mouldy crust of bread; and after visiting such a beautiful place and receiving such marked attention, their cold, dark homes would be more cheerless and uncomfortable than ever. It is like Dead Sea fruit to the eyes of the famishing wanderer; cheering and strengthening him for a moment, only to leave him disappointed and disconsolate when he attempts to pluck it.[3] It serves also to show how wide is the gulf between them and plenty, making them discontented, envious, and criminally desperate.

Without the least doubt, some of the subscribers to that dinner-fund were the next day rebuking some of the childish recipients of their benevolence for charging one or two cents more than the usual price for blacking boots, or for trying to sell them the daily paper.

4

The large number of "Homes" which are being established in all our large cities show that the great public has a conscience, and that it so far repents of its misdeeds as to adopt this method of returning to the rightful owners some of its ill-gotten gains. There are "Homes" for "Drunkards," "Consumptives," "Old Ladies," "Old Men," "Colored Men," "Reformed Women," "Little Wanderers," "Bootblacks," "Newsboys," "Worn-out Servant-Girls," "Indigent Hack-drivers," "Sewing-Girls," and "Poorhouses," with hospitals for the afflicted poor, and asylums for the blind, the insane, and the crippled. These institutions are usually endowed by some benevolent or "charitable" man, who gives a large sum of money toward the immortalization of his little name. In these "Homes" no sufferer is admitted as a matter of right, but all are constantly, and oftentimes offensively, reminded of their dependence. One of the most absurd requests ever made was the petition of an old man to be admitted into an institution which his penurious employer had founded, and where the petitioner wished to be treated "like a proprietor." Yet his earnings for twenty years, except the small percentage necessary to pay his temporary expenses, had been put into that institution by his employer.

There can be no doubt that these institutions are of vast importance to the welfare of society in its present condition, and that these gifts, no matter what the motive may be that influences the giver, are a blessing to such unfortunate persons as cannot otherwise obtain from the world their just dues.

Considering these "Homes" a necessity, then, so long as law-makers are bought, and votes are quoted in the political market like stocks in the marts of finance, the only reform in which the few justly disposed can directly engage is that of reorganizing these "Homes" upon the principle that the poor should not be treated as suppliants, but should be entitled to the same consideration and the same privileges which would be conceded to a wealthy grandfather who, although living upon his own money, has become too old to take proper care of himself.

A review of some of the methods now pursued in the management of "Homes" will show the necessity of reform and the difficulties which reformers will be obliged to encounter.

First: the charity of the trustees or managing boards begins too far up the scale. In many cases which have been brought to my notice, the managers have selected superintendents for these institutions whose only qualification for the position lay in their unfitness for anything else. Political blockheads, dozy bankrupts, or broken-down spendthrifts are caught up and given the position of an overseer out of "charity," while the invalids and needy poor are for the same reason placed under an incompetent's care. Such superintendents could not, if they would, make the place a *home* for the inmates, and are perpetually annoying them with his careless, senseless, or wilful disregard of their tastes and desires.

Even in those institutions where the most able overseers are found there will be discontent arising from the sense of dependence and the wounded pride which must be felt by every worthy recipient of charity.

Second: the openings and anniversaries are celebrated with too much pomp and ceremony. When a "Home" has been prepared for the reception of inmates, there is a "dedication" to which all the great men are invited, and where, with bands of music, feasting, speeches, and perhaps cannon, the event is ushered in with the greatest show of enthusiasm. The newspapers herald the birth of the new institution, ministers preach upon it, and with loud-mouthed acclamations the world insanely hails it as an evidence of human progress.

With each anniversary the celebration is repeated. Orators tell the inmates how poor they are, and how kind are the donors, while fashionable ladies flaunt their insulting silks in the faces of the dependants, or shake their perfumed lace handkerchiefs at the prison-like procession of paupers.

When visitors come there is a feast and a great parade; and this occurs often, for men strangely pride themselves on the number of paupers, drunkards, and cripples they have in the community, and invite every influential stranger to make these "Homes" a visit. On such occasions the unfortunate inmates are drawn up for inspection, while curious eyes note their movements just as children watch elephants in a show of wild animals.

Third: there should be no public meetings of the board of directors and no published rules. The board of directors of a "Home" now meet in some hall or at some fashionable hotel, and there, in the presence of the reporters for the press and such other spectators as choose to attend, formally vote that the inmates of their institution "shall not be out evenings," or that some other new regulation shall be adopted. All the people for many miles around know of the "resolves" of that body through the press, and charity in the public estimation becomes a matter of business to be regulated, resolved, debated, voted, possess certain by-laws and humiliating rules. The wishes of the board having been formally communicated to the overseer, he procures a "regulation card," on which the rules are plainly printed, and affixes it to the posts, doors, corners, and gates. "Thus far shalt thou go and no farther" is suggested by them;[4] and even though they be the most simple rules, the printing and posting of them destroys every sense of contentment and takes away every *home* feeling which might have existed before. It is no charity to cast the needy into prison.

5

A few examples may serve to illustrate this subject further. I once knew a worthy deacon who was so noted for his charity and sympathy that he was made an overseer of the poor, with funds at his disposal and a large salary for himself. His whole business was confined to the alleviation of suffering among the poor. It so happened that he owned a tenement in which resided an old lady who was a very industrious, honest woman.* He came to the conclusion that the rent was too small, and notified the lady of the advance. To this she protested, saying that she could not afford to pay it in her reduced circumstances; and finally told him that she should move out. At this the overseer of the poor began to reason with her, and after estimating the cost of removing the coal which was just brought in, and of moving her furniture, he showed that the outlay would more than balance the difference between his rent and that of his neighbor. This convinced her and she kept the tenement, although she was well aware that the owner cunningly waited until the win-

---

*Mrs. Parboly. See page [82].

ter's supply of coal was in the cellar, and then took advantage of her situation to get more rent for his tenement than other men received. This man was himself an "institution," and showed the tendency of the whole system. He could give in charity, but oppressed his tenants to obtain the money.

The poorhouse system in the United States, which creates an office worth from $1,000 to $2,000 a year, and is the cause of endless political squabbles, is sufficiently well known to the public. All those cases where paupers have died from the effects of abuse, where they have been buried without coffins or clothing because the grave was all that the town appropriation—five dollars for funeral expenses,—would furnish, and the enormous bills of expense entered and paid each year for comforts which the paupers never received are read about and commented upon nearly every day. Hence I pass over that in silence.

Two years ago two benevolent ladies of wealth, having an earnest and honest desire to contribute toward some charitable object, adopted this most excellent plan. A large house was purchased and fitted up with exquisite taste and at considerable expense, having carpets, gas-lights, a piano, and all the recent improvements in the way of heating and cooking. They then secured a matron who was well known to the projectors as a kind and efficient housekeeper, and gave her the entire control of the house.

To this house girls were invited to come and board upon the co-operative plan, each paying her share of the expenses at the end of each week. They were all shop-girls, whose earnings were small, and who could not find a comfortable boarding-house the price of which was within their means. By the assistance of the ladies, who were not—and I think are not—known to the boarders, the provisions were purchased at the wholesale prices, and the cost of living very much reduced. In this way poor girls secured a boarding-place at a cheap rate, and had a home in which they were all proprietors to a certain extent, and where they could receive their company and do their work with the same ease and freedom that they would find in their own father's house. Even the name of a boarding-house was discarded, and the girls led to regard the place as their private residence. No one, passing the door of that modest mansion, would ever dream that poor sewing-girls were able to occupy it, or that more than a single quiet family resided there. Here was true charity. By it no laziness or improvidence was encouraged, while the assistance which it gave to those who partook of its benefits prevented poverty and obviated the necessity of a shameful life, making the girls cheerful, healthy, and permanently virtuous.

One glaring example of the mismanagement of a "Home" attracted my personal attention a few years since, and as it shows the hardships to which the natural aristocrats of the world are subjected through the jealous rivalry of the usurping line of money-kings, I feel that it should be inserted here. During the war with the Southern States there were established in the cities of the North a class of institutions called "Soldiers' Homes." In that movement the city of Boston was a leader. Rev. Phineas Stowe, the "sailors' friend," with the assistance of a number of benevolent ladies,—women being considered of little consequence, the press is not supposed to give their names,—started the enterprise of establishing a "Home" where wounded soldiers would receive the best of care and more skilled medical attendance than they would have at their own homes.[5] This project did not meet with much favor until the attention of the city authorities was called to it, through negotiations for a building which the city owned and which Mr. Stowe wished to secure. The city council then voted to give the use of the building for the purpose, and as their proceedings were all published the attention of the public was called to it. At the same time the managers were obliged to ask for more assistance, owing to the large number of applications coming in from deserving soldiers.

The soldiers were very popular then; and the politicians, seeing that there was a chance to ride into office upon that hobby, slyly and surely undermined the influence of the originators, at the same time squeezing themselves into office. A board of directors, an executive committee, a long list of vice-presidents, together with numerous officials, were elected, or rather proclaimed, to have control of this "Home." This made it at once a great political machine, and with marvellous zeal the aspirants for office kept tugging away at the ponderous crank. The building was one of the finest mansions in an aristocratic portion of the city, and its dedication was one of the most important events of the day. Great men, great speeches, great guns, great bands of music, and great crowds. It is said the enthusiasm was so great that the soldiers present who had wounds wept for joy, while those who had none wept for shame. However that may be, the wounded soldiers were praised, applauded, and feasted until they thought the "whole world had gone crazy." I do not say that it was anything more than they deserved, but it was a love far too hot to retain its fervor.

In the selection of a superintendent the board of managers were rather unfortunate. For the first one did not fulfil either his own or his friends' expectations, while the second was discharged for some fault known to the board.[6] It happened that one of the active workers in this enterprise had a friend who was an "old chum" in the stage-driving business. The claims of this "old chum" were successfully advocated before the managers, and the professional stage-driver installed as third superintendent. Now the two "chums" were naturally very unlike. The patriotic member of the committee was a natural aristocrat, and fought his claim to nobility with such perseverance that he had risen from a stage-driver to be one of the most respected financiers and railroad managers in the country. He was an able, generous man, and was looking forward with reasonable hope to a seat in Congress. But the other was a man who was said to have reached his level as a stage-driver; and one who was as much out of place above his position as others are below it. He was most singularly unfitted for the position, from the fact that his sympathies were all against the cause for which the soldiers fought, and he could have nothing in common with them. What they respected he despised, and what they loved he hated.

As the State had now come in with its assistance,** he was given a salary of $1,300 a year for himself and family, besides their expenses, and had the entire control of the establishment. Keeping the expenses down as low as he could and avoid any loud complaints, he

---

**Appropriation of $20,000.

managed to save five hundred dollars more during the year than his predecessor had done, and that amount was generously added to his salary. The second year, "the State gave another appropriation," and

"All went merry as a marriage-bell."[7]

(This quotation applies to the superintendent and his political supporters,—not by any means to the soldiers.) In the spring of 1867 there were sixteen of the maimed soldiers in the "Home" who had so far recovered as to desire a change. They wished to go out into the world and earn their own living. To these broken and scarred young men the "Home" offered no inducements, nor made any provision for their future livelihood. It had accomplished much as an alleviator of bodily suffering, but it was to leave those who came under its roof as destitute when they left it as they were when they arrived. Under such circumstances, those who had recovered sufficiently were anxious about their future.

By the assistance of friends, six of them secured scholarships in the New England Conservatory of Music, of which Mr. Tourjée was the director, and in which their tuition was reduced to half price. Ten of them were admitted gratis into the classes of G. A. Sawyer's Commercial College, and began their studies with the most lively zeal.[8]

When their purpose became known, however, the superintendent took a sudden dislike to them, and seemed to regard their efforts to get an education as a personal insult to him, and endeavored, through the application of the State law, excluding from the "Home" such as received State aid or government pension, to expel these students. But the Governor of the State, to whom the law gave the power to send twenty-five soldiers to the "Home," delegated these sixteen, and it was supposed that they would be allowed to board there, and receive medical aid during their course of instruction.

But the superintendent had made up his mind that they should be driven out before the course was complete, and for reasons that cannot be explained, by reference to any laudable motive, began to insult them, by taunting and otherwise annoying them. He called them "beggars," and "greedy livers upon charity," or words to that effect, and spared no pains to shame them into submission. But they had begun a work upon which all their hopes of life depended, and with the counsel of friends, they determined to stay until they could go out free men,—not beggars.

I will not record in detail the actions of that superintendent, as they involve others in his disgrace; but so determined was he that those young men should not have the education that they desired, that he pulled all the political wires at his command, and with other secret means, secured the alliance of a few prominent politicians, who promised to sustain him in whatever he should undertake to do. So, on the plea of insubordination, he ordered the boys to leave the "Home," and on their refusal to go without an order from the Governor, at whose request they were there, he called in a posse of police to enforce his orders. Then, without resistance, and after one little fellow had said to the police-sergeant, "We have been soldiers, and know our duty; we will not make any disturbance," they were taken to the station-house, and stayed in that receptacle for drunkards and vagrants during the night. Strange spectacle! Wounded patriots, with one leg or one arm, or otherwise maimed, quartered in a jail in the liberty-loving city of Boston for no offence but that of attempting lawfully and peacefully to get sufficient education to earn their own livelihood!

Then the friends of the soldiers, to some of whom the superintendent of the "Home" had often applied the epithet of "common scrub-girls," undertook to do what the State Institution, without a political battle, would not do. One wealthy lady, whose goodness cannot be too highly praised, took four of the boys into her house and treated them as her own sons, while they pursued their studies.

The whole number fulfilled the expectations of their warmest friends, and secured good positions when they left the schools. To-day every one of them is making his mark in his chosen profession, and I expect to live long enough to see some of them among the greatest and most influential business men of that city.

Meanwhile, the "Home" gradually falling into disrepute, and unable to obtain a State appropriation for the impostors and beggars whom it harbored under the pretence that they were soldiers, closed its career in silence and disgrace; having an end sadly in contrast with its brilliant beginning. Would that I might record the end of every other institution of the kind which, for political power, administers temporary aid, and prevents its inmates from ever becoming useful and ornamental members of society!

6

There are three classes of charitable institutions that cannot be denominated "Homes" which are intimately connected with the subject of this chapter, namely, educational, moral, and religious charitable institutions; such as are endowed by will, or otherwise, in order to admit persons who could not otherwise afford to attend. That such institutions are founded for a good purpose, and accomplish much toward the elevation of mankind, there is no doubt; but the question sometimes arises, "Does the end justify the means?" and in many cases we are obliged to decide in the negative. A few months ago one of the wealthiest clothing-merchants in the United States left a very large sum of money for the purpose of founding a Female College. The conditions in the will, however, were such that the college could not be of any use to the present generation. Taking into consideration the fact that he made his money from the work of thousands of poor sewing-girls, whose wages were hardly sufficient for daily sustenance, it seems quite unjust that the money which they have earned should be bequeathed to a college which will benefit neither them nor their immediate posterity. The sum of the whole matter is this,—the sewing-girls have been made, with well-earned wages, to endow a college, bearing their employer's name, and in the construction, regulation, or benefits of which they and theirs have no voice.

Moral charitable institutions are often termed "Brotherhoods"; and include such organizations as the Odd Fellows, Masons, Knights of Pythias, Grand Army, Knights and Daughters of St. Crispin, and kindred societies. The present structure of society renders such associations necessary, and they seem to be the only organizations which start with the right foundations. The Odd Fellows and Masons instil the principle of natural equality, and give alms to their suffering brethren as though the recipients were justly entitled to them, and could claim them as a matter of right. Hence the great popularity and usefulness of those excellent orders.

It has been urged against the Knights of St. Crispin, that they were unreasonable in demanding the same pay for a poor workman that they do for a good one. The persons who make these objections do not appear to understand that it costs the poor workman just as much to live as it does a person who is skilled; and are not willing to acknowledge that the skilled workman in that order gets as much *less* than his value as the unskilled hand receives more.

Every order which has for its fundamental principle the right of all men to a livelihood, and the necessity of brotherly love and charity, has begun at the foundation, and cannot fail to benefit society.

Charitable religious institutions are, as a general rule, beneficial in the existing circumstances, and no one with an earnest desire for human welfare would wish them abolished. But to this there is one prominent exception. I have no fault to find with a church as a church; but I make deliberate war upon the "church kitchens." It is a little doubtful if the "house of God" is just such an edifice as it ought to be; when its carpets are too rich, its cushions too soft, its music too delicate, and the preaching too profound for the poor, coarse-dressed man or woman who strays within its courts. But if divines agree that the poor should take their religion from a different loaf, and that the pouring of money into a man's trousers pockets puts brains into his head, it may be presumption in me to question their decision. Yet I venture to assert that the audiences who attend these "branch chapels," or "church kitchens," and who are provided with that edifice by the wealthy society, because the church itself is too nice a place for them to enter, are as capable of conducting themselves properly, and of appreciating an able sermon, as one half of the giddy "doughheads" who can be seen every Sunday in their damask-decked front pews.[9]

If there is any sin in the world, those preachers who pretend to expound God's word, knowing their mental and physical unfitness for it, will have something to answer for at the judgment-seat.[10] Especially guilty are those who send such inefficient instruments to do a work which they well know the minister to be incapable of performing. It is deliberate wickedness to deal out mouldy bread from a table which lies heaped with the best and richest viands of His eternal goodness.

This, however, is done weekly in the "kitchens"; and, as if the poor in worldly goods needed poor preaching and poor religion, a house is built for that purpose, in which nothing but the poor article is dealt out. The influence of these measures tends strongly to drive away those whose strength of mind influences their associates, and to disgust the great mass of the poorer classes with everything connected with religion.

The exhausted and worn laborers, who enter the church after a week of unremitting toil, need stimulus, while they who have lived in ease will require only plain food for the Sabbath day. The tired workman needs a more talented man to preach to him than is required by those who are fresh. But church "kitchens," as a rule, have none of the mental food which the weary can relish, and are dull, monotonous, prosy, unmeaning, and soulless.

7

It often happens that the most charitable are never heard of by the world, while those who stand between the giver and receiver are the subjects of unstinted praise. I have often been reminded of this, when I have seen a few well-disposed individuals endeavoring to secure the funds or "contributions in kind" for some benevolent enterprise. It is the custom in the city of Boston to give Thanksgiving, Christmas, or New Year's dinners to the poor people, and a committee of several persons undertake the management on these occasions. The first, and often the only place to which these committees apply is at the great market around Faneuil Hall. There, among those marketmen who rise at three o'clock in the morning and work until six in the evening, these committees usually obtain all the contributions which they desire. Beef, pork, chickens, turkeys, fish, and oysters, in immense quantities, are always given, and although there are hundreds of such dinners during the year, these honest, industrious marketmen never refuse when they are persuaded that the cause is a good one. Yet the world seldom hears of their charity; nor do the newspapers applaud their generosity. On the contrary, the public is ever complaining that it has to pay such high prices at the markets, and wonders why the marketmen do not get rich. This is also the case with Fulton Market, in New York, where the appeals for material aid never cease, and where the newspapers never tire of praising the collectors of these gifts for their enterprising charity.

8

I have often wondered why there had been found no benevolent individual whose interest in the horse-car drivers and conductors was such as to lead to a bequest in their favor. From six o'clock in the morning until midnight they pursue their wearisome, monotonous task, being more exhausted after the same number of hours than are the laborers in the field. Accidents happen to them, and no one seems to care. They are paid very poorly, but it attracts no comment; they are deprived of employment when aged or crippled, and receive no aid.

Again, another class have been wholly overlooked by the founders of charitable institutions, namely, the waiter-girls and cooks in the bakeries and confectionery establishments, who work fifteen hours a day. At present they form a very respectable portion of the female employees in Philadelphia, Albany, New York, and Boston, receiving from two to three dollars a week; and yet, like the female printers, they are not regarded by the public as entitled to any respect or needing any assistance. They earn as much more than they receive and are as often in want as are other laborers, yet none of their unpaid wages have been returned to them in "Homes," colleges, or pensions.

It will not be expedient for me to go into an enumeration of all the classes who "give everything and get nothing," for their name is legion.[11] The world is full of injustice, and we can hope to annihilate but a small portion of it. We are, however, under no less obligation to eradicate as much of it as we can.

CHAPTER 13

Natural and Unnatural Aristocrats

Representatives of Nature.—Who Save the Communities.—Examples of Nobility.—Names of Prominent American Aristocrats.—The Darker Side of the Picture.—Anecdotes of Unnatural Aristocracy.—No Peace with Ill-Gotten Gains.

1

It is refreshing, after long contemplation of vice, cruelty, and injustice, to turn our eyes for a time upon the opposite picture, and thoughtfully ponder upon wisdom, benevolence, and intellectual greatness. It is inspiring to see, through the clouds of battle, some portions of the great army scaling heights and winning victories, though the beholder may have been already hopelessly defeated. Some of Nature's noblemen do win the battles of life, and are able to reap all the advantages which success vouchsafes; and but for their presence in the executive departments, the halls of legislation, the courts of law, the marts of trade, and the higher social circles, the world would be wholly lost to righteousness and God. They are "the salt of the earth," and, sprinkled here and there through society, they prevent its entire corruption, although in some localities even the "salt" fails to save it.[1]

These great representatives of Nature's royal family show by their ability and goodness what might be expected of all their relations on the side of genius, could the rightful claims of all be successfully defended. Those men and women to whom Nature has given that mental momentum called genius, as a signet of her favor, have given to the world all its civilization, all its enlightenment, and everything of value which it possesses. In all great emergencies, when nations are in danger, there is no inquiry for a moneyed or family aristocracy, no desire for persons whom circumstances have made, but for men in whose souls there is natural greatness. It matters not from what rank or station—whether a "cow ranch" or a palace—provided they are inspired with the zeal, courage, and discernment necessary to manage the helm. Such men almost without exception appear on the field unexpectedly.

Mankind will not go to Nature and learn of her; so they disregard the constantly recurring examples, and look for leadership first in other aristocracies and in the highest social circles of mankind. But it is seldom that the man for great emergencies is to be found there. He is stowed away in some sly and humble corner,—Nature knows where,—and when the occasion calls he pops into notice like the puppets in Punch and Judy.[2] Sometimes people laugh, and think that he is a real puppet because of his antecedents; but time and mighty events show them their mistake.

It is no proof, however, that because the number of successful ones is so small that the number of great men and women is also small. For who knows how many Cromwells, Washingtons, Websters, are held in reserve for occasions which never come, for revolutions which do not occur.[3] When from an army of a million there springs one leader able to insure victory, it is no proof that there are not a thousand others equally capable, of whom the world never hears. So in civil life there are men of science who make no discoveries, men of letters who write no masterpieces, men of financial ability who have no money, benevolent men and women who have nothing to give, women of culture, oratorical power, statesmanship, and judgment who never leave the kitchen,—all for the lack of a favorable opportunity to use the talents which God has given them. Like the great marble-quarry which is full of beautiful statues and imposing monuments, it can be of no use to the world until the layers of earth are removed, the stone broken, and the chisel applied. Although thousands lie unnoticed below, let us be thankful that any of the inspiring statues have seen the light; and may the gratification which we feel while gazing on those already quarried and utilized make us the more zealous in the work of exhuming others!

2

A few months ago a poor girl who had no home, and had lost her situation as a seamstress, applied to the great natural orator whose name is connected with so many modern reforms, and requested him to give her some assistance. He was generous enough to give her money, but with it he gave such words of comfort and such useful advice that she went away from his door feeling as if he had given her a fortune. She afterwards said to me: "O, I cannot express my gratitude to that great man, not for the money he gave me, but for the directions which he said would ever prevent my being in want again! I can work and suffer cheerfully now, for I see that there is hope even for me."

A factory-girl called upon the family of the well-known Senator and General from Massachusetts on a matter of business, and she was received with all those courtesies which mark the character of every noble man or woman. But there was a lady visitor at the house, whose aristocracy was founded entirely upon the dollar, and as she came sweeping into the parlor, and noticed the presence of the humble factory-operative, she curled her lips and scowled with contempt; at the same time, gathering up her rich silks and haughtily marching from the room.

I shall not soon forget the look of pity which came upon the face of the kind-hearted wife of that great man as she gazed after the retreating bubble of conceited pride. Neither shall I cease to rehearse to myself those burning, cutting words of rebuke which came from the good woman's lips when the haughty heir of a dastard's fortune appeared at the tea-table: "The poor are better than the proud, the industrious better than the idle, the producer is of more importance than the spendthrift, and a woman in calico is as great in the sight of God as she that trails her laces and silks."

In Pittsburgh, Pennsylvania, in 1850, there was a wealthy banker who had retired from an active life in New York, and who seemed at that time wholly resigned to a life of quiet, unostentatious pleasure. Every afternoon he walked through the low streets of the city among the families of the iron-workers, and would step in at this door and that to inquire after the welfare of the tenants. None of them ever knew where he lived or what his station in life until after his death, although the greater part of his time during the last years of his life was spent among those poor people. He always had money to relieve real suffering and shrewdness to detect an impostor, and his face became as dear to the poor denizens of hovels as it was to his own family. Every day, as the hour arrived when he usually made his appearance, the women would put on their best dresses, carefully sweep the rooms, and send the impatient children out upon the door-steps to welcome the visitor with shouts and clapping of hands. Some of these children grew up under his fatherly care, and many were assisted by him in obtaining an education or in learning a trade who are now influential members of society. He regarded the poor of a certain street as his especial charge, and his contributions, advice, remonstrances, and daily presence changed the appearance of the entire street. It became clean and tidy, the children more neatly dressed, the faces of men and women were more cheerful, and the police-officers whose beats crossed that street declared, at his death, that after his charitable visits became regular they had not been obliged to make a single arrest among the inhabitants of that particular locality.

He was a prince; and the good he accomplished will never cease to affect society. He raised the fallen, cured the sick, educated the ignorant, cheered the downcast, and gave to the needy. What more could man do?

There are a few nobles toward whom the eyes of humanity now turn, who, although they have doubtless sometimes succumbed to avarice and condescended to occasional injustice, have well proven their right to the positions which they hold. Among the living representatives of this class in our land will be found General Benj. F. Butler, as a defender of the factory-girls; General Henry Wilson, as a supporter of workingmen's rights; General O. O. Howard, as the advocate of freedmen's education; Theodore Tilton, as an earnest, though inconsiderate advocate of woman's suffrage; Henry Ward Beecher, as a liberal thinker and champion of free speech; Hon. William H. Seward, as a statesman; George Peabody, as a friend of humanity; Longfellow, Whittier, and William Cullen Bryant, as poets; General N. P. Banks, as a successful workingman; General U. S. Grant, as a soldier; and Horace Greeley, as an editor.[4] To these might be added a large number of "lesser lights"; but the communities in which they reside know them, and will be reminded of them when these pages are read. Upon such men no war is made. They have a "divine right" to the thrones they occupy, as they seem to have been made for the express purpose of filling the influential stations in which we now find them.

3

Historians do not tire of praising Cincinnatus, the Roman warrior and statesman, who saved his country, and, when his task was done, left every office to work in his garden. Yet there are men in this day who make the same sacrifices, and who leave public circles from which it is as difficult to break away now as in the days of that illustrious Roman. The son of a very wealthy family, having acquired a complete college education and inherited his immense fortune, had the good sense to see that his nature was such that he could not remain in the aristocratic circles of Boston and be happy. There was nothing in common between him and his frivolous, fastidious associates, and he determined to leave the mansion and the counting-rooms for a home upon a farm. In order to fit himself thoroughly for his chosen work he went into the interior of Vermont, and hired out to an old farmer for a year. There, without making known his great wealth, wearing the coarse frock, cowhide boots, old hat, and coarse flannel in which his co-laborers dressed, he diligently pursued his laborious search for practical knowledge. He ploughed and sowed, hoed and trained, cut the hay and gathered it into the barn, entered the grainfield to reap, dug potatoes, cut down the corn, cared for the horses and cows in winter, with not a single murmur or a sign of shirking in any way his share of the hardest and coarsest duties of the farm.

When his year of labor was done, and he considered himself well acquainted with all the duties necessary to carry on a large farm, he purchased one in the interior of Massachusetts, married a well-educated, but penniless orphan-girl, and settled down to a peaceful farmer's life. To-day he can be found on his farm, among a number of well-paid and happy laborers, following perseveringly his favorite avocation, although his old companions are flying hither and thither like moths in the halls of city trade, attracted by this glitter and then by that, and being scorched by all.

I recall a young woman of great wealth, and who by her relationships was entitled to the highest place in the fashionable society of the great city. Back in the country there was a little village where she loved to go, and where she took the greatest pleasure in visiting the farm-houses, riding in carts, and caring for a favorite pony. She loved to be among the laboring people, and with the farmer, the blacksmith, or the carpenter she felt equally at home. The free air, the hills, the mountain streams, the cattle, the school-children, the fruit, and the grain all had a charm for her which she could not find in the city. Nevertheless she was ever the brightest one of her circle when she appeared in fashionable life; and had such an attractive, winning manner as to command the attention and respect of every one.

When she had come to the conclusion that she must marry and adopt some settled plan for life, it was indeed a hard question to decide,—the country or the city. But the betrothed, the relatives, the property were all in the city, and she reluctantly turned back to the pavements and sidewalks. She wept when she bade the old scenes farewell with which she had spent so many pleasant days, and sobbed as she glanced in at the forge of the blacksmith where her pony had so often been shod.

After marriage she and her husband went to England, and while there they were made the guests of an English lord. It happened one day that there was an agricultural show near the lord's residence, and at her request the party attended the exercises. The farmers were ploughing when the titled party entered the grounds; and to the astonishment of the people, and especially of the lord, this lady took a plough and held it across the field, turning the cleanest and neatest furrow of all the competitors.

Fitted by nature for a farmer's wife, happiest among rural scenes and among country people, she still shines on in the city,—a dutiful wife, a kind mother, and a discontented member of fashionable aristocracy.

I cannot leave the subject of true aristocracy without making reference to three examples of natural nobility among those who have gone to their graves. Would that I could refer to all, and speak the thankfulness which I feel toward every one who has done himself and his nation honor. But the three to whom I refer were persons who came within the narrow borders of my acquaintance, and of them I may be better able to speak. Theodore Parker, Starr King, and Anson Burlingame were each of Nature's own line, and to this were added all of the graces and mental ornaments which culture and varied experience can produce.[5]

Theodore Parker in his early life, while picking berries to purchase his first Latin Grammar, and working at odd jobs to obtain the rudiments of an education,—afterwards one of the most comprehensive and most thorough,—showed unmistakable evidence of his natural ability. But it was in his later years, when he had conquered himself and undertaken to defend every injured class, that his talents showed the brightest. Then, while defending the secretion of Burns, the negro fugitive, in 1854; while saying stout words for the poor working-women of Boston, originating effective schemes for the relief of the poor, and bravely defying any and every law which conflicted with God's abiding decrees, he exhibited a greatness of soul and a goodness of heart unequalled in the ranks of his own time.[6]

Of Starr King, who hesitated not at any personal sacrifice where the welfare of mankind was concerned, and who seemed inspired with new and fresh thoughts rising with each occasion, I cannot speak too feelingly. He was your friend, my friend, and everybody's friend; and with a mind seemingly as broad as his heart was large, he lived and died in the service of his God and his fellow-men.

Of Anson Burlingame, who used to sit in his law-office and in youthful weakness defy the Whig Party, who was one of the first to defend the slaves, and at the same time the most able defender of New England industry that the country found, I can only add my word to the acclaim of millions. He was a workingman in a twofold sense, and while the world criticised, blamed, and hindered, he still believed in his mission and in his own ability to perform all that was given him to do. He rose above the occasion, reached into the future, and, grasping pillars which the short-sighted men of the day could not see, he drew himself so far forward as to be the leader of nations.

To these three natural aristocrats, who gained the places they deserved, and by good works proved their title to nobility, I would direct the attention of my readers, that the world may see and know what it is losing by preventing the advance of others like them.

4

It is a great leap from the men of whom I have just spoken to those who must now be introduced; yet without the examples the impression might not be made, nor the inferences drawn, for which this book is written. Unnatural aristocrats! There are thousands of whom I might speak, but a few shall suffice, and they shall be only such as are known to me.

A wealthy manufacturer of Massachusetts, with an earnest and honest desire to make a great man of his son, took just the course with his boy that would make him anything but what the father wished. Instead of putting him into practical life and utilizing the little natural talent which the boy possessed, he kept him in school or at watering-places for several years, after which he sent him to Europe to get a "finished education." But the father died, and the son was left an heir to an immense amount of property. The young man's mother was less careful in the use of her influence upon him than his father had been, so that he became a good-for-nothing aristocrat of the unnatural order.

When he became twenty-one years of age, his birthday was celebrated with a brilliant and costly display, fit for a state ball in honor of the Queen. It was whispered about in the aristocratic circles* long

---

*New York.

before the day came for the ball, and with much gossip and impatience the residents in the "fashionable quarter" awaited the invitations. The great mansion in which the young man resided was not large enough to accommodate the guests, and would not admit of a favorable display of the waste which it was proposed to make; so a large and well-furnished hall, with its anterooms, &c. was engaged.

Soon the costly cards were ordered from the engravers, displayed on silver plates, handled by delicate fingers, scrutinized by enraptured eyes, while the whole aristocratic world stood on tiptoe looking over the receivers' shoulder. How many disappointed ones! Aristocracy shed more tears over the non-reception of those cards than it ever did over the woes of humanity. Never was there such a *furore*, never such a party, never such exhibitions of nonsense![7]

The favored ones at once set about the arrangement of their toilets, and the trade in laces, costly silks, diamonds, and rubies received a marked impetus for several weeks. Fashionable dressmakers for once received their dues (not the work-girls), and there was a little chance for profits. Toilets were arranged for that occasion costing from ten thousand to forty thousand dollars, while the demand for new carriages, stylish livery, perfumery, and *rouge* was even greater than that for dresses. It was to be—and was—the most costly party ever given in the city. Ten thousand dollars' worth of flowers were used in the decoration of the hall, where costly fountains were made to play in sweet arbors and curious lamps to swing in floral archways. A paradise it was; and but for the contrast between the pure flowers and the hearts of the guests, it would have been a heavenly place. What a gorgeous sight! Millions of dollars displayed in a single evening in a single hall. No one cared about faces, no one thought of intellects, as brains and *natural* personal beauty were at a discount, while money for the time was worshipped. How much wine was drunk, how many deceitful bits of flattery exchanged, how much envy, how much hatred, how much pain, felt on that great occasion, the press which described the dresses did not say.

A few years elapsed, during which the young hero of that costly party, lauded by all who went to his reception and hated by all who did not, married a rich wife, engaged in a commission-business, where the goods of the great factories passed through his hands. His wealth was said to be fabulous, and his conceited display was in keeping with his reputation.

"Failed for nearly three millions!"—how these words stung the ears of stockholders throughout New England! In two years, with two fortunes to support him, he lost all his wealth, and while he had large sums of money in his hands,—or supposed to be in his hands,—the company with which he was connected failed for nearly three millions.[8] Were the unfortunate bankrupt the only person concerned, we might rejoice at the distribution of his money, but in his fall he involved others, and no sooner did the factory stockholders know of the failure than they reduced the pay of the operatives. Twenty thousand of the workmen "struck," but the discouraged stockholders felt like losing all or making themselves whole again, and the strike failed to accomplish anything. The cause of all this display, loss, and suffering was an "*unnatural* aristocrat."

Thirty years ago there was a strike among the workmen and girls in a New England factory, and one of the grave offences afterward laid to their charge was the giving of "three cheers for the frog agent," while the agent of the mill passed the strikers on his favorite gray pony, looking neither to the right nor the left. It was a strange title to give a man of his wealth, and is, doubtless, meaningless to many who have heard of that traditional "frog agent."[9] He was a proud, conceited, arrogant man naturally; but a visit which he made to Europe, on which occasion he associated with the lords, and looked upon the operatives of England from their aristocratic standard, doubled his respect for himself, and lessened his regard for working-women at the same ratio. When he assumed his duties again as agent, he tried to enforce a rule which obliged the operatives to go to the mill without hats or bonnets, in imitation of the English working-people, who were too poor to possess such useful portions of ornamental wearing apparel. He made up his mind at one time, that it was vulgar for him to have his office within the sound of the mill-machinery, reminding him constantly of mechanics and their low occupation; but instead of removing the office, he ordered all the windows to be closed in the mill. To this the overseer protested, saying that the operatives and the cotton must have air. The agent then said that "an inch of air" at each window would be sufficient, and refused to make any further concession.

The overseer, failing to execute an order so obnoxious to the girls, the agent himself marched in to execute his own commands. But while he was pulling the window down in a part of the mill where a large, muscular New Hampshire girl was engaged in dressing thread, he attracted her attention. She started from the machine with her hands thick with "sizing" starch, and exclaiming, "What! only an inch of air in a free country!" pushed him aside, threw up the window with a slam, and then marched the sheepish, starch-covered agent to the stairway, bidding him to consider whose air it was that he was shutting out.

Failing to shut in the noise of the mill, he turned his attention to the frogs, which were said to disturb his day and night repose with their "vulgar peeps." One day he cruelly ordered his servant to kill them all by pouring in lime; and, to prevent the use of the spot by immigrating "peepers," he hired men to drain it. This, of course, furnished amusement for the operatives, while it increased that hatred which culminated in a strike and the agent's removal.

The son of that distinguished agent inherited much of his father's arrogant spirit; and as his abilities did not give him much opportunity to appear in public circles, he displayed his selfishness among the servants and members of his household. He was ever afraid that his domestics would show him some disrespect, and at the same time, like his father, had not the courage to resent an insult even from them. One day he asked the busy parlor-girl why she did not say "Sir," and inquired if she meant to disrespect him, or omitted the word from ignorance; to which the impudent girl replied that she did not know or care which, as she thought too little about him to trouble herself with titles.

He went to an intelligence office and hired a professional cook, and gave the keeper of the office a fee of seventy-five cents. But when the cook refused to black his boots, wash the windows, brush his clothes, and attend to other work, he permitted her to leave, and went to the intelligence office to demand a return of the fee. The keeper objected, saying that she had done her duty, and earned the money; but as he threatened to use his influence with the authorities to revoke her license, she gave back to the rich man the sum of twenty-five cents, to avoid further injustice. His treatment of this woman was a key to his policy with regard to the operatives in those mills where he was represented by stock, and to such as he is due many of the strikes which have so often occurred.

5

I remember a mayor of a large city, whose aristocratic pride was of the most arrogant kind, and to whom it was the greatest hardship to converse with his own employees. Whenever he received a communication from his servants, they stood at a respectful distance; and if he had a letter or other missive for them, he always tossed it to them, and turned hurriedly away. One of the severest ordeals through which he is said to have passed was the official reception as mayor of a military company of which his coachman was the captain. This wealthy aristocrat, when the proposition was made to establish a free school for girls, strenuously opposed the measure, as it would be placing washerwomen's daughters on the same plane with those of the wealthy; and he feared that the education of such girls would only teach them to "set traps for rich men's sons," and thus bring misfortune upon the upper classes, whose sons, he thought, should always marry equals.

I recall two stockholders who visited the cotton-factories in which they were interested, but who knew nothing of the processes of manufacture. One of them saw a young man lying down upon a box in the "steam-room" to rest himself, after exhaustive labors upon the scalding cloth. The stockholder passed on to the office and demanded that the man be discharged. On returning with the agent to point out the man, all were so busy that the stockholder could not recognize the man, so, after looking about for some time, he pointed out a man in another apartment as the person he saw "shirking," and a hard-working, honest fellow was discharged by the agent, in spite of undeniable proof that the man had not been in the steam-room that day. The other stockholder saw some broken threads in a loom, and, noticing at the same time that the girl was seated on the window-sill, ordered her discharge; notwithstanding the fact that the broken threads did no harm, and the operative was one of the best in the factory. They had money in the mill, and wished to display their power.

There was a wealthy man living in a New England city whose income was very large, but who would not allow his wife the funds to provide the commonest necessaries of life. The wife tried to support herself and him by keeping a common boarding-house, and I have seen her ragged and barefooted, weeping as if her heart would break, because she owed a bill which she could not pay, and the cruel creditor had threatened to present it to her husband. She was an abject slave, and she was as afraid of his wrath as she would have been of an angry tiger. Still he was a moneyed aristocrat, and was recognized as a leader in financial circles. He had wealth and comfort; while his own wife was suffering in ragged clothing, with insufficient food, and broken by body-racking toil.

The most despicable, useless, aimless of all unnatural aristocracies is that of the hereditary sort. There does seem to be some little excuse for pride and display when a person has by his own efforts obtained wealth or position; but to arrogate to one's self great importance because he happens to be the descendant of some one who was noble is to an American mind one of the silliest things which a man can do. Yet there are very many American families who have nothing whatever to pride themselves on except their *descent*, who nevertheless look upon their family as on creatures too pure and holy to mingle with the "vulgar herd."

I knew a family—not many years ago—who claimed to be the descendants of an English duke; and a person, sitting in their parlors and seeing their haughty airs, would be almost persuaded that they had *done* something of which they might consistently be proud. They were not the associates of any other line of aristocracy, and despised self-made men. The gentleman of the house passed his time in idleness, taking his breakfast at ten o'clock, going to the club-house at twelve, and returning at two and a half o'clock for dinner. At five o'clock the elegant carriage with the costly span of horses dressed in gold-mounted harnesses was brought to the door by the servant, and the family went out for an hour's drive. After tea there was a party, or an opera, or a theatre, at which the evening could be spent. This gentleman never read anything but his "store-book," although his library was filled with the choicest literary productions. He spared no money in the decoration of his mansion, and from kitchen to garret it was furnished in the most costly style. There was nothing about the appearance of the mansion which would indicate that the owner was penurious, nor did they think in the club that this was his character. He was peculiar. Anything that was aristocratic he did generously because his ancestors did so, but in anything which did not involve his family pride he was close and unreasonable. He never took into his employ a person who had been a domestic in any other aristocratic family, because it is the custom among people who become suddenly rich to hire old servants to regulate the household and give it such an appearance as they have seen in other families. He took care to oversee everything himself, and knew and interfered with the business of all the servants alike. Although he purchased everything freely that could add to the personal appearance of any of the family, paid two thousand a year to the dressmaker, and large sums to the fashionable hairdresser, yet he seemed to begrudge to all the family a sufficient supply of food. Two little nieces, who had been left to his care by a wealthy sister, were decorated with every costly ornament, and when taken out for a ride, dressed in their velvets or furs, they were pointed out by the people as a beautiful and happy pair. But by his orders they were fed on "hash-and-bread" from day to day, and limited in their supply of that. Many a time the sweet little sisters went out in state to ride without sufficient food to keep them from crying with hunger. He allowed the servants to have only a sufficient number of plates and other dishes to supply the persons actually employed, thus preventing them from inviting any of their friends to dine. In this he had the support of his proud wife; and one day when a small turkey had been taken from the dining-room where seven persons partook of it, to the kitchen where six more picked at it, she scolded and discharged the cook for not saving some slices for breakfast. He declared that he could not afford dessert for the little girls unless they ate more heartily of "hash," and would not permit a servant to use the starch or soap without paying for it. When a cake was placed upon the table and a portion remained after the meal, he would ingeniously mark it to see if the waiter-girl took a slice. He purchased a medicine-bottle for use as a wine-decanter, in the glass of which was cast the name of the maker. When he had drank his last glass of wine at dinner, he took his pencil and, noticing the letter which marked the surface of the wine within, wrote the name of the letter in his diary, hoping in that way to detect any theft of his wine. It was his nature to attend to little things, and although he exhibited considerable mechanical skill and could have been an excellent carpenter, yet with all his wealth he could not get above the level of his domestics, nor occupy his thoughts with more weighty matters than their concerns.

Another striking example of the natural unfitness of some men for wealthy positions came under my observation a few years ago. A man worth four millions of dollars, living in a palace, and moving in the most "aristocratic" society, was nevertheless so narrow-minded and selfish that he felt at home with none but the humblest people. His principal occupation was in overseeing the employees about the house, and it was unsafe for the cook to bake a pie, the parlor-girl to dust the furniture, or the "kitchen colonel" to move a barrel of provisions, without the millionnaire's consent. He always made his regular "rounds" from attic to cellar two or three times during the day and night, and knew just how many provisions and how much coal had been used, how many pieces washed, and how often the washerwoman had taken rest during the forenoon. When the man came for soap-grease, old umbrellas, old boots, hats, or rags, the owner of the mansion would attend to the measurement and sale himself. He would sometimes barter over a pound of soap-grease or a pail of swill until the disgusted applicant would leave in anger without having accomplished his errand. One day the milkman came into the kitchen, and, seeing the finely dressed man attending to the business, supposed him to be the "kitchen-colonel," and addressed him with a familiar "good morning." The millionnaire stared at the honest milkman, and refused to answer the salutation. The milkman was seriously offended, and when he reached the gate, on his way out of the yard, he turned about, and, shaking his fist at the haughty man of wealth, bade him "come out of the house" and be taught that a milkman was as good as he, even though he was "dressed in some old fool's livery"! Whereupon the proprietor rushed out and engaged in a rough-and-tumble fight with the driver of a milk-cart.

Two maiden ladies, who had seen the richest side of high life, and who lived together in Boston a few years ago, were the wealthiest and at the same time the unhappiest human beings to whom my attention has ever been called. They were so selfish that they disliked to have their own sisters visit them when their presence added a farthing to the usual household expenses. They teased the cook, who could find plenty of employment on the same street for four dollars a week, to remain with them for three. Haughty, overbearing, and stingy, they made the house as unpleasant as possible for themselves and all who came within its walls. While they were cutting down the wages of the domestics, and begrudging bread-and-butter to their nearest relatives, the great rooms in the second story were filled with large trunks and boxes, in which were stored hundreds of costly dresses, imported laces, corsets, silks, shawls, cloaks, bonnets, and many articles of jewelry of immense value. Five thousand dollars had been paid at one time in duties on dress goods purchased in Europe for them. But the accumulation of forty years lay in those trunks, moulding, rusting, and decaying; while the waiter-girls could not afford a calico dress or a new bonnet of the value of a single inch of that wasting gold lace which lay above stairs. The oldest lady became very childish, and in that state—which was pitiable to behold—she would wish for joys and comforts which the poor children only know, and mourned that she was so unfortunate.

After her death the relatives were over three weeks in exhuming the costly wardrobes and in distributing the valuable property which had been miserly buried from sight for so many years. Who would be an aristocrat

"For fleeting joys like these"?[10]

I remember an old man, who in the days of his youth and middle age was a severe taskmaster, a purse-proud associate, and a disagreeable member of the household. To him there was no greater insult than that offered by employees who attempted to address him unbidden. He never gave the least sign of recognition when he met his domestics on the street, and was a tyrant as far as it is possible for man to be in this free land.

But with declining years came declining strength. His mental vigor left him, and at last he became a childish lunatic. While in that condition his former coachman, who, notwithstanding the abuse he had received, was true to his employer, waited upon him and provided him with all the little luxuries of which he knew the invalid to be fond. The old man imagined himself to be in an institution of some kind, and was ever in fear of displeasing the overseers. As if in retribution for his own arrogance, he became a prisoner in his own house, and believed that he must pay the same homage to those around him that he had once demanded of others. He imagined the coachman to be his "keeper," and obeyed him with the greatest show of respect. One day, in conversation with a visitor, the old man declared himself exceedingly pleased with the institution, but said that he was troubled about the title which he should give his "keeper."

"I have called him the Judge," said the invalid, "and it pleased him some. I called him the General, and he likes that; but I believe that he is the most pleased when I address him as the Doctor."

Thus for years that old man lived on, never daring to find fault with his food, or to omit the "Sir" when he addressed his coachman, or to move an article of furniture from the place where his keeper placed it. In which of these two positions—in health or in sickness—was this man the most to be respected?

Years ago, a poor boy, possessed of considerable natural talent, and having by various means obtained the necessary instruction to be able to enter college, found himself unable to proceed further without considerable assistance. At that time he had attracted the attention of a lady who held a high position, and who to this day is remembered for her nobleness and generosity. She interested herself in his behalf, and, going to a wealthy neighbor, she told him the boy's history, at the same time asking for aid. The man took his purse from his pocket and presented it to the lady, asking her to take therefrom all she needed. But she refused, saying that she "put her hands in nobody's purse but her own," and requested him to give such an amount as he deemed best. Whereupon he gave her one hundred dollars, and bade her come for more on the first occasion.

With such assistance the boy passed through his college-days, and entered the arena of active life as an essayist and poet. To him to-day the eyes of millions are directed, and his praises echo over the whole world. Yet, alas! not one word does he say for the poor boys who are now in the position he once held, nor will he stoop to converse with the laboring ones around him. That on which he flatters himself least is his greatest merit, while that on which he prides himself most is a curse to him and humanity.

6

When the war between the States began, there were few stronger sympathizers with the seceding portion anywhere than were to be found among the manufacturers of the North. They were the last to come into the ranks of government supporters, and but a weak ally when they did "accept the situation." They gave their moral support to slavery before the war, and so great was their influence that the leading men of the North followed for a time wherever they led. Edward Everett, when called upon to be present at a mass meeting in Faneuil Hall, where it was proposed to indorse Charles Sumner and resent the insult given him by Preston Brooks, refused to lend his influence, and suddenly concluded that "he had retired from active life."[11]

While the people became more and more convinced of the evils of slavery, the wealth of the land became more and more devoted to the perpetuation of that institution. Opposed to the war to the very last moment, the manufacturing corporations did not give their aid or sympathy until the mighty uprising of the masses forced them into the current. Even then there were men who would neither be coaxed nor driven. One of the largest factory-owners in the Eastern States declared that he would disown America—what a calamity, surely!—if war was made, and in 1862 he went with his family to Europe in disgust, declaring that he could not live in such a contemptible nation. The haste with which he returned in 1865 indicated that the nation was only contemptible so long as he made no profits, and was most lovable indeed when the close of the war sent back the slaves of wages to his mills.

7

Which is of the most value,—a man or a horse? Nearly every reader would answer that question without hesitation in favor of the man. But such an answer would rule the speaker out of the society of some unnatural aristocrats. For there are men in America who love their horses better than they do mankind, and who would make much greater sacrifice to save a favorite beast than they would to save the lives of a dozen human beings. I once made a visit to the residence of one of this class of aristocrats, and I was greatly surprised at the care which was taken of the horses and the little attention that was paid to humanity.

The building into which I was ushered when invited to see the horses seemed to me much more like a palace than a stable,—a great building, painted and decorated like a dwelling, with a neatness about it which is not found on every lawn. The first apartment which we entered was the "reception-room," where costly furniture of richest parlor description was tastily arranged, and where an immense number of gold-mounted harnesses were hung around the walls behind glass cases. Here guests were received by the chief groom, and treated to such refreshments as the occasion might require.

The next apartment was reserved exclusively for harnesses, and in it could be found samples of every kind and variety. Here the most fastidious could find a "rig" suited to his taste.

Then came the carriage hall, where twenty-three different styles of carriages were shining in new coats of paint and varnish. Buggies, sulkies, barouches, carryalls, market-wagons, chaises, and miniature coaches were arranged in rows so as to exhibit the velvet linings, the downy cushions, and the thousand-dollar robes and lap blankets of ermine, sable and seal-skin.

In the division of the stable where the horses were kept we were shown a long hall like those seen in hotels, with doors leading to the right and left. These doors opened into the "sleeping apartments," where the horses could be seen standing in straw to their knees, with no halters upon their heads, and each occupying a large square apartment by himself. These rooms were ceiled with the best timber and oiled, over which were fastened gray, coarse blankets to make the stable tight and keep the horses from marring the beautiful finish.

Everything that could be done by a large number of grooms was done for the comfort and health of the animals, anticipating in nearly everything the dumb brutes' slightest wish. Having good food and plenty of it, a nice, warm room, with a soft bed, close-fitting blankets, and regular exercise every day, those beasts might well be considered a happy, contented class of beings. Two hundred and fifty horses, varying in value from five hundred to fifteen thousand dollars, were owned and feasted by a single family. The children purchased candy to feed their favorite ponies, while the parents stood by and taught them "how to be kind to beasts."

As we turned away from the building and bade the good-natured superintendent adieu, the bell of the factory near by began its peals, notifying the operatives that the dinner-hour had come. As the factory and the stable were owned by the same man, I stopped by the great gateway as the flood passed by, to watch the manners and see the dress of the working men and women. Their appearance was sadly in contrast with that of the horses. There were bare heads, bare arms, and nearly bare feet. Little children trying to hide their benumbed fingers under scanty rags, young girls shivering and hungry, old men and old women hastening to their meals of bread and pork,—all in need of sympathy, and all in poverty compared with the condition of the horses; yet no one cared whether these creatures were supplied with food or clothing, and no one complained of the wealthy owner for thus neglecting and abusing his human cattle. The interest on the money lying idle in horse-flesh and stables would have kept two hundred of those needy ones in comfort and happiness, and would have assisted in giving to society educated, thoughtful, and profitable men and women.

CHAPTER 14

Labor Reform

*Lack of Thought.—How Politicians Lead the People.
—The Lessons of the War.—Organization of
a Labor Reform Party.—No Leaders.—What the
Laborers Demand.—Less Hours.—The Respect
of Thinking Men.—Just Legislation.*

1

The time was, not many years ago, when the employee who received his regular wages never ventured to inquire into his employer's business, nor questioned the equity of his pay, provided that he obtained a sufficient amount to defray his necessary expenses. It mattered but little to him, as far as right was concerned, whether the pay was small or great, if he obtained the sum for which he agreed to labor. No one dreamed that he was earning more than he could get in an open bargain, or that the profits of a business should have any consideration in the bargains for employment of workmen.

The intelligent workmen of America then, notwithstanding their boasted superiority to the same classes in England, Russia, and Germany, were in a mental thraldom as strong as it was subtle. The farmers of New England twenty years ago always laid the latest congressional speech which appeared in their weekly paper under the old family Bible, and preserved it for the Sabbath or a rainy day, when it could be carefully devoured and partially digested. The longest and most intricate speeches were the subjects of his greatest admiration, and the orator to whom the newspaper gave the largest space was the farmer's nominee for the next Presidency. It never occurred to him that he himself could ever be a government officer, and year after year he voted for town, county, State, and national officials, permitting his judgment to be easily controlled by the aforesaid paper or by some remarks of his pastor.

Then, it was thought necessary to make very costly displays during the canvass for the election of presidents, and on such occasions as the election of Jackson, Taylor, Tyler, Harrison, and others, millions of money were wasted in noise and idle show. The author remembers the canvass of 1856 when in the New England States there were enormous sums expended in torchlights, fireworks, and banners for the avowed purpose of "awakening an enthusiasm" for General Fremont.[1] It was necessary to do this in order to impress the unthinking masses of the greatness and popularity of the candidate. Men, however, were then intelligent, and claimed to be public-spirited, but they did not *think*. To them liberty was an inheritance, paid for by their fathers and handed down to them as a mere keepsake, of which no one would dream of robbing them; they calmly accepted it, and talked and voted as if the candidate were all there is of interest in political campaigns. Liberty and justice were, as they thought, secure. Even the great men, like Webster, Choate, and Everett, cared but little for the reasoning powers of the working classes, and pursued such a course as would be the most likely to win the influence of the wealthy classes. Hero-worship was the controlling sentiment. As Tom Brown, the shoe-boss, voted, so voted his employees; and the side which the dealer in town espoused was the party of Tom Brown, and the political opinion of some favorite orator made the opinion of the city dealer.[2] Each depended upon some one higher in office or in social standing for the necessary guidance in all political affairs. Even a "selectman" in the smallest mountain town was generally an object of veneration to every one of his constituents.[3] Hence it was necessary only to bring sufficient influence upon the leaders to obtain an election to any office.

Political discussions were then carried on only by little knots of men on the street-corners, in the bar-rooms, or in the social evening-parties. When a great man addressed the "citizens," they insensibly sided with him until his rival followed. There were no discussions on such occasions among the hearers. They accepted or rejected the proposition at the time, and, unless provoked by some extraordinary cause, would not venture to deny the statements of either party. Such wordy controversies as did occur were such as related to the character of a candidate, or the integrity of the party, without a reference, except in the most vague and unmeaning way, to the contestants' rights. In short, every white man supposed that he had all of his rights, moral and political, and deemed the arrogance of the wealthy and pride of the officials to be a part of "nature's great and grand design."

2

The late Civil War brought nearly as many great changes in the North as it did in the South. The soldiers, who were called upon to go and fight for the nation, found that their liberties were to cost something. The man who, in the draft for soldiers to supply the army, heard his name called as the first check was taken from the marshal's wheel, and who found that he must go and leave a wife and eight children, and thus pay well for the little comfort which he and his had enjoyed. When the name of his rich neighbor was called, he saw the wealthy stockholder pay a sum of money and go home a free man, and he then, for the first time, perhaps, in his life, saw what an unjust power the law placed in the hands of the wealthy.

Through years of untold hardship and danger the poor man toiled on, undergoing cheerfully the sacrifice; for with each new tax the value of liberty increased. He found that he must fight and dare in order to retain his own liberty, while attempting the liberation of others. He found time in camp, or on picket, or in the hospital, to solve the question which so often arose to the lips of the soldier, namely, What is this all for? *"For liberty we suffer,"* said the leaders. But this reply had more meaning after sieges, battles, and forced marches than it ever seemed to have before, and the man who had voted many times so thoughtlessly began to ask himself what "liberty" meant. Accepting that statesmanlike definition, "the greatest good of the greatest number," he could not fail to see that there were other classes besides the negroes of the South who had not such liberty as "the greatest good of the greatest number" demanded.

He saw, too, that his old neighbors were promoted to official positions for which they were less fitted than himself, and was compelled nearly every hour to pay military salutes to men whose station in life was socially no better than his own. This brought about a great revolution in the matter of hero-worship, and the holder of an office became simply an individual; surrounded by none of that dignity, and possessed of none of that mysterious greatness which the soldier had before imagined to belong to official position.

There, too, the citizens of different localities were unavoidably thrown together by the tactics of war, and the soldiers from Maine and Minnesota, Massachusetts and Pennsylvania, New York and Illinois, all stood side by side on the field upon an equality. Their common cause created an interest in one another, and by the interchange of ideas all became in a measure acquainted with the manners, people, and natural features of the whole country. They found everywhere the same great gulf between the rich and the poor which the founders of the nation had hoped to cover with the laws against titles and hereditary aristocracy, and felt how much more they had to pay for their liberty than did the law-protected man of wealth, who sat in his home and smoked his cigar, while a hired substitute fought his battles. Trial and woe made them jealous of their rights, and *the masses began to think.*

3

After the war there was a great reaction; their experience with proud officers, and their new views of life made them difficult to lead. They had little or no respect for the person of an officer, and felt that they were as much entitled to govern as any one. The laboring men had not overlooked the necessity for organization, neither had their irreverence for the officers decreased their respect for the law. The law was everything, and in the making of those laws they had an equal share. Before, the laws had been so constructed as to strongly favor capital; the plan of permitting supply and demand, pay and profits, to regulate themselves had been most grievously interfered with, and such measures had been established by law and custom as to increase the power of capital tenfold.

The necessity was at once apparent for either a return to the equitable state of "no law," or counter laws must be passed to defeat the purposes of those already established; and upon this work they entered with a will. As early as 1863 a movement began in Pennsylvania, and from that time until 1871 there was little or no rest. The pioneer in the movement was William H. Sylvis, an iron-moulder of Pennsylvania, who felt so strongly the need of labor reform that he worked himself into an untimely grave, while attempting to organize the laborers of the nation.[4] The National Labor Reform Congress at Philadelphia in 1869 was held pursuant to his call; but about three weeks before the time set for the meeting God called him hence. His successor, Richard F. Trevellick, is a shipwright by trade, and, like his predecessor, a nobleman by nature.[5]

Thus we see that the only three real leaders which the Labor Reformers have had have come from the ranks of actual laboring men. An iron-moulder, a shipwright, and a shoemaker, in actual toil, stepped from the dingy shop into the halls to initiate a movement destined to revolutionize this country, and have an influence upon like movements in Europe.

That there has been a great necessity for leaders, and a lack of available men in the ranks of the laborers, is apparent to the most casual observer. The reaction has carried them too far, and the workmen, although they desire to organize, have a prejudice against being led. More than this, the men and women of real merit have been too modest to assume a leadership without being forced into positions, while the attempts of silly politicians to lead them have only served to disgust them more deeply than ever with all office-seekers of every class. The whole movement in America has been characterized by no leadership except in the cases mentioned, and has had its rise entirely with the masses. No one has preached reform and organized the converts; no great Jove has arisen to hurl his lightnings at sleepy mortals; but, as if by instinct, all the laborers in all the States moved at the same time toward organization and reform. Conventions, lyceums, and "lodges" were organized in different States, and with remarkable concert of action the laborers of different sections of the country counselled together for a campaign in favor of "liberty" in its truest and best sense. The party took the form of two great divisions,—one declaring its principles to be the election to office of none but such men as can show calloused hands; while the other was unwilling to vote a comrade into office, and permit him to draw $5 or $10 a day, while his constituents, who were earning only $1.50 or $2 a day, were just as well qualified to govern as he. These apparently discordant elements did much toward the elevation of the party, as they both tended directly toward the creation of a strong desire among the laboring classes for education.

The man who, before the excitement began, spent his leisure hours in the bar-rooms or on the streets, became interested in the improvement of his mind, and regularly attended on the meetings of the order to which he belonged, and abandoned the dram-shop to pore over a book, or peruse the Labor-Reform periodicals which the discussions called into being.

This result, which has opened a door for the entrance into the arena of such as have been endowed with natural genius, will soon furnish leaders who will possess both of the required qualifications; namely, calloused hands and great minds.

4

It may be interesting to the reader to know what are some of the objects which the organizations of laborers hope to accomplish. There are many different opinions, plans, and aims; but all of them are included in the general demand for such rights as will give to natural ability its needed culture, and guarantee a recognition of Nature's aristocracy wherever its representative noblemen may appear. They purpose to begin that mighty reform which is destined sooner or later to overturn the inefficient pretenders in mortal aristocracy and substitute everywhere the generous, good, and great from God's own natural line.

To offset the unwise legislation in favor of capital, the laborers ask for a reduction in the hours of labor. They claim that such laws will insure the education of the laborers, and reduce the number of criminals and useless non-producers.

There is no more labor performed now while the few workmen labor twelve or fifteen hours a day than the demand renders necessary. Hence the reduction of the hours of labor would increase the demand for laborers. The workman, although he would do his work much better, could not do as much work in eight hours as he has done in fifteen. The reduction in the hours would oblige manufacturers, merchants, and farmers to employ a larger number of persons. As nearly all the laboring people are now employed, they must of necessity find workmen among other classes. The non-producing hangers-on, such as bar-keepers, small speculators, "fancy men," and other pests of society, with the beggars and poorhouse occupants, would be irresistibly drawn into the ways of industry, there being then work enough for all.[6] The fearful evils which idleness brings upon society, making thieves, drunkards, and libertines of men naturally fitted for higher and better stations in life, would, in a measure at least, be avoided; while the laborer who now supports this enormous body of men and women would have the cost of their living for himself. There can be no doubt that honest, well-paid labor, which is not a state of slavery, would empty the jails, as the present sentences expire, and reduce the necessity for poorhouses, hovels, charitable institutions, and houses of assignation.[7] A reasonable amount of labor elevates the workman as much as an unreasonable amount degrades him; and if it were made reasonable by law, it would also be respectable. Then no person of any ability or natural honesty would pride himself upon "getting a living without work," and none could say, when in the courts of justice or in rags, that they owe their degradation to a lack of honest employment.

The workmen of to-day would be incalculably benefited by this reduction. The efforts which they are now making to obtain education, and the way in which their spare time is now beginning to be occupied, indicates what use they would make of their opportunities had they more time and less fatigue.

Short hours will enable the workman to perform his duties without so exhausting his vital energies as to make it impossible to study or to enjoy thoughtful amusement. Books, lectures, newspapers, discussions, or creditable plays can have no attraction for exhausted men and women. Such persons need something which will require little or no thought; and in this can be found the reason why the laboring people patronize so many silly shows and love bar-room jokes.

The exhausted system craves stimulating drink, and hundreds fall into a drunkard's grave for no other reason than that they are overworked. There is at present but little opportunity for the cultivation of the mind by reading or study, and it is a wonder that the laboring classes of America have retained as much intelligence as we now find among them. Discouraged by insufficient pay, deadened by arduous toil, worn with the cares which debt and uncertainty throw upon them, and filled with envy at the sight of others whom fortune or friends have placed in positions of wealth and ease, they must lead an aimless, ambitionless life unless endowed with more than the ordinary strength of mind; and they show a greatness which is surprising, when, in the presence of these counter-influences, they can take sufficient thought to see their degradation and have the courage to point out the remedy.

5

These Reformers ask for a hearing. They believe that something may be learned of them as well as of others, and that their experience in a measure offsets their lack of education. The most illustrious men of the world have been such as were "good listeners," and could find something instructive in every man's conversation. We need more of those men in America. Mere theorists are an encumbrance to society. Like faith and works in spiritual matters, theory and experience in political affairs must always go together.[8] The workingmen have the experience, and by organizations and discussions are taking the necessary steps to secure the theory. Like Henry Ward Beecher's book-farming, where the beans seemed to come up the "wrong end first," the book theories regarding capital and labor have served only to complicate and render impracticable the whole question.⁹ The workmen wish to furnish the *facts* for the foundation, and let the structure rise from them, instead of taking theories for corner-stones, and hewing the facts to suit their shape and size. They will not accept any theories that are not compatible with the following facts, which they are struggling hard to get before the world:—

Labor is capital. The capital of the working men and women does not receive its just proportion of the profits when united with the capital of the wealthy.

Whenever the workmen have been granted an opportunity to educate themselves, they have become valuable members of society, and have given such inventions to civilization as have added tenfold to the comforts of human life.

Legislation has heretofore given its exclusive favor to wealth; and whatever progress the laborers have made, or whatever rights they have obtained, have been gained in direct opposition to capital protected by law. There is no opportunity for "self-regulation" so long as legislatures interfere. If they make laws for one side, they must for the other.

Eight hours of labor, with four hours of study or healthy recreation, will soon increase the skill of the operatives, so that they can earn nearly as much in eight hours as they now earn in twelve; and, like the sewing-machines and other improvements, they will cause a greater demand for the work of their hands.

Opportunity for reading and observation given by limited hours of labor will create a desire for the refinements of society, and make them a class of profitable consumers.

Children, who go to school six hours in every day, earn as much in the remaining six hours as they do during the entire day when they are not in school.*

Organized "strikes" and labor associations have had a wonderful effect in preventing riots, in advancing education, and in developing the best parts of the workman's nature. No mob riots have ever occurred, either in England or in the United States, where the

---

*Massachusetts Statistics of Labor.

workmen were sufficiently educated to be able to sustain a close organization.

No working man or woman, after having entered upon the discussion of the subject, is willing to accept any terms short of such remuneration as they would be entitled to under a strict and impartial system of co-operation, where every laborer is supposed to be a participator in the profits of the business to the full extent of his capital (labor) invested.

The laborers pay as dearly for their liberty as do any other class, and appreciate the benefits of a liberal form of government as well as other members of society.

6

I cannot pass this subject without adding a word to the arguments already advanced with regard to those great monopolies which law-protected capital is creating. It was thought by the statesmen of the age just passed, that the granting of certain rights and privileges to corporations, which gave them such power as to defeat any attempt of single laborers or associations of laborers to compete with them, was unwise and dangerous. What would they have said if they could have foreseen the enactments which in our day have made railroad, land, ship, and telegraph companies into mighty monopolies that threaten to overturn our whole system of government? The public domain is given away to railroad corporations in tracts as large as France. Great subsidies are granted to private enterprises, and the earnings of the poor man are used to rivet his own chains. The workman upon a telegraph line finds when it is complete that he must pay one hundred per cent profits for sending a message announcing the death of a friend. The former employee of a railroad company learns that a passage over the road is as much greater than a just rule would permit as his wages were less than what he earned; and that with the great land-grants and exclusive charters he is charged double the price which would have been asked on a road built without public assistance or protection. In the face of all this he is met at the doors of the legislatures with the cry that "labor and capital must regulate themselves."

Nothing will remedy this evil but the representation of labor in the halls of legislation. The laboring men can regulate it, and the laboring men *will* regulate it. They will have the power as soon as they learn how to use the means already in their possession. When discussion and study shall have created a desire for reading sufficient to make the subscription-lists of our daily papers show a majority of names which belong to workingmen, the press will at once be with them. With the power of the press, educated leaders, and an earnest purpose, too independent to be purchased and too vigilant to be deceived, the *majority will rule*, and the majority are working men and women.

CHAPTER 15

Woman's Suffrage

Woman's Rights.—Woman's Sphere.—Using the Talents Which God Gave Her.—History of the Suffrage Movement in America.—Margaret Fuller.—Why the Rich Do Not Want the Ballot.—Who Need It.—Conclusion.

1

The exact meaning of the word "rights" has never been definitely settled, and the expression "*woman's* rights" only serves to render its import more vague and complicated than when standing alone. You want your "rights." I want my "rights." White men want their "rights," and black men want their "rights"; but in the whole list there is nothing so indefinite as woman's "rights." Men and women stare at each other with an expression of nothingness, whenever the subject is mentioned. "What *can* woman want more than she has got?" Some venturesome wights, who seemed to think that an unmeaning or foolish reply is better than none, have made good Pope's remark, that

"Fools rush in where angels fear to tread,"[1]

by making some of the following statements: "Women want the right to go to the polls with the men," "They want to go to war," "They wish for the chance to rule," "They desire to be placed in positions for which they are unfitted," "Woman wants to vote merely because she has not had the privilege," "Woman is discontented in her proper sphere," "She wants the right of doing man's work," "She wants to oblige her husband to do the housework while she devotes her attention to the farm, the factory, and the warehouse,"

"She wishes to perform impossibilities," &c., &c. The more absurd and impracticable the proposition the more convinced have these buffoons been that it was just what the women the most desired.

"Woman's rights," however, have never been defined, and never can be defined in any one or any series of books. The needs of one woman are not the wants of another, and the desires of one class can find no sympathizers in any other class. They can unite on no certain remedy as applying to every class, because there are no certain wrongs that apply to the whole sex. Some are blessed with everything they desire; others have nothing. Some are forced into higher positions than they can fill; others are far below their natural station. While one is favored, another is slighted; and oftentimes that which makes one happy makes another miserable.

It cannot be supposed that there is a remedy for all the wrongs which women suffer; but the measure which seems to promise the greatest results is that of Woman's Suffrage. By this means women are placed on a political equality with men, and have nearly an equal chance with them of receiving a recognition of such natural talent as they may happen to possess. The agitators demand *universal freedom*. I do not believe that the thinking women of to-day desire or expect the passage of laws which will *oblige* them to do man's duties. They demand the liberty to do that for which Nature seemed to have intended them when she endowed them with intelligence and bodily vigor. No human law can change their physical stature or enlarge the size of their brains; but the absence of restrictive laws may afford them an opportunity to cultivate their brains and strengthen their physical stature. Neither do I think that laws or their consequences could ever make women as a class the mental equals of the men as a class. But when there are women, as often happens, with brains as large, with minds as strong, and with physical stature as enduring, as can be found in the ranks of men, I would not suffer a law to exist which prevented such a person from occupying an equal place with the men of her ability. I would open the whole stage to free competition from every class, and award the crown to the successful ones without regard to age, sex, or nationality. *No law should prevent the use of a single talent which God has given to man or woman.* The woman whose tastes take her to the bedside of the sick, with her who feels that she has the ability to defend the right upon the rostrum, should be protected and encouraged. If there were found in the ranks of women some who were able and willing to shoulder a musket or accept the position of a sea-captain or police-officer,—as absurd as it seems at first thought,—I would not deny them the privilege. The few women that have been soldiers, sailors, and detectives have no more "brought disgrace on their sex" than the tailors, hospital nurses, and bakers have injured the fair fame of the men. It needs no argument, however, to establish the truth of the axiom which recognizes the propriety of doing that for which one is best fitted; and woman's suffrage will serve no other purpose but that of giving equal opportunities to those equally endowed.

2

The Woman's Suffrage movement is the outgrowth of civilization, and is also the more immediate result of a recent retrograde movement among the political and social leaders of enlightened society. In the earlier ages of the world physical strength determined the superiority, and women with the weaker classes of men were held in bondage. But little attention was paid to mental qualifications for leadership, for *muscle* was the master. In that field woman had her "rights," and we often read in history of Amazonians like Boadicea, to whom were accorded leadership on account of their physical power.[2] Then came the age of chivalry, when, for the lack of other causes of contention, the lovers of bloodshed and war agreed upon assuming a protectorate over the weaker sex; each man looking upon the whole class as his immediate charge. After endless quarrels and murders in attempting to do for woman what they would not let her do for herself, the men gave up the task, and woman relapsed into her former obscurity and servitude. But the advance of civilization, while it rejected the idea of serving woman merely because she was the "weaker sex," increased man's respect for her gentleness and natural kindness of disposition.

The Pilgrim Fathers, when they came to America, did not hesitate to bring their wives and children with them across the stormy sea; but they were, nevertheless, so far advanced that they respected and honored true womanhood. Years passed, and this respect increased, until the men of New England gave to their wives and daughters the lightest and neatest part of the family labor, considering the house and its keeping more fitted to their ability, while the men undertook to perform all the out-door work, which required physical strength and endurance. It was done as an equitable division of labor, and among other duties the men undertook the care of town and colony affairs. There was no intentional injustice, and the woman had no thought of asking a vote for the purpose of protecting rights which had always been accorded to her without question.

There were husbands for all the ladies, and it was a sin and disgrace to be an old maid; hence the men felt that every woman could have a protector, who could defend her in case of any attempted injustice. They meant no evil themselves, and did not surmise that their successors would harbor thoughts of selfishness and wrong. Woman did not feel that she was deprived of any rights, because she had no occasion to exercise them.

The war of the Revolution of 1812, and the campaign in Mexico, left many widows and husbandless maids, and for the time awakened some interest in the rights of women who had no male protector; but as that generation passed off the stage the sexes were again equalized, and comparative harmony restored. The effects of the Mexican war, as slight as it was in the light of subsequent events, had not ceased entirely to be felt in the New England States when the discovery of gold in California, and the unprecedented "Western fever" induced the emigration of a large number of young men from the Eastern States. They could not entertain the thought that the women whom they loved should be exposed to the hardships which they expected to endure, and so they left the women at home while they went out by thousands "to make their fortunes." Thousands never came back, nor sent back for the girls whom they left behind; and a large surplus of female population was found in all the Eastern States at the next census. Then came the war with the South, and tens of thousands went into the field never to return, leaving behind them wives and daughters who had depended solely upon their support. The soldiers fell, and the bereaved women were left without protectors and with but a very little means of sustenance.[3] Then it was that frail women, placed at the head of families, were obliged to pay taxes on their little homes, according to assessments the justice or injustice of which they had no political power to question. They were subject to expensive delays by the "red tape" behavior of officials, in whose election, unfortunately, they had no voice; and were obliged to send their children to schools where they had no influence, either with regard to the discipline or the plan of studies. In short, they were obliged to do all of a man's work, and all of a mother's; under the double disadvantage of being physically weak and of possessing no political influence that would entitle them to respect. Many a widow has been slighted and harshly treated when she applied for pension, or tried to do a man's business, because the unprincipled official did not wish to bother with a person who could give him no vote.

3

When the surplus of women became so great, and it was evident that a large number must either starve or find some permanent employment, there arose the question as to how far a woman might with propriety proceed with a man's work. Thousands must live and die single, and there was no provision made by custom or law for this class of human beings. They must encroach upon the domain before held in exclusive possession by the men. Long before the war this question presented itself, and had been decided by many in favor of clerkships and teaching. In order to obtain any foothold in this exclusive territory, the women were obliged to repeat the action of those who, at the beginning of the factory system, attempted to obtain places in the mills. They accepted anything that offered itself, and took whatever pay was tendered them; which in some instances was exceedingly small. Notwithstanding they knew that their predecessors had received thrice the amount which they received, they never found any fault, so glad were they to obtain anything. Thus a precedent was established which, as it soon passed into custom, could not be broken without the assistance of the law. To this number of poorly paid working-women was added the host of widows and orphans left destitute by the war. The market for woman's labor was crowded to repletion with anxious applicants, and because they were in such sore need the speculating employers refused to pay them more than enough to sustain life. Great fields of labor, untilled and unthrifty, lay all around them, the bounds of which they could not pass, and men were becoming rich on salaries paid for work which women could perform equally as well as the men; but those offices were political offices, and none but voters and controllers of voters could be admitted. Farms were in need of tillage, mills were lying idle, and great enterprises were dormant for lack of man's labor, while the men who should have been caring for them were in offices which women could just as well have filled had they been qualified voters.

4

The first great advocate which woman's suffrage found in this country was Margaret Fuller Ossoli.[4] The vast emigration of the men from England, and the sad situation of the women had awakened some enthusiasm there; but, unlike the movement in this country, it had leaders, but no followers. Here there were plenty of followers, but no distinguished leaders. Through all the agitation upon the Woman's Suffrage movement in this country there has never been another advocate of its principles so uncompromising and so pure-hearted as Margaret Fuller Ossoli.

Her remarkable life and her unswerving fidelity to principle are too well known to the American people to need a repetition here. How she labored and wrote, talked and persuaded; how she pitied the imprisoned "victims of a debased civilization"; how she labored, while in Rome, in the preparation of a history of the Revolution of 1848; and how with her husband, Count d'Ossoli, she was wrecked in sight of land and with her valuable manuscript lost to the world forever,—are facts in the history of America's great and good. She was one of Nature's noblemen, combining the comprehensive mind of Webster with the culture and polish of Everett.

I remember being in attendance one evening on a lecture delivered by a woman upon Margaret Fuller's life, and the speaker, after saying much in praise, summed up her entire speech in the closing words: "Her life was a failure." In the audience, unbeknown to the speaker, sat the mother and brother of the unfortunate genius about whom the words were uttered, and the old lady turned to the brother, saying, "If you do not get up and reply to that lecturer, then I will." But the man needed no urging, and he calmly arose in his seat, and in a clear, sweet, unimpassioned voice said: "The lecturer has said some beautiful things of my sister, but she also states that her life was a failure. Could the life of that woman have been a failure, who was the staff and stay of a widowed mother, who refused advantageous marriage in order to be able to give her two brothers a college education, and who wrote "Woman of the Nineteenth Century"?[5] The applause which greeted him showed plainly where lay the sympathy of the audience.

Her life was by no means a failure. That great mind, which could sing her little boy to sleep amid the breakers that scattered the wreck, and encourage the sailors to face death when even they were without hope, has left its impression in her writings, and on her disciples who remain. Biographers may call her an "egotist," may assail her as they choose; the time will come when she will be appreciated, and when the great reform, which she almost unconsciously originated, will claim the homage and respect of every civilized nation on the face of the earth.

It was pleasant indeed to find on the sixtieth anniversary* of Margaret Fuller's birthday so many able women who were willing to take up the work where she left it.

Such strong, sensitive, judicial mind as that of Elizabeth Cady Stanton, such eloquence and independence as Mary A. Livermore displays, such culture and originality as marks the efforts of Julia Ward Howe, are just the elements which insure success.[6] Above all this, however, is the faith they have in the cause, and their apparently conscientious behavior.

---

*Meeting of the Woman's Club, Boston.

5

To-day in New England—and it is only there that women are so numerous as to be at present much neglected or oppressed—there are three great classes of women with whom this question has to do, namely, the aristocratic, the middle, and the working classes. The aristocratic class do not want the ballot, and declare that they "could not be forced to vote"; the middle classes concede that the ballot is plainly a right, but avoid the question, by saying that woman does not need it; while the laborers see in it a remedy for many of their ills, and are anxious to obtain it.

The daughter of an aristocratic family, beginning in infancy, is supplied with every comfort and pleasure which money can furnish. Books, dolls, toys, and pictures fill the hours of childhood; while visits, games, parties, music, and the dull pleasures of a private school return day after day in ever fresh variety as the weeks of girlhood pass. When after seventeen or eighteen years of a happy life have gone, during which time she has never been without devoted and wealthy friends to do her bidding and satisfy every wish, she is suddenly placed in the marriage market by her relatives. A splendid and costly entertainment is provided, and nearly all of the young men and young ladies of her class are invited to participate in the ceremonies of her "coming out." If very wealthy she at once becomes a prize, set up for the best or the richest or the shrewdest or the most noted young man in society. The race begins at once, and although the young lady most concerned may look on with considerable interest, yet she has little or nothing to do with the regulations which are to govern and decide the race.

The young man who has seen the lady and thinks that it is best for him to attempt to win her, calls at her house late in the afternoon. He does not ask for her, however, nor mention the object for which he calls, but sends his card to the young lady's mother, and requests her presence in the parlor. If, during the interview which follows,—when he tries his utmost to be agreeable to the old lady,—the young lady is introduced to him, or encouraged in his presence to converse with him, he concludes that he is regarded with favor.

He asks permission to call again if all parties seem to be "exceedingly pleased," but at each subsequent interview some member of her family is present, until such time as the suitor has become by common consent the betrothed husband. Then a formal engagement is made, the world is notified, and no restraint is placed by guardians upon the movements of the young couple. The young gentleman thinks it to be his duty to wait upon his affianced bride with unceasing care and devotion, and watches her footsteps with the greatest vigilance lest she be annoyed or injured in some way.

Then follows the marriage, the parties, the presents, the tours, and sensations, after which she becomes the mistress of a mansion where her word is law, and where she is ever protected and cared for by numerous hired domestics. In all the journey of life, she holds in her hands the imperial power which money and position supply, is educated to no work, taught to avoid working men and women, and told by all that it is vulgar for a lady to do anything but oversee the servants, receive callers, and stitch upon fancy work. In her presence no man would venture a word upon politics. Such women naturally look upon the idea of going to the polls with a promiscuous crowd of men and women, and having only the same number of ballots that a servant has, as something repulsive and very much to be feared. In their blissful ignorance of the world and its ways, the ballot is a very undesirable thing. They have nothing to gain by it, while it might cause them a great deal of trouble. That they have a duty to perform to those whom it will benefit cannot be impressed upon their minds, because the whole tendency of their education has been to give them the opinion that they are beings higher and nobler than they who work; while in some few cases the lower classes are treated by them as a nuisance to be abated on the first occasion. There are more of those ladies who have no part or interest in the government, and who regard any participation in politics by a lady as an exhibition of coarseness or vulgarity, than there are of "low Irishwomen" who would not understand the meaning of a vote. Either would use the ballot with great awkwardness until the faulty education of the one and the ignorance of the other were overcome by experience and care.

6

Omitting any extended notice of the middle classes, who incline toward one or the other of the two remaining divisions as circumstances happen to influence them, and who take but little pains to advocate woman's suffrage, although they all recognize the natural right of every sane woman to the ballot; I will refer to the women who see their degradation, and feel their chains, but cannot escape.

The factory-girl, who enters upon her work when ten or twelve years of age, has none of the friendly care and none of the comforts which the wealthy daughter possesses. She is treated neither with politeness nor consideration. She must go to the agent herself, and without favor or advice, make her own bargain with him. She must hire her own board, buy her own clothes, earn her own money, and attend personally to all her affairs of business, whether they call her to the street, the counting-house, or the parlor. She has no difference shown her there because she is a woman; and she must work as hard and do her task as well as a man, or, like him, be discharged, without ceremony or apology.

Treated in every respect like a man, governed by the same strict rules, and as often obliged to defend her property or character, she receives only about one half of a man's pay, and none of his "perquisites." She is placed in a position where she is exposed to calumny, temptation, and crime; with no weapon to defend herself, and no friends to act for her. Her contact with the world and her experience in affairs of business gives her an independence of character and a knowledge of her rights which, under present circumstances, serves only to aggravate her discontent. She feels the power of the law, and knows full well that many of her trials are due to unjust enactments which she might amend if she had an equal right with the half-witted loafer who is employed to do "odd jobs." If you should ask her opinion about the delicacy of going to the polls to vote, or with regard to the reasons why she would vote for specified measures, she would say that the polls could not be a worse place than those which she is obliged to enter every day, and that she is as able to discuss questions of politics, takes as many papers, and has as much interest in public affairs as any of the men who work beside her.

Factory-girls are always politicians; they must discuss something; and in the absence of fashionable balls, dinner-parties, new styles, and the amusements of high life, they turn their attention to the solid affairs which concern the welfare of State and nation. They see the deceit, double-dealing, and fraud which enter into politics, making men miserable as well as women. They are cognizant of the dangers that beset the nation, and of the measures which would avoid them; but they can only sit and weep while politicians concoct their schemes for plunder and advantage.[7]

7

The lady clerks and accountants, who form a large proportion of the women employed in the non-manufacturing towns, are obliged to care for themselves and do their own business. In Massachusetts there are thousands of orphans, both in factory and store, who began very young, and have had no assistance of any kind in providing themselves with the comforts of life. Many began as little "cash girls," and from the time they shrinkingly entered the salesroom for the first time, they have been constantly schooled in the severest trials of life. Engaging in men's business, they became as efficient as men; and although they so unjustly receive but one half the compensation which men would receive, have been successful competitors with them in every mercantile department into which they have been permitted to enter.

I remember a row of little girls who were seated on the edge of the platform during a meeting of the "Dover strikers," and who appeared to me to be too small to be away from home without a guardian. Leaning over so as to call the attention of one of the nearest of the group, I asked her what she could be doing there. "O," said the lisping child, "*I ese on der sthike.*"

Two little girls who had been turned out of employment by a refusal of the other employees to attend to their duties, went into a confectionery shop, where one proposed to purchase some candy;

but the smaller one, who was about six years old, advised the elder to save her money, and added: "You know we are on a strike, and there is no certainty about the time when we shall earn any more!"

"I know," said the other independent child, "but the money I've got is my money. I earned it, and I'll spend it as I see fit."

Beginning thus in their youth, and continuing through life in the same course, they become, by force of circumstances, intelligent women, endowed with a large amount of practical knowledge, and its excellent helpmeet, good old-fashioned common sense.

The most favored and at the same time the most abused class of clerking women are those who have succeeded in obtaining situations in government offices. Their pay is usually better than that of many other women, but their weakness and lack of political power exposes them to the insults and despicable chicanery of any political rascal who presumes to attack them. If they had votes to cast, no such assaults would ever be made upon them. There might be political quarrels, jealousy, and hate, but for every actual wrong there would then be the same means of redress which the men have.

A short time ago a member of the United States Congress arose in a branch of that august body, and accused all the girls in the employ of the Treasury Department of crimes which cannot be rehearsed here. Why he should spend his temper, time, and breath in thus accusing the wives of wounded soldiers, the daughters of deceased generals, and virtuous supporters of invalid parents and children, can only be accounted for by the fact that his associations elsewhere had been such as to destroy his respect for women in general, and kill every sense of shame which he might otherwise have possessed. The untruth of his statements was so apparent to all that the people of the country laughed at him, and excused him as the Yankee did the donkey, because "he did n't *know* any better." It may be that some of the government offices employ female clerks whose reputations are not good, and if so, it is the fault of the men who vote and who hold the offices. But this could be said of but very few in the departments at Washington compared with the whole number, and those would not remain in office, and continue to sin if woman had sufficient political influence and the opportunity to meet in Congress the few debauched and unprincipled representatives who keep those disreputable persons there. Neither would those defenceless women, to whom a good name is everything, have been permitted to mourn and weep under the insult, without a single word of defence from among that host of talented lawgivers.

On the evening—I should say, *night*—of the 22d of February, 1870, a great number of the fashionable ladies and titled men gathered at a hall in Washington to celebrate the birthday of Washington; and the description of the event, from the pen of that unrivalled correspondent, "Olivia," found its way over the country in the columns of the Philadelphia Press.[8] O the magnificent equipages and the gorgeous apparel! The most fashionable people of other cities sighed and wondered while they read. It was a ball of the "old school," and unnatural aristocrats were in their glory.

In all that company of diamond-decked ladies it is very doubtful if there was a single one who would not scoff at the idea of woman's suffrage. They had more than their rights, and were satisfied to trail their silks and coquette with their jewelled fans, while thousands in that same city were without a good name, without friends, and without proper sustenance, for the very reason that these ball-goers possessed such a wealth of display.

At that same time the umbrella and parasol girls of New York were on a strike, attempting to obtain a slight approach to a just compensation for their work. One of them seeing "Olivia's" description of the ball, exclaimed as tens of thousands have done before,—

"Oh! why was I born? It does seem as if God cursed the poor and always favored the rich!"

I doubt not that the effect of that display upon the desponding hearts of poor working-girls was the indirect, if not the direct, cause of many of the suicides which followed in such numbers so soon after.

Do you ask if woman's suffrage would remedy these evils? We all know that it would remedy a great many of them; and I doubt not that the knowledge of woman's political principles and the power for good which she would possess has hindered the movement much more than the fear of evil has done. The great and good have never opposed the elevation of society and the advancement of woman; the little and the bad have always done so.

CONCLUSION

In the inscrutable course of nature, men and women are endowed with special mental and physical qualifications, fitting them for certain stations in a perfect state of human society and unfitting them for others.

In the present condition of the world very few men or women reach the exact station for which they appear to have been designed; while some are so far misplaced as to cause much wretchedness and crime.

So uncertain are we as to the time when, or the place where, great and noble women will be born that the only safe and just plan is to so regulate our laws that all the men, women, and children may have the full advantage of their natural genius.

In order to accomplish this there must be an entire lawful equality between all mankind, and the facilities for mental and physical culture must extend to all alike.

With the aid of such laws and assistance the great will rise to their stations untrammelled, while the little will fall to theirs,—making a complete and harmonious whole.

But as we cannot look for perfection nor hope to rid the world entirely of evil, we will not attempt in our weakness to right at once all the wrongs which we find in the world.

For some evils, however, resulting from the unnatural condition of society, we can plainly, unmistakably, see the remedies; one of which is, *practical co-operation* between the laborer and the capitalist, and the other is *woman's suffrage*.

The first will give to working men and women alike the means to assist themselves into the spheres of labor for which they are fitted, will alleviate much suffering, and eradicate much evil. Without it education is a curse to many, as it creates desires which can never be satisfied and leaves them to a poverty, the full misery of which they are sufficiently enlightened to realize.

Woman's suffrage gives to women who are specially gifted the opportunity to assume their proper stations in the political affairs of the nation. It is not expected that many will leave the kitchen, or the parlor, or the bedside, or the desk to assume the badge of office, for few of them are fitted for it. Woman will never rule, or aspire to rule, those who are better qualified for office than she. But there are crimes to prevent, fallen women to raise, poverty to alleviate, ignorant people to educate, and justice to do, which have not been done under the exclusive franchise of the men, and which in all probability woman would accomplish if she had the power that the ballot gives.

Suffrage, taken aside from the good it would accomplish, is due to woman as an act of the simplest justice. She is taxed for her property, but has no voice in the use of those contributions to society. She is arrested for breaking laws which were made without consulting her. She is tried before judges and juries who cannot understand or appreciate a woman's weakness or temptations, and is often driven into further crime, and at last buried in the holes of a "potter's field," because of the unwise decisions of her male judges. She is often at the head of a family, owing to the death of her husband, and though intrusted with a man's cares and responsibilities, she has none of man's political power. In fine, she is under the continued oppression of many foolish and injurious laws, which man wilfully or ignorantly made, and which he wilfully or carelessly refuses to abolish; to none of which has she ever been asked to give her consent, although a hundred and fifty thousand of her sex in the United States must live and die under those laws single and unprotected.

Not, however, to one law, not to one class, not to one people, do I ask the reader's entire attention; but rather to all those measures which will do justly by all those men and all those women, wherever they may be found, who can show an undisputed title to an honorable rank in Nature's Aristocracy.

Notes

1. NATURE'S ARISTOCRACY

1. *shades*: Ghosts, spirits.
2. *Merrimack*: The Merrimack River flows from New Hampshire into Massachusetts. It provided water power for many of the early textile mills in cities such as Manchester, New Hampshire, and Lowell, Massachusetts.
3. *those persons to whom God has given five talents*: See Matt. 25:14–30 (Authorized [King James] Version; hereafter AV).
4. *poorhouse*: A publicly supported institution where poor and homeless people lived. *hod*: An implement for carrying mortar and bricks.
5. Dressing-room workers prepared the warp beams and reeds for the looms in the weave rooms. Most early nineteenth-century textile mills were water powered.
6. *belt*: Water-driven turbines and flywheels conveyed power to belts that drove the spinning mules, looms, and other machinery. *bobbin-boy*: Bobbin boys and girls worked in the spinning and weave rooms replacing empty bobbins with full ones.

2. THE BEGGARS

1. *cars*: Railroad cars.
2. *State or Wall Street*: Boston's State Street and New York City's Wall Street, financial centers.
3. *Broadway*: A main thoroughfare in New York City.
4. *Beacon Street*: A fashionable street in Boston's Beacon Hill neighborhood.
5. "All the world's a stage, / And all the men and women merely players" (Shakespeare, *As You Like It*, act 2, scene 7, lines 139–40).
6. *farthing*: A coin worth one-fourth of a penny.
7. *head of the corner*: "Jesus saith unto them, Did ye never read in the Scriptures, The stone which the builders rejected, the same is become the head of the corner" (Matt. 21:42 [AV]).

3. ONE GRADE ABOVE THE BEGGARS

1. *The poor ye have always with you*: "For ye have the poor always with you" (Matt. 26:11 [AV]).

2. *God's will shall 'be done on earth as it is in heaven'*: "Thy will be done in earth, as *it is* in heaven" (Matt. 6:10 [AV]).

3. *mansion prepared for such as her before the foundation of the world*: "Come, ye blessed of my Father, inherit the kingdom prepared for you from the foundation of the world" (Matt. 25:34 [AV]). "In my Father's house are many mansions. . . . I go to prepare a place for you" (John 14:2 [AV]).

4. *were confirmations strong as Holy Writ*: "Trifles light as air / Are to the jealous confirmations strong / As proofs of holy writ" (Shakespeare, *Othello* act 3, scene 3, lines 322–24).

5. *ambrotype*: An early kind of photograph.

6. *Indian pudding*: A pudding made from cornmeal, milk, molasses, and sometimes other ingredients.

4. CRIME AND NOBILITY

1. *thank God that we are not as other men*: "The Pharisee stood and prayed thus with himself, God, I thank thee, that I am not as other men *are*" (Luke 18:11 [AV]).

2. Collins may be referring to the following passage from Theodore Parker's "A Sermon of Poverty," in *Speeches, Addresses, and Occasional Sermons*, comp. Theodore Parker (Boston: Ticknor and Fields, 1861–67): "I never see a poor man carried to jail for some petty crime, or even for a great one, without thinking that probably, in God's eye, the man is far better than I am, and from the State's prison or scaffold, will ascend into heaven and take rank a great ways before me" (1:335).

3. The original reads *from Wellie, She knew the arts*; presumably *from Wellie. She knew the arts* is meant.

4. Alexander Pope (1688–1744), English poet; John Dryden (1631–1700), English poet, playwright, critic; George Gordon Byron (1788–1824), English poet; Percy Bysshe Shelley (1792–1822), English poet; Felicia Hemans (1793–1835), English poet; Thomas Moore (1779–1852), Irish poet; Lord Alfred Tennyson (1809–1892), English poet; Henry Wadsworth Longfellow (1807–1882), U.S. poet; Thomas Carlyle [the original reads *Carlisle*; presumably *Carlyle* is meant] (1795–1881), Scottish author, critic; Joseph Addison (1672–1719), English author, statesman; Victor Hugo (1802–1885), French poet, dramatist, novelist; August Wilhelm von Schlegel (1767–1845), German author, scholar, or Friedrich von Schlegel (1772–1829), German

philosopher, critic, writer; Walter Scott (1771–1832), Scottish novelist, poet; Charles Dickens (1812–1870), English novelist, journalist.

5. William Blackstone (1723–1780), Joseph Chitty (1775–1841), and Rufus Choate (1799–1859) were prominent attorneys and legal authors.

6. See Hymn 250 beginning, "There's a light in the window for thee, brother," in *The Western Harp: A Collection of Social and Revival Hymns*, 3rd. ed. (St. Louis: P. M. Pinckard, 1867) 230–31.

7. *the "Prisoner's Friend"*: Henry C. L. Dorsey (1824–1898) of Pawtucket, Rhode Island, was a benefactor of prisoners and the poor.

8. *the Prodigal Son*: See Luke 15:11–32 (AV).

6. SHOP-GIRLS

1. *Tantalus*: In classical mythology, a king who insulted the gods and after death was punished in Hades with perpetual hunger and thirst.

2. *dry-goods*: Textile fabrics, sewing notions, and related items.

3. *horse-car*: A railway car pulled by one or more horses; *omnibus*: a public vehicle for transporting passengers.

4. *Needlewomen*: Seamstresses earning their living by hand-stitching. *machine-girls*: Women earning their living by working at sewing machines.

5. *bushel-women*: Perhaps the same as *bushelers*, those who repair clothing. *baste-girls*: Workers who do the loose, preliminary stitching together of garment pieces.

6. *normal schools*: Schools for the training of teachers, especially elementary school teachers.

7. *sabbath-school*: A Christian Sunday school.

8. *who does the best his circumstance allows*: "Who does the best his circumstance allows / Does well, acts nobly; angels could no more" (Edward Young, *The Complaint: or, Night-Thoughts on Life, Death, and Immortality*, 5th ed. [London: R. Dodsley, 1743], Night 2, lines 91–92, p. 44).

9. *the spirit is willing*: "the spirit indeed *is* willing, but the flesh *is* weak" (Matt. 26:41 [AV]).

10. Cf. the Lesson (or Parable) of the Widow's Mite, Mark 12:41–44; Luke 21:1–4 (AV).

7. JOURNEYMEN TAILORS

1. *They Grind the Face of the Poor*: "What mean ye *that* ye beat my people to pieces, and grind the faces of the poor? saith the Lord God of hosts" (Isa. 3:15 [AV]).

2. *jour.*: Journeyman, skilled artisan, day laborer.

3. *iron goose*: Tailor's iron with a curved handle.

4. *fails up to make money*: To "fail up" is a New England slang term meaning to fail financially, go bankrupt.

5. *potter's field*: A burial place for poor or unknown people.

8. SERVANT-GIRLS

1. *When the cry of the working-women of New England finds lodgement in the ears of the wealthy housewives*: Cf. "Behold, the hire of the laborers who have reaped down your fields, which is of you kept back by fraud, crieth: and the cries of them which have reaped are entered into the ears of the Lord of Sabaoth" (James 5:4 [AV]).

2. *Give me liberty, or give me death*: Words attributed to the American Revolutionary patriot Patrick Henry (1736–1799).

3. *Governor Andrew*: John A. Andrew (1818–1867), Massachusetts governor from 1861 to 1866.

4. *the Waverley novels or Pope's poems*: The Waverley series of novels by Walter Scott were very popular in Europe and the United States. The poetry of Alexander Pope was also widely read.

5. Daniel Webster (1782–1852), U.S. orator, constitutional lawyer, politician; Edward Everett (1794–1865), U.S. politician statesman, orator; Lafayette (1757–1834), French general, statesman; Andrew Jackson (1767–1845), U.S. president; Millard Fillmore (1800–1874), U.S. president; perhaps James Bruce Elgin, 8th Earl of Elgin (1811–1863), English governor of Canada.

6. *his great 7th of March speech*: On March 7, 1850, Daniel Webster delivered a speech to the Senate favoring the Compromise of 1850. He advocated measures that strengthened the fugitive slave law and allowed newly acquired territories to determine for themselves whether to permit slavery.

9. THEN AND NOW OF FACTORY LIFE

1. *summum bonum*: Latin for "the greatest good."

2. Although mill working conditions in the 1830s and 1840s were far from easy, they deteriorated in later decades with speed-ups, wage reductions, and the like. Nostalgic memoirs of the early "golden age" were published not only by Collins but by other former mill women. Titles include Harriet Hanson Robinson's *Loom and Spindle; or, Life among the Early Mill Girls* (1898), Lucy Larcom's *An Idyl of Work* (1875) and *A New England Girlhood: Outlined from Memory* (1889), and Eliza Jane Cate's "The Old Mill at Amoskeag," *Peterson's Magazine* (1866).

3. Samuel Slater (1768–1835), U.S. manufacturer. The Pawtucket mill produced cotton yarn.

4. Sir Robert Peel (1788–1850), English prime minister, statesman.

5. Anthony Ashley Cooper, 7th Earl of Shaftesbury (known as Lord Ashley) (1801–1885), English politician, reformer; Richard Oastler [the original

reads *Ostler*; presumably *Oastler* is meant] (1789–1861), English labor reformer, abolitionist; Michael Thomas Sadler (1780–1835), English politician, reformer; Thomas B. Macaulay, 1st Baron of Rothley (1800–1859), English essayist, politician, historian; Charles Grey, 2nd Earl Grey (1764–1845), English statesman, prime minister.

6. Philip Grant (d. 1880), English weaver, editor, author, labor reformer.

7. Henry John Temple, 3d Viscount Palmerston (1784–1865), English statesman.

8. Henry P. Brougham, 1st Baron Brougham and Vaux (1778–1868), British politician, lawyer; John A. Roebuck (1802–79), English politician; John Bright (1811–89), English statesman, radical.

9. The English author Charles Dickens visited Lowell in 1842 and published his impressions in chapter 4 of *American Notes for General Circulation* (1842). Collins derived her quotation (slightly changed from the original) from this chapter.

10. *that General*: Perhaps U.S. General and President Andrew Jackson, who visited Lowell on June 26, 1833, and viewed a procession of factory women.

11. *the goose which laid the golden eggs*: A fable attributed to Aesop, warning against the dangers of greed.

10. HOW COTTON IS MANUFACTURED

1. Elihu Burritt (1810–1879), U.S. peace activist, reformer; Abraham Lincoln (1809–1865), U.S. president; Nathaniel P. Banks (1816–1894), U.S. soldier, politician.

2. *circumstances do not make men, but men make circumstances*: "Man is not the creature of circumstances. Circumstances are the creatures of men" (Benjamin Disraeli, *Vivian Grey: A New Edition* [London: H. Colburn, 1826–27], vol. 4, bk. 6, chap. 7, p. 260).

3. *teter*: Also spelled "teeter" or "teater," this is the game of seesaw.

4. The actors Junius Brutus Booth (1796–1852) or his son Edwin Booth (1833–1893) and Charlotte S. Cushman (1816–1876). Costar has not been identified.

5. *Lawrence*: Lawrence, Massachusetts.

6. *the 11th of January, 1860*: The Pemberton Mill collapse occurred on January 10, 1860.

7. *My Father's house is built on high. . . . I'm going home, to die no more*: From the Methodist Episcopal hymn, "The Heavenly Home," lyrics by William Hunter (1811–1877).

8. *changing works*: A colloquialism meaning the exchange of duties among people; barter, cooperation.

11. AMONG THE "STRIKERS"

1. The original reads *honest in the desire*; presumably *honesty in the desire* is meant.

2. From Massachusetts, *Report on the Statistics of Labor*, 1st ed. (Boston: Wright and Potter, 1870), by Henry K. Oliver. Collins's quoted passage is slightly altered from the original.

3. Massachusetts, *Report on the Statistics of Labor*, 170 (with minor changes).

4. The original reads *no "strikes." and run*; presumably *no "strikes" and run* is meant.

5. Newell A. Daniels (1828–1904), shoe worker, labor leader.

6. William J. McLaughlin of Ashland, Massachusetts, was the International Grand Sir Knight of the Knights of St. Crispin from 1868 to 1871.

7. *Coolies*: A term denoting Asian (usually Chinese) immigrant laborers, now considered derogatory.

8. The original reads *the jour.s. The jour.s*; presumably *the jours. The jours.* is meant.

9. *the granite hills*: The White Mountains of New Hampshire.

10. See: "Death's stroke he gave no coward's alarm. / But he smiled, and died in his messmate's arms. / . . . We proudly deck'd his funeral vest / With the Starry Flag upon his breast! . . [sic] / We gave him this as a badge of the brave, / And, then, he was fit for a sailor's grave" (Eliza Cook, "The Sailor's Grave," broadside [Boston: Horace Partridge, 1860], lines 7–8, 13–16).

11. David G. Farragut (1801–1870), U.S. admiral.

12. *the attack on Mobile*: During the Civil War, Farragut and his forces defeated a Confederate fleet at Mobile, Alabama.

13. *the same thing thirty years before*: In March 1834 and in the winter of 1836–37, the Dover factory women struck to protest against wage reductions.

14. *petticoat overseer*: Presumably a female overseer.

15. *many bright gems which the world has not seen*: Compare to, "Full many a gem of purest ray serene / The dark unfathom'd caves of ocean bear / Full many a flower is born to blush unseen, / And waste its sweetness on the desert air" (Thomas Gray, "Elegy Written in a Country Churchyard" [1751], *The Golden Treasury of the Best Songs and Lyrical Poems in the English Language*, selected and arranged with notes by Francis Turner Palgrave, bk. 3, rev. ed. [London: Macmillan, 1897] 173, lines 53–56). This stanza appeared on the title page of early issues of a Lowell factory women's magazine, the *Lowell Offering* (1840–45).

16. Shakespeare, *Hamlet*, act 1, scene 5, lines 166–67.

17. Perhaps Philip Grant and Anthony Ashley Cooper (Earl of Shaftesbury), *The Ten Hours Bill: The History of Factory Legislation* . . . (Manchester, England, 1866); James Ward, *Workmen and Wages at Home and Abroad* (London, 1868).

18. *mule-spinners*: The mule was a spinning machine created by the British inventor Samuel Crompton (1753–1827).

19. *hobbies*: Favorite projects or ideas.

12. CHARITABLE INSTITUTIONS

1. *carding-machine*: A machine that smoothes and aligns the fibers before they are spun into thread.

2. *the "Cradle of Liberty"*: Faneuil Hall, Boston.

3. *Dead Sea fruit to the eyes of the famishing wanderer*: Cf. "Like to the apples on the Dead Sea's shore, / All ashes to the taste" (George Gordon Byron, *Childe Harold's Pilgrimage* [1812], canto 3, verse 34, lines 303–4). "Like Dead-Sea fruits, that tempt the eye, / But turn to ashes on the lips!" (Thomas Moore, "The Fire-Worshippers" [1817], lines 939–40).

4. *Thus far shalt thou go and no farther*: "And said, Hitherto shalt thou come, but no further: and here shall thy proud waves be stayed?" (Job 38:11 [AV]).

5. Phineas Stowe (1812–1868), pastor of the First Baptist Bethel Church, Boston.

6. The original reads *friends expectations*; presumably *friends' expectations* is meant.

7. *All went merry as a marriage-bell*: A common expression.

8. Eben Tourjée (1834–1891) founded the New England Conservatory of Music, Boston, in 1867. George A. Sawyer's Commercial College was located at 274 Washington Street, Boston.

9. *doughheads*: Blockheads, stupid persons.

10. *judgment-seat*: See Rom. 14:10; 2 Cor. 5:10 (AV).

11. *their name is legion*: "And he answered, saying, My name *is* Legion: for we are many" (Mark 5:9 [AV]).

13. NATURAL AND UNNATURAL ARISTOCRATS

1. *the salt of the earth*: "Ye are the salt of the earth" (Matt. 5:13 [AV]).

2. *Punch and Judy*: A comical puppet show featuring a husband and wife, Punch and Judy.

3. Oliver Cromwell (1599–1658), English statesman, general; Daniel Webster (1782–1852), U.S. legislator, orator.

4. Benjamin F. Butler (1818–1893), U.S. attorney, military leader, politician; Henry Wilson (1812–1875), U.S. senator, vice president; Oliver O. Howard (1830–1909), U.S. military leader; Theodore Tilton (1835–1907), U.S. journalist, reformer; Henry Ward Beecher (1813–1887), U.S. clergyman, preacher; William H. Seward (1801–1872), U.S. lawyer, government official; George Peabody (1795–1869), U.S. merchant, financier, philanthropist; John Greenleaf Whittier (1807–1892), U.S. poet, novelist, journalist; William Cullen Bryant (1794–1878), U.S. poet, editor; Ulysses S. Grant (1822–1885), U.S. military leader, president; Horace Greeley (1811–1872), U.S. newspaper editor, politician.

5. Theodore Parker (1810–1860), U.S. clergyman, transcendentalist, abolitionist; Thomas Starr King (1824–1864), U.S. author, clergyman, orator; Anson Burlingame (1820–1870), U.S. congressman, diplomat.

6. *Burns, the negro fugitive*: Anthony Burns (1834–1862) was a fugitive slave from Virginia, who was recaptured but finally freed in 1854 by some Bostonians, mostly African Americans.

7. *furore*: Latin word meaning furor, madness, frenzy.

8. The original reads *three millions*; presumably *three millions.* is meant.

9. *frog agent*: The agent of a Dover, New Hampshire, factory where the workers struck in 1836–37 to protest against a wage reduction.

10. *For fleeting joys like these*: Cf. "O fleeting joys / Of Paradise, dear bought with lasting woes!" (John Milton, *Paradise Lost* [1667], Bk. 10, lines 741–42).

11. After delivering a powerful Senate speech against slavery in 1856, Charles Sumner (1811–1874, U.S. senator, abolitionist) was brutally beaten by Preston S. Brooks (1819–1857, U.S. representative) in response to Sumner's criticism of Brooks's uncle, Andrew Pickens Butler (1796–1857, lawyer, U.S. senator).

14. LABOR REFORM

1. John C. Frémont (1813–1890), U.S. explorer, military leader, politician, 1856 Republican presidential candidate.

2. *shoe-boss*: The owner of a factory where shoes were made.

3. *selectman*: In all New England states but Rhode Island, an elected town official who serves as a chief administrator.

4. William H. Sylvis (1828–1869), U.S. iron worker, labor leader.

5. Richard F. Trevellick [the original reads *Trevelick*; presumably *Trevellick* is meant] (1830–1895), U.S. labor leader, reformer.

6. *fancy men*: Slang term for men supported by prostitutes' earnings; pimps.

7. *houses of assignation*: Brothels, houses of prostitution.

8. *faith and works*: Cf. "For by grace are ye saved through faith; and that not of yourselves: *it is* the gift of God: Not of works" (Eph. 2:8–9 [AV]). "What *doth it* profit, my brethren, though a man say he hath faith, and have not works? can faith save him?" (James 2:14 [AV]).

9. *Henry Ward Beecher's book-farming, where the beans seemed to come up the "wrong end first"*: Book-farming is discussed in Henry Ward Beecher, *Plain and Pleasant Talk about Fruits, Flowers, and Farming* (1859). "Have you discovered any new way of growing beans wrong end up . . .?" (Robert B. Roosevelt, *Five Acres Too Much* [1869], 185).

15. WOMAN'S SUFFRAGE

1. "For Fools rush in where Angels fear to tread" (Alexander Pope, *An Essay on Criticism* [1711], line 625).

2. *Amazonians like Boadicea*: In Greek mythology, the Amazons were a band of female warriors. Boadicea (or Boudica, Boudicca; d. 61 AD), the queen and ruler of a Celtic tribe, led a revolt in England against the Roman Empire.

3. The original reads *protectors: and*; presumably *protectors and* is meant.

4. Margaret Fuller (1810–1850), U.S. intellectual, transcendentalist, writer, feminist. She married Giovanni Angelo, Marchese d'Ossoli, in 1849.

5. *Woman of the Nineteenth Century*: Margaret Fuller's book is entitled *Woman in the Nineteenth Century* (1845).

6. Elizabeth Cady Stanton (1815–1902), U.S. leader of the women's rights movement, suffragist; Mary A. Livermore (1820–1905), U.S. suffragist, editor, author; Julia Ward Howe (1819–1910), U.S. author, suffragist.

7. *they can only sit and weep*: Compare to "By the rivers of Babylon, there we sat down, yea, we wept, when we remembered Zion" (Ps. 137:1 [AV]).

8. *that unrivalled correspondent, "Olivia"*: Olivia was the pen name of Emily Edson Briggs (1831–1910), a correspondent for *Forney's (Philadelphia) Weekly Press*.

In the Legacies of Nineteenth-Century
American Women Writers series

The Hermaphrodite
By Julia Ward Howe
Edited and with an introduction by Gary Williams

In the "Stranger People's" Country
By Mary Noilles Murfree
Edited and with an introduction by Marjorie Pryse

Two Men
By Elizabeth Stoddard
Edited and with an introduction by Jennifer Putzi

Emily Hamilton and Other Writings
By Sukey Vickery
Edited and with an introduction by Scott Slawinski

Nature's Aristocracy: A Plea for the Oppressed
By Jennie Collins
Edited and with an introduction by Judith A. Ranta

Selected Writings of Victoria Woodhull:
Suffrage, Free Love, and Eugenics
By Victoria C. Woodhull
Edited and with an introduction by Cari Carpenter

To order or obtain more information on
these or other University of Nebraska Press
titles, visit www.nebraskapress.unl.edu.

www.ingramcontent.com/pod-product-compliance
Lightning Source LLC
Chambersburg PA
CBHW030340240426
43661CB00052B/1692